Fundamental Principles of Lean Manufacturing

Fundamental Principles of Lean Manufacturing

BY

Shigeo Shingo

Originally published as *Fundamental Principles of Continuous Improvement*, copyright 1977, by Nikkan Kogyo Shinbun Publishing Company, Tokyo, Japan.

English translation © 2009 by Enna Products Corporation and PCS Inc.

Enna Products Corporation
1602 Carolina St.
Unit B3
Bellingham, WA 98229
Telephone: (360) 306-5369
Fax: (905) 481-0756
E-mail: info@enna.com

PCS Inc.
809 S.E. 73rd Ave.
Vancouver, WA 98664
Telephone: (360) 737-1883
Fax: (360) 737-1940
E-mail: info@pcspress.com

Printed in the United States of America

Library of Congress Control Number: 2009938688

Library of Congress Cataloging-in-Publication Data
Shingo, Shigeo, 1909-1990
Fundamental Principles of Lean Manufacturing
  Includes index.
  ISBN 978-1-926537-07-8
  1. Continuous Improvement 2. Lean Manufacturing 3. Operations Management

TABLE OF CONTENTS

FOREWORD

Who is Dr. Shigeo Shingo and what does he have to do with the Toyota Production System? Anyone that is serious about Lean Manufacturing knows of Dr. Shingo, mostly because of his invention of SMED, which dramatically reduced setup times for equipment. What is less well known is his overall contributions to TPS. Actually his contribution to TPS is clearly that of the trainer of Toyota's engineers and is intertwined as one of the originators of TPS along with Mr. Ohno. I do know that Dr. Shingo was an industrial engineering genius who fully understood all the intricacies of TPS and made many important contributions — one of which was SMED.

When Dr. Shingo went to a work place and observed it, he was looking through the eyes of a TPS master. He saw waste at a level of detail few of us can imagine. From his own accounts it seems that, unlike the vague questions that many Toyota experts in TPS ask, Dr. Shingo would jump in and provide his analysis of the situation and make suggestions for improvement.

What we can learn from Dr. Shingo's more overt approach to process improvement is the way a true TPS master thinks. He is not shy about pointing out the waste and telling us about his solutions. In clear and concise terms, with detailed tables of numbers and figures, he describes a few key concepts and then deep examples of those concepts in action. This book follows that format. The number of rich examples is remarkable and the time it must have taken just to prepare the illustrations is mind blowing to authors such as myself.

Obviously TPS should be learned by doing; but as a backup, if that is not possible, most of us learn through case examples. Well here they are — for every major TPS concept you have ever heard of.

I began thinking about what Dr. Shingo does in this book in terms of my 4P model in The Toyota Way. The two Ps most heavily populated in the book are process and problem solving. In this book we learn how a true sensei thinks in the context of solving problems. The problem solving drives process improvement using lean tools. This sequence is very important. Dr. Shingo did not "implement lean." He solved problems. In the process of solving real manufacturing problems he drew on what we now call lean concepts and tools.

Let us use an example from Dr. Shingo's book of when he was involved with one of the early model plants to implement a Kanban System. In the 1970's, Toyota Gosei was under pressure by Toyota to increase quality and decrease cost and they selected one plant to be the model for a Kanban System. A model plant experiments with some methods, makes it successful, and becomes a model for others to learn from. We all know what Kanban are — those clever little cards that tell you when the customer is ready for you to ship another bin of parts. All it takes is the right information and some way to print the cards, right? Dr. Shingo writes that there are a set of known prerequisites in order for a Kanban System to work:

1. Continuous production
2. Stable production volume
3. Streamlined and stable production processes
4. Invariable quality
5. Thorough operational understanding
6. Defects are addressed immediately
7. Establishment of clear defect criteria
8. 5S
9. Schedule is managed by Kanban
10. Swift and thorough execution of all decisions
11. Short set up time
12. Preventative maintenance and rapid machine repair

Dr. Shingo reports that Toyota Gosei worked diligently to achieve these conditions before they implemented the new Kanban System, but condition 12 was not adequately satisfied. In 1972 they launched a vigorous TPM campaign, but the data showed that the biggest cause of equipment downtime was setup time. Since they were moving to small lot production the number of setups increased, which limited machine availability. That is when Dr. Shingo became involved to help reduce setups, and they were able to make the Kanban System function smoothly.

There is a chain of logic from a Kanban System to efficiently delivering material Just-In-Time, to a complete overhaul of the plant. This was necessary to ensure stable and reliable production to reducing setup times in order to have sufficient equipment availability. Dr. Shingo shows how interconnected the whole system is. Many of us have been involved with companies that fail to understand this and "put in Kanban" only to see it fail. Dr. Shingo did not see a manufacturing plant as an opportunity to try out new lean tools, but as a complex system with inherent problems that need to be diagnosed and solved one by one.

I think the greatest value of this book is an opportunity to learn how a master sensei thinks about operational improvement. We see how Shingo thought both about macro-improvement of value streams, and micro-process improvement. This is not a book about soft-side issues — people, leadership, and philosophy are notably absent from this book. Dr. Shingo was an engineer's engineer. It is how he looks at the process, the questions he asks, and the solutions based on the philosophy of TPS that he contributes. I should say that the philosophy is implicit in his discussions — which is clearly to strive for excellence. The vision is zero defects and zero inventory, at the lowest possible cost.

Dr. Shingo addresses all the fundamentals of operational excellence like quality principles, one-piece flow, and SMED. He does so in a logical manner, and always with detailed examples and explanations of the reasons why. The photos, diagrams, and explanations make you feel as if you were at the shop floor. I suggest as you read this book you learn from the details, but also step back to reflect on the way of thinking of one of the geniuses behind Lean Manufacturing.

Jeffrey K. Liker
Professor, Industrial and Operations Engineering
University of Michigan

INTRODUCTION

Dr. Shigeo Shingo is perhaps best known as the developer of quick changeover, Poka-Yoke and Non-Stock Production, and as one of the original architects, along with Taiichi Ohno of Toyota, of what has come to be known as Lean Manufacturing. Lean methods have been used world-wide by hundreds, if not thousands of companies in both the manufacturing and service sector to save millions of dollars through the elimination of waste, employee involvement in workplace improvements, and the elimination of defects and errors.

This is by far the most technical of Shingo's books. However, of all of the Shingo books, it gives the reader the most wide-ranging overview of Shingo's contributions to modern industrial engineering and Lean, many not found in any of Shingo's previously published works. To those new to Shingo and his works, this book offers an excellent introduction. To old friends of his concepts, this book not only offers a refresher course, but also unveils approaches to plant improvements like transportation, delay, capacity and flow analysis, not previously available in any English translation of Shingo's works.

A caution for the reader – It would be easy to scour this book for the tools and techniques discussed, and not for what Dr. W. Edwards Deming called "profound knowledge." Too much of what passes for Lean Manufacturing today is not what Shingo calls "fundamental improvement", but the somewhat "incidental" improvement that comes from the blind application of Lean Manufacturing tools. Consultants sell and teach these techniques using wonderful simulations and games, and students go back to the plant floor or the office and try to apply them without understanding their own production or business system, its components and the interactions between those components. Lean efforts either partially succeed or fail entirely and executives are left wondering if Lean is nothing more than the soup du jour.

Why don't other consultants have the level of success of an industrial engineering genius like Shingo? Why can't we all just go to a seminar or two, go back to our workplaces and apply the various formulaic techniques of Lean to achieve the same degree of success? Can it all be blamed on "Resistance to Change" or "Lack of Management Support?"

To find the answer (or an answer) to these questions, one needs to look beyond the titles of Shingo's books and improvement tools and focus on the actual work that Shingo did. This is best revealed in the case studies of Shingo's consulting work cited in this and other books.

The wise reader will look at each consulting case study and realize that:

1) Shingo first sought to thoroughly understand the system of production of his consulting clients – the upstream and downstream processes and their interaction. Clearly he was a pioneer of systems thinking.

2) He went to the Gemba, or the workplace, to see for himself the system in operation to thoroughly understand the "problem", how the system produced the problem, and why, despite their best intentions, his clients were blind to the cause of the problem, and consequently, to its solution. Shingo therefore understood that the "problem" encountered was unique to that system.

3) Understanding the uniqueness of the problem, Shingo then "invented" a unique solution, one that fit the system, its components and their interaction. It's my guess, although Shingo does not provide any documented follow-up, that the solution did not produce the unintended consequences of a lot of improvement efforts, and, once implemented, was met with little resistance from the client and the client's employees.

Shingo kept journals of his work with clients, later analyzing the results and by applying inductive reasoning, generalized similar specific solutions into the concepts of Poka-Yoke, SMED, Non-Stock Production and others, and published and taught these concepts so that others might begin to apply what he had experienced, learned and developed as an industrial engineer and consultant.

The wise reader will recognize though, that if labels like SMED, Poka-Yoke and Non-Stock Production did not exist, the true genius of Shingo is revealed. That genius does not lie in applying techniques. It lies instead in a thorough understanding of a problem and the system, components and interactions that created it, to form a unique, elegant and systemic solution.

What message should the Lean practitioner take away from this book?

1) Learn your system of production and business, the set

of sequential processes that comprise its structure. Start at the beginning, whether that beginning is a customer purchase order, a newly written insurance policy, the admission of a patient to a hospital, or a concept for a new product. Understand each sequential process as order becomes product delivered to the customer's dock, the policy becomes a claim and the claim becomes a payment, the admitted patient receives treatment and is discharged, the concept becomes the new product.

2) Understand the interaction of upstream and downstream processes, how products, materials, and data flow through the system.

3) Look at the "problem" as a product or a by-product of the structure and interaction of processes. Whether that problem involves delays in processing, defects and mistakes, excess inventory, or some other phenomenon, understand that it is uniquely created by the system.

4) Go to the "actual place" and see the problem for yourself. Talk to everyone connected with the process. Again, realize that the problem is unique to the system. Don't for a moment believe that you've seen the same problem before.

5) Forget all the Lean, Six Sigma and other tools and techniques you know.

6) Based upon what you've learned about the system, try your hand at inventing the unique solution that fits the unique problem and the system that produced it. That solution may involve what you already know, perhaps a combination of tools and techniques, perhaps something that doesn't yet have a label for, perhaps something profound.

Follow these six steps and maybe, if you're lucky, or if you're highly skilled, you might get a glimpse into the genius of Shigeo Shingo.

Jeremy Green, Ph.D., LSSMBB, Board Director
Emerald Valley High Performance Consortium
Eugene, Oregon

A Note from the Publisher

Every other year, since Dr. Shingo's passing in 1990, I would visit Fujisawa, Japan, and would have lunch with his wife, Umeko. Mrs. Shingo would normally take us to a marvelous restaurant; and embarrass me by never allowing me to pay for it. On a recent visit, Umeko did two wonderful things, in addition to dinning with us, she gave me one of Dr. Shingo's Japanese scrolls and also all of his old books not yet translated into English. Two years ago Collin McLoughlin, from Enna, and I published the first of these books, *Kaizen and the Art of Creative Thinking*. This book teaches the fundamentals of problem solving, similar to the P-course taught to 3,000 Toyota managers and engineers. Now, we are very pleased to publish this second book.

Hopefully before the end of this year or early next we will bring you the last of Dr. Shingo's books.

It was November 1981, on a study mission to Japan, when the plant manager, Mr. Ohta, gave me a sheet of paper with the words *The Study of the Toyota Production System from an Engineering Viewpoint* (the Green book), by Shigeo Shingo. At first, I had no idea what the paper was referring to or why Mr. Ohta gave it to me. A few hours later, in Tokyo, I called the Japan Management Associations (JMA), mentioned on the paper, to find out about the *Study*. They told me it was a book just published that month. I ordered two copies, gave one to Jack Warne, VP at Omark Industries, and both of us read the book on the airplane going back from Japan to the states.

It was the first book published in English to give the details about how the Toyota Production System worked and could be applied at other companies. After reading the book, Jack and I did the exact same thing; we ordered 500 copies of the book. Jack gave copies to all of his managers and engineers, asking them to read the book in study groups to determine how they could apply the principles at Omark. Within one year, from reading the book and applying it, Omark became the best Lean company in America; drastically reducing their inventory, re-arranging the manufacturing lines, and substantially reducing their manufacturing costs.

I sold the 500 copies of the book through my Productivity Newsletter. The Green book was difficult to read, often repetitive, called 'Janglish,' but it was very powerful for it gave us a deep understanding what Toyota was doing to be so successful. Eventually, we sold over 35,000 copies and also had the book retranslated into better English.

The following year, I want to Japan, stayed at the New Otani hotel in Tokyo, to attend a JMA conference and heard both Mr. Taiichi Ohno and Dr. Shingo speak. I introduced myself to Dr. Shingo and invited him to come to America to speak at my Productivity the American Way conferences and to visit a number of manufacturers. He agreed and for the next ten years, Dr. Shingo would visit the United States at least twice a year, lecture to thousands of managers and visit dozens of companies.

Omark very cleverly set up their own Shingo prize and had their plants each year compete against each other. At the end of each year, Dr. Shingo, on his trips to America, would visit the best Omark plant to give out the award. On one of the early trips he went from an Omark plant in Wisconsin to a Productivity workshop in Toronto. On his return to Detroit for his next consulting assignment, he was confronted by US Immigration and prevented from re-entering the states. I was frantic for in the next two weeks, we had many events lined up for Dr. Shingo. Not knowing really what to do, I called the White House and the head of the US Immigration and finally convinced an agent to let him in. "He is saving America billions and you want to keep him out. It is absurd," I shouted. "Will I get into trouble?" "If you don't let Dr. Shingo get across the border in the next few minutes, I wouldn't want to be in your shoes," I replied. Within minutes, Dr. Shingo was allowed back into the United States.

On his first visit here, we went to a Dresser Industries plant, manufacturing gasoline pumps. The plant manager gave us a tour of the plant and Dr. Shingo stopped in front of a punch press and watched a worker pick up a sheet of metal, place it into the press, press two buttons with both hands to activate the press, and remove the formed metal. Dr. Shingo asked the engineers around us to determine the value adding ratio. One engineer said, "100%," another said "75%" and another said, 50%." Dr. Shingo laughed and said only 17% of the time was value being added. "Only when the metal is pressed by the dies is value being added," he said. Then, turning to the group around him, he said, "What can you do to increase the value adding ratio?"

One engineer said, "We could put the metal on a platform, level to the press, that would rise automatically when a sheet was removed." "We could put a spring in the press to automatically eject the formed metal," said another engineer. "Great, do it!" said Dr. Shingo.

A great lesson for me was to learn now to ask instead of always telling people what to do.

A few minutes later, we stood in front of another press, which historically would take two hours to do a change-over. Dr. Shingo told them to do the change over in less then 10 minutes. Everyone laughed and some mumbled, "impossible." In the next 30 - 40 minutes, Dr. Shingo gave them many hints to speed up the change-over process. He then challenged them and told them he would come back in two hours to watch them do a change-over. He came back later, took out a stopwatch (something every IE should have in his/her pocket) and told them to proceed. They did a change-over in exactly 12 minutes. With a frown on his face, he said, "I told you to do it in less then 10 minutes." Again we all laughed.

Dr. Shingo asked me to publish his other books in English and to have them also done in other languages. The first translation and publishing project I did was *A Revolution in Manufacturing The SMED System* (the White book). Frankly, I did not know what I was doing. I had no idea what it would cost to publish the book. I paid for two translations, the first done in Japan was unusable, the second by Drew Dillon was superb; including the illustrations and editing, it cost over $100,000. If I knew in advance, I probably would not have gambled, but as they say, "ignorance is bliss." The book eventually sold over 100,000 copies and represented close to $10,000,000 in business for Productivity Inc. I would guess that this White book has been the most important book ever in terms of the money saved by the world's industries, probably hundreds of billions of dollars.

There has been a foolish argument over Dr. Shingo's worth to Toyota, but surely there should be none where it comes to how

Dr. Shingo has helped the world. He was absolutely dedicated to teaching us. He knew what the information was worth to the industry but never cared how much he got paid. Even his poor health would not prevent him from coming to America and visiting his clients in Japan. Mrs. Shingo would travel with him, pushing his wheel chair and making sure he got his Japanese food.

One year he was to keynote the APICS conference in Las Vegas. Early that morning, I came to his room to help him to the stage. I bought four bananas for him to use in his introduction, but without any breakfast, I ate one of the bananas. He stood up in front of the 3,000 attendees, turned, looked at me sitting behind him and told the audience that he was devastated for he had based his speech on four bananas and this Bodek had eaten one, messing up his calculations. My face became bright red and after the roar from the crowd, he told them that we shouldn't have to pay for the skin of a banana. The banana skin is a waste. He said the same about manufacturing, "We shouldn't charge our customers for our wastes."

His next book was *Zero Quality Control Source Inspection and the Poka-Yoke System* (the Gold book). Here he wanted to teach us that zero defects was not a myth but a reality, if we enlisted every single worker to create very simple devices to prevent defects from ever leaving the plant. He claimed that he had clients in Japan that never allowed a defect to pass on to the customer. When you start to apply these principles you begin to understand the validity of Dr. Shingo's pronouncements.

He liked to tell the story of one client being berated by a new customer for not having quality charts up on the walls of the plant. The president said to his new prospect, "Why do we need quality charts when we produce no defects?"

A year ago, I taught Poka-Yoke to a Gulfstream plant in Mexicali, Mexico with over 1,000 employees; within one year their employees developed and applied 4,000 Poka-Yoke devices to eliminate defects from the production process.

Next came the Blue book *The Sayings of Shigeo Shingo - Key Strategies for Plant Improvement*. This was a fun book filled with many of his thoughts on process improvement.

Around this time, knowing Dr. Shingo's value to the world, I tried, unsuccessfully, to get him the Nobel Prize for Economics. Maybe they declined, since Mr. Nobel was famous for blowing things up by using nitroglycerin, while Dr. Shingo was noted for improving productivity and quality, were diametrically opposite in values. But fortunately, shortly later, I met Dr. Vern Buehler at Utah State University who agreed to do his best to get Shingo an honorary doctorate degree and to also establish the Shingo Prize for Manufacturing Excellence.

At least once a year, Dr. Shingo would hand me a Japanese language book of his and tell me to publish it in English. So without any thought or hesitation, I did, and then came the Black book, *Non-Stock Production: The Shingo System for Continuous Improvement*. This Black book was not easy to read but of very great value and I hope it is on the reading list of every management and engineering school in America.

Those doubters to Dr. Shingo's participation in Toyota's Success should read all of his books. A few years back, when Mr. Toyoda, chairman of Toyota, was in China at the dedication of a new Toyota plant, he turned to Ritsuo Shingo, president of Toyota China, and said, "Without your father's help Toyota would surely not be where we are today."

Around the early 1990's we published two other books of Shingo's, *The Shingo Production Management System - Improving Process Functions* and, *Modern Approaches to Manufacturing Improvement: The Shingo System (Manufacturing & Production.)* This later book, edited by Professor Alan Robinson, was a compilation of Shingo's earlier books to be used especially by college students.

I asked Dr. Shingo at lunch in Fujisawa, a few months before he died, "Who invented The Toyota Production System, you or

Mr. Ohno?" "I did for I was Ohno's teacher," he replied. And according to Mrs. Shingo, Ohno directly contacted Dr. Shingo and asked him to come and teach at Toyota. I concur on Dr. Shingo's statement for he conceived, in the 1940's, the idea that operations were separate from process allowing, Ohno and others to understand the need to focus on the elimination of all non-value adding wastes. I do not intend in any way to deny the power and genius of Mr. Ohno, who conceived most of the concepts that built the Toyota system.

I once asked Nakao and Iwata, they brought the Kaizen Blitz to the West and worked for over 10 years with both Dr. Shingo and Mr. Ohno, "Who created JIT, Shingo or Ohno?" Their answer, "Which came first the chicken or the egg?"

What I especially like from Dr. Shingo's books is that he likes to teach us from his experiences, from his stories. I once took him to Grenville Phillips in Boulder Colorado, a manufacturer of vacuum testing equipment. Dan Bills, the president, asked Dr. Shingo to go through their entire production process from design to shipping. It was taking them four days to produce a product and the defect rate in final inspection came to 97%.

Each department presented problems to Dr. Shingo and he would start off with the five "whys," getting the engineers and managers to think about the root causes of their problems. Many of the defects were produced by a woman inserting chips into the IC boards, and then placing the boards into the solder. First, Dr. Shingo asked why the lights in the room were so bright. "Because so many of our errors originate from this process we raise the lighting to help the operator's see." "But, the bright lights create glare on top of the board; you want light to come from the bottom of the board to see the holes more clearly," he said.

He then looked at the solder baths and asked, "What could cause errors from soldering?" One engineer said, "Changes in the temperature." "Right," Dr. Shingo said, "But what would cause the temperature to change?" After further investigation they determined that the solid solder, instead of slowly entering into the solder bath would drop in chunks causing the temperature to drop. Their answer was to reduce the incline so that the solder would continuously be feed into the bath.

Dr. Shingo spent three days at the company. Three months later the lead time dropped from four months to four days and their defect rate was reduced from 97% to 3%. Yes, just careful study his books and get groups of people to read them chapter by chapter and ask each other, "How can we apply his knowledge here?"

Please use this book, in your teams, and follow Dr. Shingo's advice and Do it! You will surely see the miracles happen.

Norman Bodek
Co-Publisher

RECOGNITION

One of many memorable encounters from my years of traveling with Shigeo Shingo took place at a sprawling aircraft manufacturing plant in Missouri. Our hosts had paid lavishly for Dr. Shingo's visit and although they claimed they wanted his help in solving a changeover problem, they seemed eager most of all to impress him. Even though Shingo asked that he be taken immediately to the site of the problem, the plant manager insisted on giving him a tour to dazzle him, apparently, with the might and magnificence of his manufacturing facilities.

Shingo didn't dazzle easily. He loathed, in particular, being expected to admire technology because it was big or fast or expensive and he wasn't bashful on this occasion about letting our hosts know how he felt. As the plant manager launched into ecstatic praise for a massive milling machine, Shingo waved his hand to cut him short.

"I've seen big machines before," said Shingo. "Unless you have some problem with this one, I don't want to hear about it."

The manager was undeterred. "We're getting to that," he replied. "I just thought you'd like to see some of our equipment along the way." Shingo turned to me and uttered a sharp remark that he immediately asked me not to translate into English. Then he started walking away.

"All right," said our guide, capitulating. "We'll show you where we'd like some help." And we all began walking again.

A minute or so later, though, Shingo abruptly halted in front of an automatic stamping press whose operator was sitting on a chair next to the machine.

Shingo turned to the plant manager and exploded. "Who told that operator to do his job like that?" he demanded. "There's nothing wrong," our guide answered. "He's one of our best operators. He's monitoring the machine to make sure it runs well."

"Nonsense!" Shingo barked. "You don't make a machine run well by watching it. You're wasting that man's valuable skills!"

The plant manager reddened and fell silent. For once, he had no ready answer and seemed almost chastened. Yet it was unclear that he had grasped what Shingo was getting at. In Shingo's view, the real waste wasn't in the monetary loss of paying a man to do something unnecessary. It was in failing to separate mechanical functions and human functions, with the attendant loss of potential and demeaning of both worker and management.

"Idiots!" Shingo muttered to me as we walked away. Then

he added, "Don't bother to translate that. They wouldn't understand."

It was a striking image: a small man in a dark suit seeing through to the essence of things.

Dr. Shigeo Shingo was a romantic. He was very much a realist, too, of course. No one who ever met him could doubt that. He knew nuts and bolts better than anyone and unfailingly impressed those who met him by his casual mastery of particular techniques and technologies. At the end of the day, though, the practical business of improvement always, for Shingo, came down to matters of principles and ideals: scientific thinking, zero defects, zero inventory, instant changeovers.

Shingo was a romantic in the deep sense that he pursued perfection with single-minded passion. Rejecting as complacency the smug "realism" of engineers and managers who specialize in knowing what *can't* be done, Shingo looked beyond the world of best fits and relative advantages to show us the way to perfection, how to change machines over instantly and eliminate defects entirely. Of the little English he spoke, his favorite phrase, it seemed, was "fundamental change."

Even some of Shingo's most successful disciples and heirs shrank from the master's insistence on perfection. Yoshiki Iwata, when asked about Shingo's concept of "non-stock production," smiled indulgently. "I have never seen a production system without inventory," he said.

Yet Shingo, the super-realist, returned to ideals again and again.

For him, specific improvements were merely tokens of broader and deeper principles that apply to the improvement of any process. He wrote books filled with examples, but had no intention of keeping anyone dependent on recipes or "best practices." Shingo wrote, consulted and lectured to help others internalize powerful underlying ways of thinking and seeing that, in the end, are more powerful than any recipe.

Dr. Shigeo Shingo liked to tell that his career was decided in 1929 when he read in Frederick Winslow Taylor's *Principles of Scientific Management*, that the close study of work could improve the lives both of workers and their employers.

There is deep irony here, for while the "Scientific Management" movement spearheaded by Taylor led American industry to unprecedented gains in productivity, it also helped poison labor relations in America for many decades. In Japan, meanwhile, the ideas of Taylor traced a rather different path, where the uncritical worship of "efficiency" became overshadowed by the ideal of *kaizen*, or "improvement," that is to say, the elimination of work elements from which no one benefits.

Shingo didn't talk much about Taylor's many and extravagant failings, although he recognized that "scientific management," for all its promise, had in large measure devolved into a scheme for burdening workers and enriching consultants. In the end, Shingo's sympathies lay far less with Taylor than with Frank B. Gilbreth, who sought to determine the "one best way" to perform any given task and who, unlike Taylor, insisted that workers be full partners in the improvement of work. Shingo considered himself a Gilbreth disciple, striving always to make work, not faster, but easier.

A reflexive concern for workers permeates Shingo's work and teachings. His impatience with the swaggering plant manager in Missouri underscored the respect and solicitousness with which he treated workers on the shop floor.

Shingo emphasized, for example, that the success of *kaizen* — nowadays we would call it successful *lean* — depends on the fulfillment of three conditions:

1. Top management must be firmly committed and personally involved in continuous improvement.
2. Organizational mechanisms must be established to ensure that *kaizen* is promoted and sustained throughout the company.
3. The benefits of improvement must, in some form or anoth-

er, be returned to everyone in the company.

This "third key" of Shingo's is essential to his teachings. One doesn't hear about it much these days about it or, more perhaps accurately, one hears about it far more than one observes it practice. For whatever reason, lip service paid to the "wisdom of the shop floor" and to "respect for people" often finds ways to reconcile itself with the impulse to eliminate jobs and make people work faster.

Dr. Shigeo Shingo would be appalled.

But he would also be optimistic. His faith in the ultimate triumph of reasonableness was a glorious strength and he communicated it powerfully in person and in his writings. The book you are holding in your hands, like all of Shingo's works, is a call to practical idealism.

Shingo's motivating ideals are particularly relevant at a time when lean ideas and practices are flooding into health care, green enterprises, education and other domains where goals explicitly and necessarily transcend mere profit. Indeed, in these realms, too, it is easy to imagine the master still leading the charge, exhorting us to put aside quibbling over our shrinking portions and to get to work making the pie bigger for everyone.

Andrew Dillon
Former Translator/Interpreter for Dr. Shigeo Shingo

ACKNOWLEDGEMENTS

We would like to acknowledge the hard work of the following people: Satomi Umehara, for the precision of her translation from the original Japanese text; Tracy S. Epley, for his careful editing of the manuscript; and, Khemanand Shiwram for the design layout and his faithful reproduction of the original illustrations. We would also like to acknowledge our indebtedness to Mrs. Umeko Shingo, wife of Dr. Shingo, for discovering this book for us.

Collin McLoughlin and Norman Bodek
Co-publishers

I FUNDAMENTAL APPROACH TO IMPROVEMENT

There are two types of improvement: fundamental and incidental. In many cases when an improvement is implemented it does not address the real cause of a problem, only its symptoms. Yet people are content with it.

1.1 Drying Asbestos Threads

R Industries had an operation where asbestos threads used for clutch facings were soaked in resin and dried. The order of operation was as follows:

- Immerse asbestos threads in resin
- Eliminate excess resin by pressing the threads between two rollers
- Run the threads through the drying oven

There was a problem with this operation: since asbestos

threads have short fibers that are easy to sever, strong pressure could not be applied during squeezing process. As a result, the resin in the fibers was not adequately extracted after pressing.

To solve this problem the company sought a way to boost the drying ability of their oven. I visited the shop floor to add to my understanding of the situation. What I observed is shown in Figure 1.1. During this visit I was told of several improvement ideas the company had:

- Increase the oven temperature
- Install a fan in the oven
- Slow down the speed of the threads in the oven
- Increase the size of the oven by 50 percent

As we talked more about the issue it became clear to me that the threads were absorbing excessive resin—about 150 percent of what was necessary—in the immersion process. This realization spawned an idea. To demonstrate my idea I asked to conduct the following test (Figure 1.1 b):

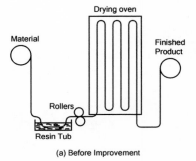

(a) Before Improvement

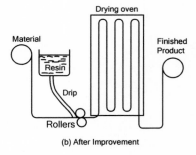

(b) After Improvement

Figure 1.1 Drying Asbestos Threads

- Drip the resin on the threads so that only the necessary amount is applied
- Use the rollers to evenly distribute the resin on the threads

This experiment was successful. Since the asbestos was not soaked in the resin the drying oven was able to completely dry the threads without any modifications to the drying process

This example shows that there are two types of approaches to improvement:

- Incidental: Use excess resin and compensate by improving the drying ability (addresses a symptom — inadequate drying)
- Fundamental: Use a precise amount of resin so that the threads can be dried with the current system (addresses the fundamental cause — too much resin)

1.2 Matching Wood Grain

One of the operations in plywood production that requires great experience and skill is matching the grain of two adjoining pieces of fascia veneer.

Fascia veneer is produced as follows:

- The log is peeled into a sheet of veneer on a rotary lathe
- The veneer is cut into pieces while avoiding knots and splits on the log
- Cut veneers are dried in a dryer
- As heating contracts veneers, cut the end pieces to make uniform
- Veneers with the same grain are sorted and placed together

Only veneers with matching grains can be used as fascia while mismatched veneers have only limited use as a backing. Correspondingly, the price of non-matching veneers is considerably lower. Throughout the cutting and drying operation, the different grades of veneers were often mixed together. This led to a critical step in the operation — sorting the veneers to properly separate those with matching grains. Since this task required the highly sophisticated skill of memorizing wood grain pattern only a limited number of people could do this job.

Since I had previously consulted with a woodworking company, I remembered that wood grains from the same circumference area have the same grain patterns throughout. Based on this knowledge I suggested a different approach.

In general a log has three or four knots and/or splits around its circumference. If there are three of them, divide the veneers in groups that correspond with the knots or splits, as seen below in Figure 1.2:

- Veneers between 1 and 2: A
- Veneers between 2 and 3: B
- Veneers between 3 and 1: C

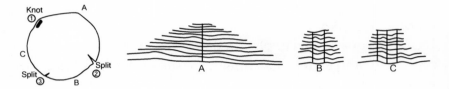

Figure 1.2 Veneer Groupings

After cutting, pile the veneers according to group A, B, or C, and maintain these groupings after each process. In order to prevent mix-ups, I devised a color-code for each group: one red line on the side of pile A, two blue lines on the side of pile B, and three green lines on the side of C.

As a result, the task of matching wood grains became much easier. The skills required for the modified operation were reduced from memorizing grain patterns to simply matching up one panel with the next. This change not only accelerated the work significantly, but also opened up the job to relatively inexperienced workers.

In the past the company had many ideas for improving the operation, among which were creating a different storage area for veneers without matches, and placing the veneers on turn-tables to facilitate handling. However, these ideas were not designed to address the cause of the problem, but merely to address its consequences or symptoms. Only by doing the latter and attacking the problem at its foundation can truly effective improvement ideas come about.

1.3 Cutting Sheathed Heater Terminals
Many electrical heaters are "sheathed heaters." A typical struc-

ture of one is shown in Figure 1.3. These kinds of heaters are produced as follows:

- Insert a heating element into a metal pipe and fill the inside with insulation powder
- Pack the powder in tightly
- The added pressure inside the pipe causes the coiled heating wire to stretch, leaving excess wire extending from either end of the pipe; cut both ends to make uniform
- Use a file and smooth out burrs created from cutting

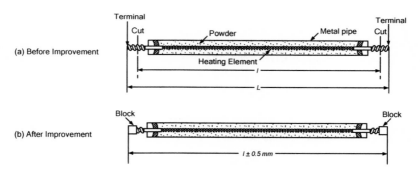

Figure 1.3 Cutting Sheathed Heaters

The heater company I was consulting for was looking for a way to simplify this process and to reduce the time it took to deburr the coil wires.

After visiting the shop floor and observing the process for a while I said to the foreman, "Do you know there's a way to completely eliminate deburring?"

"Eliminate deburring? What sort of cutting method could do that?"

"One that doesn't cut at all.'"

"Then how do you make the wire length uniform?"

"You keep the wire from expanding in the first place," I said and explained the method shown in Figure 1.3 (b). "Blocks" are placed inside the terminals to keep the wire from extending too far from the ends of the pipe. After a quick test, we found that the length of the wire was always within 0.5mm, an acceptable limit. Therefore, cutting was unnecessary with this new method.

In this case there were three improvements:

> Deburr using a better method
>
> Cut in a way that minimizes burrs
>
> Create a method that does not create burrs in the first place

Which improvement do you think addresses the root cause of the problem?

1.4 Applying Resin On Glass Wool

At one company, containers were manufactured by stacking glass wool in several layers as follows:

- Apply glass wool inside the outer case
- Apply resin on top
- Press out any air bubbles manually with a roller

The last step of removing trapped air bubbles was important: if any air bubbles remained, the strength of the container decreased significantly. Since resin is highly viscous, bubbles often just moved around or broke into smaller pieces under the roller.

Some suggestions were made to improve this process, such as rolling out bubbles mechanically instead of manually.

When I went to the shop floor, I talked with the foreman.

"It sounds like you're focusing on improving the rolling process, but I don't think that's the best approach" I said.

"What makes you say that? If we improve the rolling process, we should get better results."

"Wouldn't the best approach be to ensure that bubbles don't form in the first place."

"How is that possible? How do you keep bubbles from forming," he asked.

I told him that the order of applying glass wool and resin should be switched. The conventional method was to apply resin to a layer of glass wool. The new method was simply to apply the resin, followed by the glass wool, and then apply pressure to the wool with a roller.

Since this method places resin underneath the glass wool, it was very easy to keep air from being trapped. As a result of this discovery, the company was able to produce higher quality containers much more efficiently.

1.5 Low Volume — Mixed Model & Build to Order Production

Two of the most difficult types of production to manage efficiently are low volume — mixed model production, and build to order production. Since low volume — mixed model production requires frequent changeovers, reducing the *number* of setup changeovers is difficult. The *time* required for changeovers, however, can be reduced drastically when Single Minute Exchange of Die, or SMED (explained in a later chapter), is used. According to a survey of 400 companies that introduced SMED, the average setup changeover time was reduced by 95 percent. A setup which used to take two hours now takes only 6 minutes; an hour to three minutes.

At the companies surveyed, SMED was used for a variety of machines including metal presses, die-casting machines, plastic molding machines, machine tools, and wood working machines. In a very successful case, the setup time of an injection molder was reduced 98 percent from 6 hours and 40 minutes to a mere 5 minutes and 35 seconds.

As illustrated in the above examples, it is possible to dramatically decrease the changeover time required for low volume — mixed model production environments. In doing so, the difficulties associated with low volume — mixed model production, can be eased accordingly.

As for build to order production, difficulties always lie in balancing "*D* and *P*."

D stands for *delivery time*, the period from order to delivery. *P* stands for *production time*, the actual time it takes to manufacture a product. If a part of the production is outsourced, the production time at the subcontracted factory is also counted as part of *P*.

Having *D* less than *P* is problematic — for example, if a product is ordered for delivery within ten days but takes 15 days to produce, it obviously cannot be delivered when it is required. To avoid this, there are two preventive measures factories commonly take.

- Anticipate orders and carry work in process stock. Once the order is placed, complete the products. As in Figure 1.4 (b), the production period after the order, *P*, is now shorter than the delivery period *D*.

- Anticipate orders and carry stock of completed products. Production period *P* is zero in this case, so the delivery deadline can be anytime.

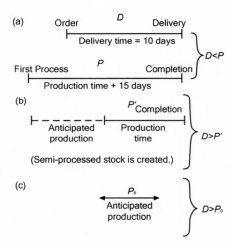

Figure 1.4 Relation Between D & P

These measures provide an effective way to meet delivery dates. However, the resulting increases in stock and decreases in cash flow both negatively impact the company. Moreover, if the production order forecast were incorrect, the company would lose its investment through work in process and finished goods inventory. This problem could be minimized by standardizing parts and products, so that they can be used for multiple purposes.

All of these approaches are based on the notion that a drastic cut to production time is impossible. But is that really the case?

Production time can be broken into two parts: processing time and process delay. According to a survey, 20 to 40 percent of production time is spent for processing; the remaining 80 to 60 percentages are spent for process delay. Therefore, if delay can be cut back to one third, it is quite possible and relatively easy to cut the production cycle in half.

In addition to process delay, there is one more type of delay hidden in production time — lot delay. That can be explained as follows:

- Process delay: An entire lot is waiting for the next process
- Lot delay: The entire lot, except for the one piece being processed, is waiting either processed or unprocessed

Lot delays are unavoidable in large lot production. However, as shown in Figure 1.5 b, it can be reduced if the lot size is decreased. And it can be minimized by reducing the lot size to just one.

As shown in Figure 1.5 b, the ratio of the time required for a one-piece flow production over that of the production time for regular lot production can be expressed as follows:

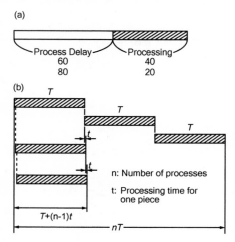

Figure 1.5 Production Period & Wait Time

$$\frac{T + (n-1)t}{nT} = \frac{1}{n}$$

(T: processing time for one lot through a process n: number of processes, t: processing time for one piece. In general, $(n-1)\,t$ is negligible compared with T.)

By switching to a one–piece flow production, the production cycle time can be reduced to $1/n$ of the cycle time for lot production. In other words, if production with five processes were changed to a one–piece flow production, its cycle would be one fifth of the time taken for a regular lot production.

By introducing one-piece flow production, Y Auto Body succeeded in cutting back their production cycle from 20 days to five days. In addition to reducing production cycle time, Y Auto Body also solved a chronic problem of bloated inventories.

D Industries also introduced one–piece flow production to their press operation and was able to reduce work in process by 90 percent. Afterward, the company never missed another delivery deadline.

Many factories believe that carrying work in process inventory is the best way to deal with short delivery periods and other unexpected factors of production. However, simultaneously shortening the production cycle *and* reducing work in process inventory is actually a far better and more fundamental approach.

CHAPTER ONE SUMMARY

When dealing with improvements on the factory floor, we tend to focus only on superficial aspects of problems rather than digging deeper to the core. However, if we do not think about the purpose that lies beyond the obvious, thorough improvements can never be achieved. It is important ask "Why" at least five times, such as "Why is this operation necessary?" Fundamental improvement becomes possible only after seeking out the true cause of problems.

II FUNDAMENTAL APPROACHES TO PLANT IMPROVEMENT

In many cases when plant improvement is conducted, only visible phenomena are dealt with. As a result, improvement is superficial and further improvement becomes necessary. To counteract this phenomena it is important to have a solid understanding of the entire system of production first in order to go beyond the superficial and carry out improvement that is fundamental and lasting.

2.1 Structure of Improvement
2.1.1 The Difference Between Driving and Repairing a Car

When I had an Industrial Engineering Seminar at Y Auto Motors, I said to the participants, "Please raise your hand if you know how to drive."

All 40 participants raised their hands immediately. I was impressed until I remembered that I was at an auto maker.

"Please raise your hand," I continued, "if you think you could fix any car problem." Only two hands were raised.

"So, you can fix anything?" I asked one of the two.

"Yes, I'm a mechanic," he said. His answer triggered laughter from the crowd.

Obviously, driving skills and mechanical skills are two very different things. Let us take a closer look at these skills to see what really sets them apart:

- Driving: Knowing rules and procedures of the road
- Repair: Understanding the essential aspects of
    1. Structure.
    2. Functionality of each part.
    3. Interaction between parts.

Repair work requires much more knowledge. In addition to structure and functionality it is crucial to understand the interaction between parts, as in "if A changes, B also changes accordingly."

Assume that there was an engine stall. In this case it is necessary to check the following:

Fuel–related check

- Is gasoline reaching the injectors
- Are the injectors functioning correctly
- Is there gasoline is the tank

Electrical–related check

- Is the distributor functioning correctly
- Is the alternator functioning correctly
- Are the spark plugs functioning correctly

Take the human body as an example. Everyday we use our bodies as we see fit. However, if we get sick or injured, we go to a doctor for help. We do this because doctors understand the structure of the body, the functionality of each part, and how the parts interact. Most of us who are not doctors are completely ignorant about these aspects of our own body. Knowing how to use one's body and knowing how to treat an injury are very different, just as driving a car and being able to repair it are different. However, we sometimes entertain the delusion that since we can drive, making repairs should be easy.

The same can be said with respect to improving plant operations. People sometimes falsely assume that since they operate a factory everyday, fixing problems and making improvements should also be as easy. In reality, if we are serious about true plant improvement, we have to start by understanding the entire system of production.

2.1.2 System of Production
Production consists of two interwoven actions called, "processes" and "operations."

Processes: The action of raw materials into finished products (flow of items).

Operation: The actions of people and machines on materials (flow of people).

In this sense, the structure of production can be explained as a network of processes and operations.

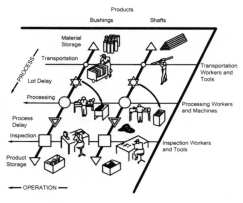

Figure 2.1 Structure of Production

Take a look at the example of a process flow below:

1. Raw material is stored.

2. Material is moved to the side of a machine.

3. Material waits by a lathe.

4. Material is processed by lathe operator.

5. Finished products wait.

6. Finished products are inspected.

7. Finished products are stored.

As this shows, materials go through five process steps: processing (raw material to finished products), inspection, transportation, delay, and storage.

An example of an operation flow would be:

1. Material handler A transports pins and bushings.

2. Lathe technician B processes pins and bushings.

3. Inspector C inspects pins and bushings.

In principle, operations consist of the human activity required to process materials into products. However, humans use machines to assist them so any machine activity is also considered to be a part of operation.

This flow of processes and operations exists at any type of plant. Take a look at the processes from a variety of factories below:

- Confectionery plant: a flow in which raw material (corn syrup) changes into final products (candy)
- Food factory: a flow in which raw material (pork) changes into final products (sausages)
- Shipyard: a flow in which raw material (steel plates) changes into a final product (a ship)
- Laundry machine factory: a flow in which raw material (sheet metal) changes into final products (laundry machines)
- Auto factory: a flow in which raw material (steel bars) changes into products (crankshafts and eventually to cars)

No matter what products are manufactured, the concept of processes and operations can always be applied. When problems arise these two channels can always be used to address them.

There is a common misconception regarding operations and processes that I would like to address here. It is sometimes explained that process is a production activity broken into large units, whereas operation is a production activity broken into small units. However, this is not true at all. Whatever the unit of analysis is, an operation is an operation, and a process is a process. For this reason the word "process ability" is not appropriate. The proper term is "the ability of resources (human and machine) to operate a process."

2.1.3 Conflict between Processes and Operations
Although production is the result of processes and operations working together, the two often conflict with one another. Take a look at these cases:

> Factory 1—An order came in with a rush delivery. So the factory stopped production of the products that had been in progress, changed setups, and began on the new order. As a result, overall processing time was longer than necessary. This is an example of processing functions given too much priority over operational functions.

> Factory 2—Since lot sizes were small and setup change-overs were frequent, this factory typically consolidated six months or orders for a product into a single production run This strategy reduced process time, but resulted in processing delays for other products, causing the company to miss delivery deadlines. This is an example of operational functions given too much priority over processing functions.

Problems of unbalanced processes/operations like the above are not uncommon in factories. Those in charge of sales and scheduling in factories tend to think of production from the standpoint of processes, while those working on shop floors always think from the standpoint of operations.

In other words, customers benefit from process activity and factories profit from operational activity. Prioritizing by process means that delivery dates come first. However, in doing so the efficiency of the operation could be adversely impacted. On the other hand, prioritizing by operation gives priority to efficiency.

However, giving too much importance to operational concerns may result in late deliveries to customers.

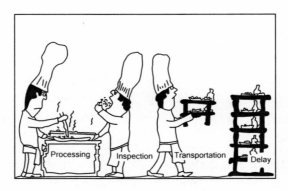

Figure 2.2 Four Functions of a Process

In the end, the key to successful production activity is balancing and creating harmony between process and operation.

2.1.4 Four Phenomena of a Process
A process was explained as an action by which raw materials are transformed into finished products. This transformation is comprised of four phenomena:

1. Processing

    Altering form — changing the shape of an object by some means such as grinding and bending.

    Altering quality — changing the molecular state, or quality of an object by some means such as quenching and tempering.

    Assembly — joining multiple parts into a whole.

    Disassembly — dividing a single item into multiple parts.

2. Inspection

    Compare outputs with quality standards to

avoid making defects.

3. Transportation
   Change in location.

4. Delays
   Process delay: an entire lot is waiting for the next process, while the previous lot is being processed.

   Lot delay: Whenever parts are processed in lots, the entire lot, except for the one piece being processed, is waiting either processed or unprocessed.

Figure 2.3 Inspection, Transportation and Delays

In addition to the four phenomena above, there is the storage of raw materials and finished products. Although these are both types of delays, they are not included here since they are often influenced by outside factors beyond a company's control, and are not purely an issue of production.

Without exception, in every type of a factory — regardless of the size of production, a process will always consists of four phenomena: processing, inspection, transportation, and delays.

2.1.5 Overall and Specific Process Improvement
When improving a process there are two types of approaches: overall and specific improvement.

A. Overall Improvement
As discussed above, a process is made up of processing, inspection, transportation, and delays. Among these four, "processing" is the only element which adds value to the products. The remaining elements of inspection, transportation, and delay, only contribute to in-

creasing costs.

For this reason, the first thing to consider when making improvements is the elimination of inspection, transportation, and delays. Even if we improve methods or use better technology, the very existence of these three factors negatively impacts production efficiency. Therefore we should consider the elimination of these factors, above all else, to be the most fundamental measure of improvement.

B. Specific Improvement

Although the best improvement is to eliminate inspection, transportation, and delays, in reality it is impossible to eliminate them completely. So, after elimination efforts are exhausted, improving specific elements should be our next consideration.

When process improvement is being discussed, people often do not understand that overall and specific improvement are two stages — first overall and then specific. Furthermore, specific improvement is often considered to be the only measure possible, but this is simply not the case. Therefore, we should always be aware of the distinction between these two types of improvement and their order of priority.

2.2 Active and Passive Improvement of a Process

The two stages of process improvement — overall and specific — when viewed from a different angle can also be classified as active and passive. As such, there are active and passive improvements to each aspect of process functions: processing, inspection, transportation, and delay.

2.2.1 Process Desktop Experiment

The following desktop experiment of a process is an effective demonstration of the various phenomena involved in a process, and the meaning of active and passive improvements.

18

(A)

Process	Method	Question	Answer	Worker	Time	Individual time
①	Mental calculation	4 + 7 + 9 + 1 + 3	24			
②	Mental calculation	①X 6 ÷ 7	21			
③	Abacus	②+135 + ①+215 - 328	67			
④	Calculation by writing	③X 4 ÷ 55	5			
⑤	Abacus	④+②+③+ 230 -①	299			
⑥	Mental calculation	⑤X 2	598			
⑦	Mental calculation	⑥÷ 4	150			
⑧	Slide rule	√⑥X⑦	300			

Round off to the nearest whole number

(C)

Process	Method	Question	Answer	Worker	Time	Individual time
①	Mental calculation	9 + 15 + 21 + 14	59			
②	Mental calculation	①X 2 - 58	60			
③	Abacus	②+ ①+411 + 185 - 508	207			
④	Calculation by writing	③÷ 2 X 9	932			
⑤	Abacus	④+ ①+②+ 85 +③	1343			
⑥	Mental calculation	⑤X 4	5372			
⑦	Mental calculation	⑥÷ 6	895			
⑧	Slide rule	⑦X√⑥	65335			

Round off to the nearest whole number

(B)

Process	Method	Question	Answer	Worker	Time	Individual time
①	Mental calculation	15 + 2 + 8 + 13 + 15	53			
②	Mental calculation	①÷ 4 + 15	28			
③	Abacus	310 +②- 58 +①- 70	163			
④	Calculation by writing	③X 12 ÷ 7	279			
⑤	Abacus	①+③+④+ 113 -②	580			
⑥	Mental calculation	⑤÷ ③	193			
⑦	Mental calculation	⑥X 8	1544			
⑧	Slide rule	√⑦X 13	142			

Round off to the nearest whole number

(D)

Process	Method	Question	Answer	Worker	Time	Individual time
①	Mental calculation	18 + 11 + 13 + 9 + 12	63			
②	Mental calculation	(①- 32) X 2	62			
③	Abacus	①+ 811 + 98 -②+ 153	1063			
④	Calculation by writing	(③- 735)	984			
⑤	Abacus	120 + ④+ 318 - 941	484			
⑥	Mental calculation	⑤÷ 7	69			
⑦	Mental calculation	⑥X 3	207			
⑧	Slide rule	√⑦X15	56			

Round off to the nearest whole number

Figure 2.4 Format for Desktop Process Experiment

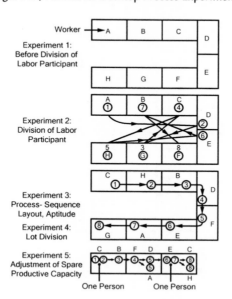

Figure 2.5 Layout for Desktop Process Experiment

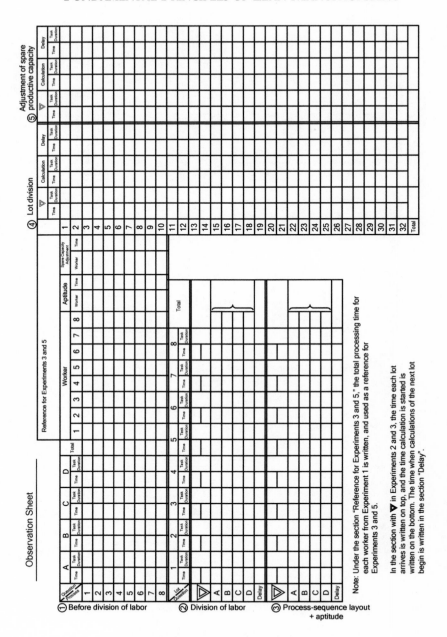

Figure 2.6 Observation Sheet for Desktop Experiment

A. Preparation and Procedure
Preparation:

- Question sheets: 8 sheets x 5 experiments = 40 sheets

As in Figure 2.4, the question sheets are formatted with four sets of mathematical problems: A, B, C, and D. Each set has 8 problems (processes) that must be solved in order since each process can only be completed using the answer from the previous process.

- Workers: 8 people (It is good to assign another 8 people as observers)
- Transportation worker: 1 person
- Planners: 1–3 people (For planning the third and fifth experiment)
- Tools: Stopwatch, slide rule, abacus (eight each), 12 blank sheets of paper (Editor's note: readers wishing to replicate this experiment can substitute a hand calculator for each abacus and a spreadsheet program on a laptop computer for the slide rule)
- Layout: See Figure 2.5
- Others: It is convenient to prepare about 11 observation sheets as shown in Figure 2.6 (Eight for observation and the rest for planning)

Procedure:
Conduct five experiments with different conditions. During each experiment measure the following times:

- Average processing time: average amount of time needed to finish one question
- Average production cycle: average amount of time it took for each question sheet (product) to be completed

B. Implementation of Experiments
Experiment 1 — Before the Division of Labor
Place desks as shown in Figure 2.5 and provide a question sheet for each of the eight workers. Everyone must solve all the questions sequentially, in the order of A 1–8, B 1–8, C 1–8, D 1–8.

When I conducted the experiment, the results were 13 minutes,

53 seconds for both processing time and production cycle (Figure 2.7).

		Time				
		10'	20'	30'	40'	50'
① Before Division of Labor		——— 13'-53"		(Average processing time) (Production time)		
		– – – – ■ 13'-53"				
② Division of Labor (Lot production)		——— ı 9'-22" (67.5%)				
		– – – – – – – – ■ 28'-56" (214%)				
③ Division of Labor (process-sequence layout, Aptitude)		——— 8'-1" (57.5%)ı				
		– – – – – – ■ 22'-7' (160%)				
④ Lot Division		——— 8'-11" (59%)				
		– – – – – – ◄ 20'-12" (146%)				
⑤ Adjustment of Spare Productive Capacity		——— 7'-40" (55%)				
		– – – – ■ 11'-13" (81%)				

Figure 2.7 Results of Desktop Experiment

In this case, all workers used slide rules, abacuses, and blank sheets of paper. The operation rate of these tools was equally low. This experiment also required everyone to use various skills — mental calculations, written calculations, and using a slide rule and abacus. It took some people a very long time to complete certain processes. There were also many calculation mistakes (disparity in quality) within this experiment.

In order to address the problems of low tool operation rate, skill requirements, and overall poor efficiency, we implemented the division of labor in the next experiment.

Experiment 2 — Division of Labor (Lot Production)
British economist Adam Smith explained the benefits of division of labor over 100 years ago.

"The division of labor simplifies labor, allowing workers to acclimate to their jobs much faster. Psychological and physical waste that occurs when workers switch from one job to another are eliminated, leading to heightened efficiency."

In this experiment, workers were arranged randomly as shown in Figure 2.5 and sheets were passed around in the following manner:

Give all eight question sheets to worker A.

Worker A calculates the answer for the first process, a mental calculation, for questions sets A, B, C, and D. After the first sheet is done the transportation worker brings it to worker D, who is in charge of the second process — worker A continues to work only on the first process of the seven remaining sheets.

As the sheets arrive one at a time, worker D works only on the second process for question sets A, B, C, and D.

Repeat this formula with the third process, calculating with the abacus, complete the fourth calculation by writing all the way to the eighth process.

Question sheets were not passed to the next worker unless all four questions, A, B, C, and D, were answered. In this sense, the experiment was a simulation of a four–piece production lot.

The result of this second experiment is shown in Figure 2.7. The average processing time (average individual calculation time) was 9 minutes and 52 seconds, or 67.5 percent of the average process time of the first experiment. The production cycle (the time it took to finish all eight sheets) was 28 minutes and 56 seconds, or 214 percent of the production cycle for the first experiment.

Due to the division of labor, individual processing time became shorter. However, the production cycle more than doubled. This is due to the delay of products, i.e., question sheets, caused by the difference in calculation time between successive processes.

If the calculation time of one process is faster than the next process, the products have to wait. Reversing our perspective, we could also say that the worker on the next process has to wait for the product (the answer) to be completed. The average processing time was shorter even after these delays were taken into consideration.

In addition to the difference in calculation time, there is another cause of the prolonged production cycle. In the first experiment, each person worked on all the processes so the question sheets stayed in one place the whole time. However, when the labor was divided, it became necessary to pass the sheets around to the various workers. In other words, transportation happened as a result of the division of labor.

For this reason if the benefit of the shorter processing time does not overcome the disadvantage of transportation, it is better not to introduce the division of labor. In this case, the processing time was 67.5 percent of the previous experiment.

$$8 \text{ people} \times 0.675 = 5.4 \text{ people}$$

This means that the processing time saved was equivalent to 2.6 people, justifying the use of one transportation worker. This experiment demonstrates that the division of labor has the following advantages and disadvantages:

- Advantages

    Increase in efficiency

    Increase in the machine operation rate

- Disadvantages

    Transportation becomes necessary

    Production cycle becomes longer

One very noticeable aspect of this experiment was the hurried movement of the transportation worker. He was constantly criss–crossing between desks trying to pass around the sheets. Although the division of labor necessitated this transportation, this inefficiency in movement actually stemmed from something else: the inefficient layout of workers.

The random layout increased the frequency of transportation runs, product delays between processes, and contributed to the prolonged production cycle. To address these issues the layout was improved to match the process sequence.

Experiment 3 — Division of Labor, Process–Sequence Layout, Worker Aptitude (Lot Production)
In accordance to the outcome of the first experiment, jobs in this

experiment were assigned to workers according to their aptitude. For example, those who excelled in mental calculations were assigned to processes requiring mental calculations. Worker layout was also changed to match the process sequence as shown in Figure 2.5.3 (p. 19). The procedure for this experiment was now the following:

> Give all eight question sheets to worker C
>
> As in the second experiment, worker C works on only the first process, mental calculation; once the first set of questions A, B, C, and D are done, the transportation worker brings the sheet to the next worker, H
>
> Worker H works only on the second set of questions A, B, C, and D.

Since each question sheet stayed in one place until a worker finished all four questions, this setting is also considered to be a four-piece lot production.

As shown in Figure 2.7, the outcome was as follows (Comparison to the first experiment):

> Average processing time: 57.8 percent reduction
>
> Production cycle: 160 percent increase

Processing time is now 42 percent less than the first experiment, and 10 percent less than the second experiment. This 10 percent was due to assignment of worker by process aptitude. The production cycle is still longer than the first experiment, but is 45 percent less than the second experiment.

This 45 percent reduction stems from the fact that calculation time of processes became more uniform as a result of providing the right jobs to right people, and products flowed from one process to another smoother with less waiting from process to process. Better layout was also a positive factor. Since workers were placed according to the process sequence, the transportation worker moved more efficiently and made fewer mistakes. Product control also became much easier.

Although the outcome was getting more favorable, the product cycle was still longer than the first experiment. This is mainly attributed to the lot production nature of the experiments. Therefore, a one–piece flow system was tried in the next experiment.

Experiment 4 — One–Piece Flow

This experiment is the same as the previous except for one aspect: lot size was reduced from four to one. Each sheet was cut into four pieces A, B, C, and D, and sent around one piece at a time (Figure 2.5 p.19). Since there were eight sheets, 32 small question sheets were created.

> All 32 sheets were given to worker C who is in charge of the first process; as C finished each sheet, it was sent to the following worker.
>
> Sheets were transferred between workers by the transportation worker.

As shown in Figure 2.7 (p. 22), the outcome was as follows (comparison to the first experiment):

> Average processing time: 59 percent increase
>
> Production cycle: 146 percent increase

The processing time was almost the same as the previous experiment, since the conditions of the operation were about the same.

The production cycle was reduced by 14 percent compared to the previous lot production, due to the elimination of lot delays (lot delays are explained in later chapter in detail).

Although these were positive results, there was one downside to this experiment: the number of transportation runs quadrupled.

> 32 sheets x 8 = 256

The transportation worker was required to move the sheets 256 times. This was only possible since the layout matched the process sequence. If it had not matched, carrying out this many runs would have been out of the question.

As this experiment shows, if the lot size is reduced the production cycle becomes shorter. However, since transportation increases significantly, proper measures have to be taken first to take full advantage of the one–piece flow system. The best measure is eliminate transportation by changing the layout, the second best measure is the introduction of a convenient transportation system, such as conveyors.

Experiment 5 — Balancing Out Processing Times

Even in the fourth experiment the production cycle was still longer than the first, which did not employ the division of labor. This was attributed to the wait time between processes. Delays occur mainly because workers in some processes have spare production capacity. A difference in calculation time is a by-product of this unbalance. This fifth experiment was designed to address this issue using the following procedures:

- Although the total number of workers is still eight, assign two workers to processes that take the most time, such as calculation by a slide rule and abacus; for processes that take less time, such as mental calculations, one worker takes charge of two processes
- Eliminate transportation by placing desks side by side — workers simply pass the question sheets to adjacent workers without using the transportation worker

Although worker aptitude was taken into account, the priority in this experiment was to equalize the cycle time of each process. Below was the arrangement (Figure 2.7 p. 22):

Process 1,2 3 4 5 6,7 8

Worker C B F AD E HG

The result of this experiment came out as follows (Comparison to the first experiment):

Average processing time: 55 percent

Production cycle: 81 percent

There was no major difference in the processing time. However, the production cycle finally became shorter than the first experiment, with a reduction of 19 percent.

This was due to the fact that delays between processes were minimized by using previously wasted production capacity and balancing the process cycle times.

This experiment reveals that using spare worker capacity is extremely effective at reducing the production cycle.

SUMMARY

These experiments as a whole can help clarify some important aspects of production:

> After the division of labor was introduced, layout became an important issue; transportation efficiency was dependent on a functional layout.

> Introducing the division of labor while taking into account worker skills greatly reduced processing time.

> Layout and transportation are issues independent of worker skills and division of labor.

> The following measures cut back the production cycle:

>> Using workers spare productive capacity.

>> Decreasing the lot size.

>> Arrange the layout to match the process sequence.

> A reduction of lot size cuts back the production cycle, even though it significantly increases transportation. Therefore, it is important to consider eliminating transportation by changing the layout; consider introducing a better transportation system, such as conveyors.

> Reducing process cycle time is effective in reducing the production cycle, however, using worker spare production capacity to balance cycle times and reducing the lot size have a greater impact.

This desktop experiment on a process has been conducted hundreds of times, in various places, with various people. In some cases the fourth experiment of lot division resulted in a shorter production cycle than the first experiment, without maximizing the labor capacity and eliminating transportation that occurred in the fifth experiment. However, the results were very similar to the experimental examples presented in this text, lending valuable credence as to the validity of the principals listed above.

2.2.2 Active and Passive Improvement of Processing
In 1948, I went to listen to a lecture given by Mr. H. He said, "The mechanical engineering courses in the universities of Japan these days are teaching useless knowledge that leaves their students with the ability to create a bunch of worthless scrap. My company produces motorcycles; when we create a cylinder, we bend a piece of sheet metal and weld the ends. We only use a grinder to polish the joint and only to maintain accuracy.

"However, this is not how cylinder production is taught at school. Instead, the students are taught to create cylinders by casting. After that, they attach the cylinder to a lathe and grind it. This is a very efficient method — of producing scrap.

"Don't you think it's wrong to only focus on cutting while overlooking what's really important, creating final products?"

I could not agree with him more. His comment resonates with the concept of Value Engineering which is gaining popularity now. I am still impressed with his foresight.

True, the purpose of production is to create products, but more important than just making them is ensuring that the products are actually functional as well. In the case of Mr. H's motorcycle cylinders, the products need to be able to withstand exploding gasoline in order to convert the energy into power.

It is unfortunate that we often lose sight of what is really important — the final product — and focus only on the methods used to produce those products. It is essential to maintain a broad perspective and to continually keep this higher purpose of production in the forefront of our minds.

Around 1945, I read an article about a coal mine in a newspaper. When the quality of coal was low at this mine, instead of being dug out, the coal layer was ignited and its energy was extracted as gas. I was impressed with this idea, which also goes along with the concept of Value Engineering.

I once held an industrial engineering course at T Mine in Shikoku, Japan. The director of the mine, who was listening to my lecture very intently, sent me the following letter six months later.

"Our T Copper Mine has been in the red for the past ten years. Directors were changed one after another to revamp the mine, but nothing was effective enough to achieve a turnaround.

"At our company, we used to judge our achievement by mining volume, which is the volume of everything that came out of the mine. Even low quality ore was dug out to meet our target.

"However, as I listened to your lecture, I realized that what really mattered was copper, not mining volume. So I stopped using mining volume as a target. Instead, I started underground sorting. In the past even impurities, which are mostly just rocks, were hauled out to increase the mining volume. Sorting was done outside and impurities were hauled back inside as fill. However, sorting is now done underground and only high-quality ore is carried out. Our mining volume did decrease; however, the wasteful practice of hauling out and returning the impurities was terminated, and the company returned to profitability for the first time in a decade. As an additional bonus, mine car shortages also disappeared."

The mining company's success lied in the realization that a large mining volume, which is a common indicator of good performance, was not their purpose. What was really important was mining copper.

The same idea holds true for processing improvement. Grinding is not the ultimate purpose of production. Hence, focusing on how to improve grinding is only a "passive improvement." Ensuring that the product functions as intended is the ultimate purpose of production. Improving a production method to improve product functionality is what is called "active improvement."

2.2.3 Active and Passive Improvement of Inspections
A. Death Certificate and Health Certificate

When I visit factories I always ask if there are any defects, and if so if I could look over their defect statistics. Statistics usually show a monthly tally of defects such as damaged products, out-of-specification products, and dimensional mistakes. Some are in the form of charts or graphs.

Although they may look impressive they only capture the phenomena of defects, not the cause. For example, these are causes of defects:

Damage: products crushed against each other

Eccentric Products: chucks were not tightened

Dimensional Mistakes: misread measurements

Only by addressing these causes are future defects prevented.

Sometimes, when you go to a meeting to discuss product quality, defect statistics are stacked high upon the table. The discussion is usually based on these statistics and the conversation generally unfold like this:

"The number of defects seems way too high."

"There are various reasons. We'll try to decrease them."

Words and promises are exchanged, but nothing specific is being discussed to address the root cause.

Every time I look at one of these defect statistics I praise it by saying, "You're producing very attractive death certificates." Creating defect statistics is similar to saying how someone died, such as, "That person died from cranial hemorrhaging" or "This person died from a heart attack." Even though it is an accurate diagnosis, it can never bring back the deceased. Diagnosis is only useful when people are alive and they get the benefit of learning what the problem is and how they can address it. The same goes for factories. Just capturing defect phenomena is not enough. Defects will decrease only after their cause is discovered and addressed.

An inspection which separates defects from non–defects is very common. This is a typical death–certificate style inspection.

B. Quality Control in Germany

While studying and touring various companies and factories throughout Germany, a fellow member of my tour group, Mr. M, asked a question at the conclusion of our tour. The answer revealed a profound difference between the way German and Japanese companies operate.

"Do you do quality control at your company?"

"Of course we do," said the chief engineer.

"I didn't see any control charts during the tour."

"Control charts? What are they?"

Mr. M then proudly explained what control charts were.

The engineer said, "I see. That's very interesting, but I have to say that the use of control charts seems to be based on a less than ideal premise."

"Less than ideal premise? What makes you say that?"

"If I understood you correctly, control charts are created and used based on the premise that defects should be addressed after they occur. In other words, it's based on the idea that it's okay to create a little bit of junk. However, our style of quality control is built on the premise that defects should not be allowed to happen in the first place."

"How do you go about doing that," asked Mr. M.

"First, we do a very strict, 100 percent inspection of incoming materials. Then, we have very high standards of machine and tool maintenance, especially in terms of accuracy. We also ask our workers to adhere to the standardized operation. We check our inspection equipment very frequently to maintain their accuracy. What's the rate of defects at your company?"

"Around 2.5 percent. What's your defect rate over there?"

"About 0.5 percent."

This silenced Mr. M and he fell deep into thought. His company was in the same industry.

As the chief engineer pointed out, quality control in Japan, which revolves around control charts, is based on the premise that defects cannot be avoided. Whereas the W Company in Germany has a quality control system that tries to eliminate defects in the first place. It is an entirely different mind-set. I toured several more companies in Germany, and I did not see a single control chart.

C. Inspections Do Not Decrease Defects

When I visit factories, I often encounter this common misconception: the stricter the inspection, the fewer the defects. At one plant, 100 defects were found in a lot of 1000. The inspection was conducted by one inspector, so the plant manager decided to add one more inspector, in theory, to make the inspection more stringent. The next day the number of defects decreased to 80. The following day it dropped further to 60. However, on the third day, it jumped to 120 (Figure 2.8).

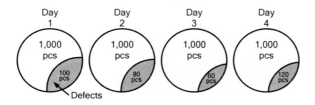

Figure 2.8 Feedback of Inspection & Defects

Stories like these are all too common—even if the number of inspectors increases, the number of defects will not decrease. Any attempt at the contrary comes directly as a result of misunderstanding the real function of inspection. In other words, it comes from not understanding the basic concept that defects are created by processing.

Making inspections stricter does contribute to boosting the effectiveness of inspection itself. If the number of inspectors is not enough and they are too busy, good products might be mistaken for defects or defects might slip through the inspection. Certainly by securing enough inspectors, mistakes like that would diminish.

However, the inspection itself has no power over how many defects are created. Defects will only decrease if the inspector notifies processing about the defects. Processing must then adopt a method that prevents the same defects from happening again. If processing does not change their methods in the face of a warning from an inspector, defects will continue to happen.

It would be very convenient if inspectors could use magic to turn defects into non-defects. Until then let us think of the process, not the inspection.

Inspections can find defects but cannot make them disappear. This will always be true no matter how skilled, or how many, inspectors there are. As long as inspections stop with just the discovery of defects, the number of defects will never go down.

D. Sampling Inspections Do Not Assure Quality
When I met Mr. Tokizane, the managing director at A Electric, he told me, "Our company has a zero defect policy. We don't want a single television that we manufacture to be defective.

"When millions of televisions are manufactured, people often think that it's normal for a few to come out defective. However, each customer only buys one television, so even if the defective product is one in a million, the customer that happens to buy that one in a million will label all of our products as unreliable. We simply can't afford to let that happen."

For whatever reason, this remark lingered in my mind. I mulled it over as I sped home on the bullet train, which made me think about sampling inspections.

So, if even a single defect is not allowed, then what about sampling inspections? After much thought, it occurred to me that sampling inspections are only a more effective means of inspecting; they cannot make quality itself more effective. In other words, sampling inspections are based on the assumption that nothing can be done to eliminate that one or two defects out of thousands.

Around 1951, when I was working at Japan Management Association, Mr. H from N Electric asked me if I knew what quality control really was. I answered, "It's carrying out effective inspections and eliminating defects, isn't it?"

"No, you have to use statistics," he said, and went on over the course of a few hours to tell me about control charts, how to design experiments, and statistical sampling. At the end of it all he said, "Even if you do a 100 percent inspection there's no way can be thorough enough. That takes too much time and trouble. It's much better to introduce a sampling inspection which has the backing of statistical science."

Since that conversation, I had believed that sampling inspections are better than 100 percent inspections. However, the remark of Mr. Tokizane opened up my eyes —"*Even a single defect is not allowed to end up in the customer's hands.*"

Sampling does make the method of inspections more efficient but it can never assure that all defects will be found. In order to assure quality, 100 percent inspection is superior.

The downside of 100 percent inspections is that of time and trouble. Therefore, when switching from a sampling inspection it is necessary to come up with a more efficient 100 percent inspection.

A sampling inspection can be used if there is no method for a 100 percent inspection. Even in this case it is important to recognize that sampling inspections have an advantage over 100 percent inspection only in terms of efficiency. They cannot assure quality, as total inspections do.

If people understand this correctly then perhaps many new ideas for better 100 percent inspection methods might be created.

E. Development of Defect–Eliminating Inspections

As mentioned before there are two types of inspections — ones that find defects and ones that eliminate defects. There are also two means of inspections — 100 percent inspections and sampling inspections.

In this section, I will explain how to achieve a defect–eliminating inspection with the various examples presented below.

B Industries is a manufacture of rubber seals. When I met the chief inspector, Mr. Y, he told me, "We send our products to our parent factory but they often find defects and send an entire lot back rejected."

I said to him, "Mr. Y, there are only two reasons why defects are found at the parent factory. One, they find defects that you somehow missed, and two, they don't accept the products that you think are acceptable. For the type of products you make, it's necessary to use limit samples since a visual inspection is used. Do you use limit samples?"

"No, we don't use them," the chief inspector said.

"Well, you need them. Unless you and your parent factory have the same inspection procedures and limit samples, your inspection is essentially meaningless, no matter how strict it is."

Mr. Y went to the parent factory soon after this conversation and made an agreement on inspection procedures and specifications for limit samples. It turned out that there were some discrepancies in both areas.

After his factory started using the newly established inspection procedures and limit samples, an entire lot never came back rejected again. Mr. Y let me know about this improvement and added that he intended to also reduce overall defects.

When I visited him at the factory the following month, he came to me beaming, "Listen, defects have dropped by 80 percent!" We were both overjoyed at this news.

I went to the factory floor later to check on a different issue. While I was walking, I happened to pass by the vulcanization presses and saw a box by the machines filled with defects.

I asked a worker nearby, "There seems to be a lot of defects. Was there some kind of a problem today?"

"No, lately we've had more than normal."

"Really? You mean you had fewer defects before?"

"Yes, the inspections have become much more strict recently. They point out even the smallest imperfections. So if things aren't completely perfect, we just throw them away in this box."

The cat was out of the bag, the only reason defects had dropped by 80 percent was because they were kept on the shop floor and never sent to inspection. In truth, the trouble with defects was just as much of a problem now as it was before.

I had Mr. Y come over to the shop floor and see what was happening. I told him, "There are only two reasons why defects would be found in an inspection — one, the shop floor and the inspectors are using two different inspection standards, or two, the standards are the same and the shop floor is missing defects that inspection later discovers. This is the same problem you had with the parent factory and it needs to be addressed the same way.

"Furthermore, even if fewer defects are found in inspection statistics, if the shop floor is producing the same number of defects, then the inspection results are meaningless."

The factory's conventional flow of processing and inspection was as follows:

1. If there is an order of 1000, raw material for 1,100 products (10 percent extra) is sent to the vulcanization process.

2. Except for obvious defects, all products produced are sent next to the deburring process.

3. On the following day products are deburred.

4. The day after that, products go to inspection.

5. If the number of acceptable product is less than 1000, the coordinator asks the shop floor to make additional products.

If there was a shortage, it created a host of problems. Even if the shortage was just for ten pieces the setups had to be changed and it took an entire hour to heat up the molds for the vulcanization process. The foreman and the coordinator often ended up in a quarrel.

"We can't do it today, it has to be tomorrow."

"OK, but we'll miss the delivery deadline."

To address the problem with the conventional method, I suggested the following method:

1. As shown in Figure 2.9, place a conveyor belt in the middle of the vulcanization presses.

2. Each press makes a set of four products at once. When one set is finished, place the products on the conveyor belt, and send them to the following process immediately.

3. After the deburring process, place the products on the conveyor and send them to the following inspection process.

4. At the inspection, stack good products according to their type on the nearby turn–table.

5. If there is a defect, immediately notify the worker in charge of the process and stop the operation.

6. The worker, foreman, and the inspector must then get together and discuss the cause of the problem. If the problem can be easily fixed, such as small scratches on the mold, grind and fix it on the spot. If it cannot be easily fixed, take an alternative measure such as retiring the use of that particular mold.

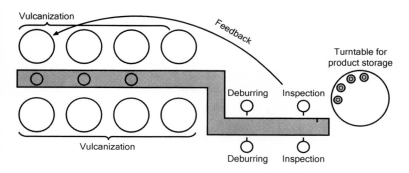

Figure 2.9 Feedback of Inspection

The company introduced this method and as a result their actual defect rate dropped by 90 percent. As this shows, defects will decrease if inspection provides immediate feedback to production, and production takes appropriate measures. This style of inspection is called an "feedback inspection," and is the type of inspection that eliminates defects.

In contrast, the conventional inspection which only finds defects is called a "segregation inspection." Putting it differently, segregation inspections are death–certificate style inspections, while feedback inspections are a physical health–checkup style inspection.

It should be noted that even with feedback inspections, defects can happen. However, the first defect will stop any ensuing defects of the same nature from happening. On the other hand in the case of segregation inspections, on the other hand, the same defects will occur again and again.

Using a medical analogy, feedback inspections are similar to a tumor being found during a routine monthly physical checkup, and then treated before it becomes more serious. Conversely, segregation inspections are akin to doing an autopsy after someone's death, concluding that they died of cancer and suggesting that they should have been treated earlier.

In order to eliminate defects, even with feedback inspections, 100 percent inspections must be used instead of sampling. Many people on the shop floor still adamantly believe that 100 percent inspection takes too much time and trouble. As mentioned earlier sampling inspections are ultimately only a more efficient method of inspecting; however, they are not as effective as 100 percent inspection at detecting and eliminating defects.

By using our brains, efficient methods of 100 percent inspections can be conceived. Do not a let phrase like, "sampling inspections have the support of statistical science," deceive you into denying the effectiveness of 100 percent inspections.

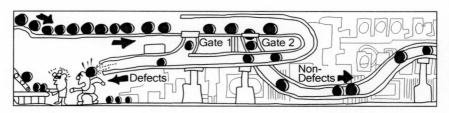

Figure 2.10 100% Inspection & Feedback

Inspection Improvement — Example 1

R Industries manufactured o–rings by compacting and shaping powder. Although external and internal diameters met specifications, the thickness was not always uniform, which was problematic.

The company produced about 10,000 pieces per day and did

"sampling inspections based on statistical science," which took 1.5 man–hours. However, defective items were still found by customers, which led to complaints. The internal defect rate itself was also high at 6 percent. So I advised the company to use the following method (Figure 2.11):

- According to product specifications, the height of an o–ring has to be 10mm ± 0.5mm — on the chute from the compacting machine place two kinds of inspection gates, the heights were set as follows:

    Gate A 10.5mm

    Gate B 9.5mm

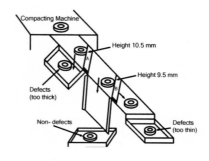

Figure 2.11 Inspection of "Stem Tight"

Products thicker than 10.5mm will be blocked by gate A and slide into one of the defect boxes. O–rings thinner than 9.5mm will go through gate B and fall into another defect box at the end of the chute. Only good products will go through gate A to be shunted aside by the minimum height allowance of gate B, to the box for acceptable products. When a defect falls into one of the defect boxes, it triggers a limit switch, a warning buzzer goes off, and the machine stops.

After this new system was introduced, the 1.5 hours of inspection labor became unnecessary. Also, the defect rate was reduced by as much as 95 percent. This drastic reduction was possible because the machine stopped at the very instant it created the defect. Engineers were able to pinpoint the cause of the defect immediately and take appropriate measures.

In the past, it was difficult for the engineers to take effective measures since they had to guess the cause of the defect. The new method effectively prevented the same defect from recurring.

A couple of years ago while I was in Europe I visited Refa in West Germany, and had a discussion about production management with industrial engineers. During the discussion I said, "Sampling inspections are only a more efficient means of inspecting; they do not guarantee the elimination of defects. Therefore, we should implement 100 percent inspections more aggressively."

Opposition was raised at once, "100 percent inspections drive up the cost."

I replied that we just need to think of ways to keep inspection cost down and presented pictures of the above o–ring inspection system and its effect. Everyone agreed that it was an excellent idea.

Inspection Improvement — Example 2

At H Company, section chief Mr. Y asked me to come see their assembly line for shock absorbers.

On the shop floor work pieces were assembled by the machine press at the end of a line of machines. When assembled products come out of the press they go through a gate set at a certain height. If a product is too high it will stop at the gate. This will activate the proximity switch and the air cylinder will push the product aside. Mr. Y told me that an inspection worker used to stand by the press doing just that before this inspection system was introduced.

"What do you think," asked Mr. Y, rather proudly.

I said, "It's working very well. However, I have to say that I don't like the basic concept this is built upon."

"Basic concept? What do you mean by that?"

"Well, it is a great method, but it's still an essentially mechanized death–certificate style inspection. Which processes create defects in height?"

"The second and fifth process," he said.

"If that's the case, why don't you place a red light in each of these processes that can warn workers when a defect is detected?

The worker can check the machine every time this happens and prevent the same type of defect.

"The system you're employing now mechanizes the segregation of defects, and probably saves time and trouble when inspecting. However, it probably doesn't do much to actually reduce defects in general."

I heard later that the company introduced a feedback system which let processes responsible for the defects know about the presence of defects. This eventually lowered the number of defects to near zero.

Inspection Improvement — Example 3

At the R television factory, assembled televisions underwent their final adjustments in two phases. First, four workers with B-level skills, B1, B2, B3, and B4 adjusted the part each was responsible for. Then the televisions were sent down the conveyor to a second set of workers with A-level skills, A1, A2, etc. These workers would make any necessary comprehensive final adjustments.

I observed the workers and noted that they all looked very busy. However, the time it took to adjust each product varied greatly for A workers. Sometimes they lagged far behind B workers even though they seemed to be in just as much of a hurry. I asked the foreman, "Why do you need to adjust twice?"

"We can't be completely confident about the quality unless workers with more than ten years of experience do a comprehensive final assessment and adjust the settings so that everything functions cohesively."

"Is that why A workers often have to readjust the settings that B workers made?"

"Right."

"If there are problems with B workers adjustments, how do A workers let them know?" I said.

"They have a meeting once a week."

"I see. Is that really effective, though? Don't they just say things like, 'This aspect of adjustment wasn't very good.' 'I'm sorry, I'll be careful about that.' If that's the case, no real improvement is happening," I said, and suggested attaching a light and intercom in front of each worker.

If there is an adjustment error, an *A* worker can call up the corresponding *B* worker and inform them of the problem. If necessary, the *A* worker should go to the *B* worker and give feedback in person.

The company implemented this method and after about one month it became clear that only one *A* worker was necessary. Furthermore, that single worker was able to easily keep up with the flow.

This was the direct result of *A* workers incorporating feedback into their operation. By immediately informing B workers of their mistakes, they transformed the inspection from one of just finding and fixing defects to one which prevents them altogether.

Defect rates can always be lowered, so long as we transform the purpose of our inspections from discovery to feedback and elimination. Nevertheless, there are still many factories that continue to use conventional defect–finding inspections and I cannot help but wonder why.

Figure 2.12 Defects and Feedback

F. Successive Checks

Inspections are used to discover defects created during processing in order to assure product quality. Sampling inspections are often used as a more efficient means of inspecting. However, they lack the ability to provide complete quality assurance. As mentioned earlier, the only way to provide complete quality assurance and prevent defects is by using 100 percent feedback inspection.

Still, the number of defects can only be reduced if the inspection gives immediate feedback regarding the specifics of the defects to the manufacturing processes and the workers at those processes are allowed to take appropriate action. For this reason, the speed of feedback becomes an important issue. The fastest way of providing feedback is via the worker doing the specific operation, which is called a "self check."

Creating a self check inspection system can be as simple as encouraging workers to be more careful, or providing them with inspection tools to do sampling inspections. Then, when a defect is found, root out its cause together with the foreman and the inspector and then take appropriate measures.

The basic concept of this method is good but in reality there is a drawback, people tend to be lenient when inspecting items that they make themselves. Naturally, inspection mistakes tend to increase.

If the inspection is objective, such as one that requires the use of a gauge, these problems can be avoided. However, if it is a more subjective visual inspection, this problem tends to be magnified.

The problem of leniency and carelessness can be addressed if the inspection is done by others. The best way to achieve this while maintaining speedy feedback is by making each worker the inspector of the previous process. I first came up with this idea of successive checks around 1945, it has since been taken up in many factories.

For example:

1. The worker for the second process inspects the job of the first before starting the second process.

2. The worker for the third process checks the job of

the second process before starting the third.

If there is a defect, immediate feedback is provided to the previous worker. This allows the worker who made the defect to learn what went wrong and adjust their machine or method accordingly before another defect is made. This style of quick, objective, fast-feedback inspection is called "successive check" and is considered a 100 percent inspection, which is critical to the elimination of defects. By using such an inspection, defect rates can be driven down significantly in a short period of time.

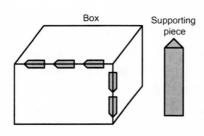

Figure 2.13 Attaching Reinforcement Material

Successive checks were introduced at L television factory. Prior to its introduction, an excellent yet perhaps overly proud worker, was in charge of gluing on supporting pieces inside boxes (Figure 2.13). A final inspector once found missing pieces and let her know. Unfortunately, the worker responded incredulously, "I don't think it's my mistake. Someone else must have taken them out by accident." Even after the inspector pointed out that there was no trace of glue, she still refused to concede that it was her mistake.

After successive checks were implemented, the next worker pointed out one day that there was one place the piece was not attached. She was able to see for herself that there was a missing piece in the box she had just finished. Of course she fixed it immediately, but it was a humbling reminder for her that even she could make mistakes. After that she became even more attentive and never forgot to attach pieces again.

"A bystander's vantage," is a phrase used often in Japan; it means that onlookers see the game better than the players. The same can be said for inspections. Workers can easily overlook obvious mistakes they have made while others with more objective eyes do not. Successive checks therefore have the advantage of objectivity as well as the advantage of speedy feedback.

At R Electric, Mr. Nishida who was chief of the television production department said, "In TV assembly, around 15 percent of our defects were the result of processing error. We used statistical control charts and other QC (Quality Control) activities and managed to reduce it to 6.5 percent, but it seemed to hit a plateau there."

At this time, my idea of the successive check method was coming fresh off the drawing board, so I proposed the method to him and suggested that his company should introduce it.

Figure 2.14 Method of Successive Checks

Since inspection was added to the regular processing, I had the assembly takt time increased by 10 percent from 30 seconds to 33 seconds.

By the end of the first month, the results were in:

- Process–defect rate was reduced to 1.5 percent
- By the 23rd day, the takt time was the same as before: 30 seconds

There are two reasons why the takt time did not become longer: 1) defects decreased, 2) inspection did not require much time and became a part of the normal routine.

I anticipated that inspection would not take long, but added the extra time initially due to my concern regarding possible complaints from the workers, such as, "how can you expect us to do extra work in the same amount of time?"

By the third month, the defect rate was down further:

- Defects found during processing: 0.65 percent
- Defects found at the end of processing: 0.016 percent

In the calculation of defect rates above, the denominator is the number of televisions manufactured, the numerator is the number of defects. In other words, if 10,000 products are manufactured and there are three defects per thousand televisions on average, the rate would be .3 percent. So, 0.016 percent was indeed a phenomenal result.

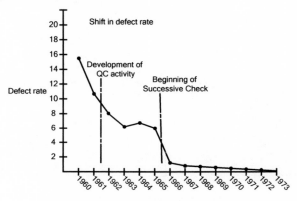

Figure 2.15 Effect of Continuous Inspection

After this success, I implemented successive checks at dozens of other factories. In general it cut back defects by 80 to 90 percent within a month, and many people told me that the same result could not have been achieved by conventional QC activities. These accomplishments were confirmation that my idea of successive checks was the right one.

Although successive checks are effective in most cases, I occasionally hear people say that the outcome was not as good as expected. In order to achieve an optimum result, the following rules must be observed:

1. The number of inspections on a single product should not be excessive.

2. If a defect is detected, take action immediately.

3. If an inspection is visual, make sure to use limit samples.

The first rule, inspection items should not be excessive, comes from the fact that too many inspections would require too much time, which may cause workers to skip the inspection altogether. Inspection items should be narrowed down to just a few items with high defect rates; while quantifying total defects should be held off until final inspection. Every inspection item should be reviewed again after two or four weeks by the same style of analysis. However, most important items and items susceptible to critical defects should always be left on the list.

The second rule is to take action immediately if a defect is detected. Successive checking does not just mean that inspections are done successively. It is also essential that the detection of a defect is communicated to the worker responsible so the problem can be fixed immediately. This can result in the need to change processing methods. To accomplish this may require that the production line be stopped.

In general, front–line managers tend to hesitate when it comes to stopping the line. However, the following reasons should provide the justification to do so:

> By stopping the line, managers can immediately spot the problem, instruct the workers as needed, and improve the situation quickly.

> The worker feels responsible for stopping the line and will be more careful afterward.

> Any temporary stoppage is offset by the reduction in defects. The loss in throughput would be larger if corrective measures were taken and the problem continued to show up.

It is just like the treatment of appendicitis. When you have appendicitis, putting ice packs on your stomach can ease the condition, but the pain is likely to come back. An appendectomy will solve the problem much faster.

The third rule is, if an inspection is visual, make sure to use limit samples. Inspecting color tone, for example, would be visual and whether or not the products meet the quality standard should be decided by a comparison to a limit sample. Even with limit samples making the correct call can be difficult if the product is close to the limit.

Figure 2.16 Visual Inspection and Limit Sample

One company adopted the following style of inspection to address the difficulties inherent with inspections in a three step operation:

- Worker B inspects the work of worker A, the operator of the preceding worker
- At the last process, inspector C checks worker B's work
- Every day after work, A, B, and C get together and talk about the day's inspections

Involving a final inspector in this way was quite effective and, a week after its introduction, disagreement on what was acceptable disappeared.

In the case of successive checks, a coworker has to judge another coworker's job. Unfortunately this can result in the effectiveness of inspections being compromised as in the following conversation:

"I don't agree that this is a defect. I think perhaps you're being too strict."

"Alright."

This tendency can be a major problem if a worker on one process has more seniority than the worker on the following process. Take the company above as an example. If worker B had less seniority than worker A, B might hesitate in pointing out A's mistakes. Even if worker B manages to point out a defect, if worker A insists that it is not a defect, worker B might feel obliged to back down.

By involving the overruling input of an inspector, worker A would have no choice but to follow B's judgment if the inspector thinks it is correct. Therefore, the addition of an inspector gives authority to worker B's judgment and helps smooth things over.

The following are examples and important requirements of successive checks:

1. Successive Checks and Inspection Items

As explained earlier, inspection items per person should be narrowed down to two or three. There have been many cases where the results were not as good as expected, simply because there were too many items to inspect on a single product.

To make an accurate flat surface in a grinding operation, red ink is first painted on the surface of an object to be ground by the machine. After that the ground pane is placed against a surface plate so that the ink on the higher surface is smudged. The smudged surface is then reground until the surface becomes completely flat. This analogy provides insight that can be very useful when trying to implement an efficient and effective successive check inspection system.

Another useful tip is to keep an inspection–item log sheet with the work instruction sheet to help keep track of inspection items. Keeping them with the instruction sheets is convenient for the worker. Moreover, keeping them as separate documents makes it easy to accommodate inspection item changes.

Using a marker is also effective means of keeping track of inspection items. After inspection each product is marked to make it clear that it was inspected. This is called a "Marker Check."

2. Increase of In-Process Defects at the Early Stages of Successive Checks

I sometimes hear people say that defects actually increase after a successive check system is implemented. Why? First of all, it needs to be understood that there are two types of defects:

- Defects detected during processes are In-process defects
- Defects detected at the end of processes are End-process defects

The number of in-process defects naturally increases because abnormalities that went undetected before are now detected by the successive checks. However, the number of end-process defects should decrease by 80 to 90 percent by the end of the first month.

In general, there are three stages to go through when successive checks are implemented:

1. In-process defects increase, but end-process defects decrease by about 30 percent.

2. In-process defects decrease by about half, and end-process defects decrease by about 80 percent.

3. In-process defects decrease by about 80 percent, and end-process defects decrease by about 90 percent.

If we understand these stages there is no reason to worry if defects increase at the beginning.

3. Seek the Understanding of Workers

When we implement successive checks, it is necessary to seek the workers understanding.

At company L, when worker A pointed out that there was a problem in worker B's soldering, worker B became upset because his mistake was pointed out by someone with less seniority in the company, and the two eventually got into an argument. In this case, a manager stepped in and they settled the argument. As this shows, successive checks can cause a problem if implemented without thorough explanation.

I heard later that worker B above was not even aware of his mistake, but he became more careful about it and made no defects after this incident.

At company H on the other hand, workers commented that it is better for a mistake to be pointed out by a friendly coworker than an inspector. The successive–check method was accepted very well there and the defect rate plummeted accordingly.

In any case, it is extremely important that workers themselves understand the rationale for successive checks thoroughly so that the right workplace atmosphere can be created.

4. Worker Care

The successive check method was implemented at Company N, an auto–parts assembler. There is a button and a red light in front of each worker that are connected to the worker at the end of the production line. If there is a defect, the worker who found it presses the button, the light in front of the worker who created it flashes, and the worker at the end of the line turns off the conveyor. The cost of this system was very reasonable.

Right after this system was introduced there was a day when the conveyor had to be stopped three times because one worker forgot to attach labels. This worker felt a deep sense of responsibility and could not come to work the next day.

A manager visited her house and convinced her to come to work by telling her that the missing labels were not her fault. After this, due to an improvement in work procedures and her efforts, she never forgot to attach labels again.

When mistakes are found some thoughtless managers blame the workers and end up saying things that have adverse effects. If there is a mistake, managers should think about why it happened and what can be done to keep it from happening again. In the case of forgetting to attach labels, there could be several possible causes such as an excessive workload or a poor stock location of labels. Of course the manager should take action, but it should be focused on improvement. Indeed, unless managers have a positive and compassionate mind-set, results will never be favorable.

5. Stopping the Line Makes Managers Aware

Company Y assembled a chassis in a way that required soldering in many processes. Since there were many soldering–related problems, the foreman often gathered all the workers and asked them to work more carefully. However, the number of defects did not go down so management decided that part–timers did not have the necessary skills.

When successive checks was introduced, it became clear that the conveyor often stopped at the fifth process. So the foreman stood behind the worker at the fifth process and observed his work for a while. This worker's method was to melt solder with the soldering iron and drip it on a spot. The foreman pulled the worker from the line, substituted a temporary replacement, then gave the worker a 30–minute lesson on soldering outside of the production line.

The worker said that the extra instruction allowed him to understand the correct method of soldering for the first time ever — that it should be poured on instead of dripped on; with that, he returned to the line. After this lesson his soldering mistakes never happened again.

Every time the line was stopped by the same worker multiple times, the foreman gave special training to that worker. By the end of the first month their defect rate had dropped by 90 percent.

One manager told me, "We thought that part–timers just didn't have what it takes, but we were wrong. We came to the realization that it was our training that was not up to par."

As this shows, by stopping the conveyor belt managers and foremen can immediately learn the location of problems. Appropriate actions that root out the problem, such as worker training, can be taken as a result. The loss from line stoppages can always be made up in a short amount of time. Therefore, I would encourage managers to stop their production lines immediately whenever defects are detected.

6. Eliminate the Need for Touch–Ups

S Industries was a factory where tape recorders were assembled. Since it was low–volume mixed model factory, an array of products needing touch–ups would often pile up at the end of the assembly line, leading to product mix–ups and shortages.

However, by implementing a successive check the need for touch–ups disappeared completely since all defects were detected and taken care of during the assembly process. Not only was the problem of product mix–up and shortage taken care of, the shop floor was much more organized as a result.

7. When Rules of Successive Checks Cannot be Followed

For every rule there is almost always an exception. At times, this can certainly be true for successive checks. Indeed, there are a few exceptional cases where the rules of successive checks cannot be followed to the letter. Examples of these situations and strategies for handling them are discussed below.

Inspection of work in the very next process is one of the fundamental rules of successive checks. However, in reality this is not always possible. In such cases, delaying the inspection can be acceptable, although the number of processes separating the work from the inspection should be minimized. Regardless, effective feedback is crucial. Therefore, feedback methods should be modified accordingly to accommodate the changes in inspection.

In important processes, an inspection is sometimes repeated in the following two processes. This is called a "double check."

When defect repairs consume too much time, one worker can

inspect for defects, while another worker can repair it somewhere else.

Sometimes, even the 100 percent inspection rule may have to be bent. When the speed of production line is fast, sampling may be the only realistic inspection option. Even so, the percentage of items inspected should be kept as close to 100 percent as possible.

Although exceptions to the rules may be required, the basic principles are still as follows:

- Conduct inspections that do not make defects
- Judgment of defects should be objective
- If a defect is found, feedback should be given to the worker responsible immediately
- The worker who created the defect has to look at it and repair it
- Inspection should be 100 percent; sampling should be avoided

Various examples have proven that successive checks following these principles can usually reduce defect rates by as much as 80 or 90 percent.

G. Self Checks Using Poka–Yoke

As mentioned earlier, successive checks are quite effective in preventing defects because of their objectivity and speedy feedback. In contrast, self–checks by processing workers themselves tend to be too lenient and can cause careless mistakes.

However, these drawbacks apply only to cases where subjective visual judgment is required; inspection of paint hues, for example. If an objective measurement is required, as would be the case for product shape or dimension, strict and careful inspection is possible even with self inspections. When it comes to the speed of feedback, nothing is faster than the feedback provided by the processing workers themselves.

Devices can sometimes be used to make objective self inspections more efficient and effective. These devices are called "poka-yoke" which means "mistake proof."

The term "baka–yoke" which means "fool–proof" was used before; however, this term could give people the impression that workers on the shop floors are fools. In fact, I once offended a worker unintentionally by using this word. When I was at the factory of R Auto Body, I said to a part–time worker, "Bake–yoke pins were attached so that you won't mix up right and left." The worker looked at me and said, "I am such a fool," and burst into tears. I learned my lesson and never used the word "bake–yoke" again. Instead, I started using "poka–yoke," or mistake–proof.

The following is an example of poka–yoke at R Industries. There was an operation in which the edges of covers are bent by a press. The appearance of the left and right covers were identical except for the placement of holes (Figure 2.17).

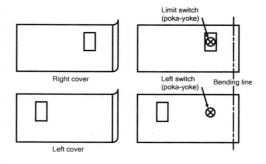

Figure 2.17 Bending Covers and Poka-yoke

The part was designed to be bent on the right side but occasionally right and left–handed components were accidentally interchanged. To prevent the press from bending the part the wrong way, a limit switch was installed on the press at the place where the hole should be. If the hole is not in that position when the limit switch is pushed the press shuts down and a red warning light comes on.

In this case the limit switch is acting as an inspector, it sends feedback to the process worker immediately with the red light. Since every part is checked, this is also a 100 percent inspection. If poka–yoke is implemented successfully, it is even more effective in preventing defects than successive checks.

Detection method / Feedback method / Application	Control Type			Warning Type		
	Contract	Fixed-number	Motion-step	Contract	Fixed-number	Motion-step
Poka-Yoke — Self Check	◎	◎	◎	○	○	○
Poka-Yoke — Successive Check	◎	◎	◎	○	○	○

Table 2.1 Classification of Poka-yoke

Poka–yoke feedback can be done in one of two ways:

1. Control type: If the method of operation is wrong, the work is obstructed and cannot be continued.

2. Warning type: If the method of operation is wrong, the worker is alerted with a buzzer or a lamp. The work could continue if the worker does not notice the warning.

With the warning type poka–yoke device the work can continue if the worker does not notice the warning. This makes the control type poka–yoke a more robust corrective device. However, the warning type can be used if the work is non–critical, or the cost of control type would be too much.

There are also three different types of detection in poka–yoke:

1. Contact–type: it checks dimensional differences based on whether or not contact is made.

2. Fixed–value type: it checks for deviations from predetermined values.

3. Motion–step type: it checks for errors in motions and sequences.

The following are examples of poka–yoke with different combinations of detection and feedbacks:

1.1 Control Type – Contact Type

This is an example from Daitou Mokko, a TV cabinet maker. In one operation four metal parts, mounts for cathode–ray tubes, were secured on frames with four screws. Then, insulation tape was placed on top. (Figure 2.18)

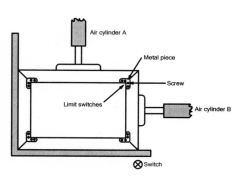

16 screws were supposed to be used but sometimes the workers forgot a few. Since

Figure 2.18 Screws & Poka–yoke

insulation tape was placed on top, the mistakes were usually not detected at the exit inspection; instead, most were found at the incoming inspection of the parent factory.

Since this was a major issue, the company implemented the following improvement:

Place 16 limit switches underneath each screw hole on the jig. Each screw inserted activates a corresponding switch.

Frames are made from four pieces – after the pieces are glued, they are pressed together by air cylinders. If all switches are not activated, the air cylinders would not release the frame, making it impossible to continue work.

Because of this set–up, it simply became impossible install less than 16 screws. In this case, the 16 limit switches acted as inspectors conducting 100 percent inspections.

The next example is from S Iron Works. This bolt manufacturer had a critical defect: doublethreaded screws. Regular screws have a single thread, but one out of every 50,000 to 100,000 screws manufactured with double threads. To use such a screw was very dangerous because it could damage the threads on other products and cause major damage. To make matters worse, doublethreaded screws were extremely difficult to find and only experienced workers were able to detect them.

Due to the potential of serious damage to customer products by the doublethreaded screws, two experienced S Iron Works workers did 100 percent inspections of all screws. However, defective screws still slipped through the inspection and it became a vexing problem for the company.

I asked a foreman, "Are there any phenomena associated only with doublethreaded screws?" The foreman said, "Yes. When defective screws are being made in a rolling machine, the screw top becomes about 1mm higher than regular screws."

"That's convenient," I said and convinced the company to attach a sensor at the die plates of the rolling machine. If a defective thread were to be created the sensor detects its higher head, closes the shutter near the product chute, and stops the machine. At the shutter, five or six screws are pooled and one of them is a defective screw.

This system made finding defects so much easier that two inspectors became unnecessary.

In addition, the machine stopped at the very point in which defects were created, so the company was able to pinpoint the cause. Appropriate measures were taken and the number of defects itself decreased significantly as a result.

In this case, the sensor was an inspector and conducted 100 percent inspections.

1.2 Control Type — Fixed-Number Type
At O Auto factory, rivets were used to assemble car frames. Each frame required 24 rivets, but there were occasional mistakes and the number would end up less than 24.

To fix this problem the company implemented the following poka-yoke system. A parts feeder first lines up all 24 rivets. As a rivet is released and attached on the frame one by one, a counter kept track of how many were used. If a rivet is not released within 30 seconds after the previous one, the assembly conveyor was shut down.

If even one rivet was missing, the conveyor stopped and the work could not be continued. Therefore, the problem of missing rivets never happened again.

1.3 Control Type — Motion–Step Type

At U Auto factory, engine oil was poured in the engines at one of the assembly processes. However, this job was sometimes forgotten and cars without engine oil would proceed along the assembly line. To address this problem the following poka–yoke was installed.

The oil for the engine oil used to be placed on a shelf waiting to be used. The oil was supposed to be poured after attaching all the parts, then the car would move on to the next process To implement the poka–yoke the oil injector was instead hung overhead using a spring. A limit switch was then installed before the next process that would automatically stop the car. If the spring supporting the oil injector was pulled, as it would be if oil was added, the limit switch would be deactivated for one cycle and the line would not stop.

2.1 Warning Type — Contact Type

At R Auto factory, metal tubes were attached on the bottom of the driver–side floor boards. One of the tubes was different from others: it had a triangular shape in order to hold electric cables inside.

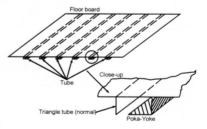

Figure 2.19 Base Plate and Poka-yoke

This triangular tube had to be attached at a certain angle. The regular worker in this process always attached the parts in the correct way. However, when someone else had to fill in for the worker, the parts were often attached in a wrong way, causing major problems.

To prevent this mistake from happening, a simple poka–yoke

device, as shown in Figure 2.19, was attached. If the triangle tube was attached in a wrong way, the floor board was raised and a red light was turned on. After this method was implemented, defects never happened again.

2.2 Warning Type — Fixed–Number Type

At O factory, there was an operation where ten pieces of insulation tape were attached inside each TV cabinet (Figure 2.20).

The tape pieces, about 8cm long, were lined up on a square bar and removed as necessary. However, when all ten pieces were not there, the mistake went unnoticed until much later.

As a counter-measure, the following simple poka–yoke was adopted. 10 pieces of insulation tape were lined up on the square bar as one group. If even one sticker was forgotten, it became very obvious to a worker since there was a remaining space on the bar. After this poka–yoke was introduced, the mistake never happened again.

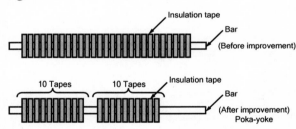

Figure 2.20 Insulating Tape and Poka-yoke

A similar improvement was made for another process at the same factory. Four television legs and assembly instructions were supposed to be placed in a small box as a set, and 50 sets were placed in a large box.

However, the parent factory often found small boxes without any instructions and made frequent requests for the company to use more caution. So, the following poka–yoke was conceived to address the issue.

- Count 50 instructions at first and insert a separator
- When starting a new large box, take out one section of 50 instructions
- If any instructions are left when the boxed is filled, it means there are a corresponding number of small boxes without instructions — open up the small boxes again to fix the problem.

This small improvement proved successful and complaints from the parent company stopped completely.

2.3 Warning Type — Motion–Step Type

An operation at H factory, inserted bushings inserted into both ends of leaf–spring suspensions (Figure 2.21). Since workers sometimes forgot to install one of the bushings, the following poka–yoke device was installed (Figure 2.22):

Figure 2.21 Inserting Spring Bushing

- When springs are unloaded from the conveyor, a limit switch is activated and the bar in front of the palette comes down where products are placed.

- The worker uses the press to insert a bushing on one end of the leaf spring, removes the spring from the press and repeats the operation for the other end. This sequence of motion activates the limit switch again and raises the bar.

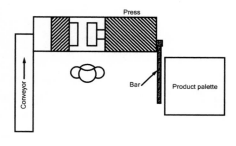

Figure 2.22 Motion Sequence Poka-yoke

- If the worker tries to place a product on the palette after inserting only one bushing, the bar is still down and blocks the motion.

In general, many poka–yoke devices are contact type, which

63

detect defects by dimensional differences. However, if a dimension cannot be used to detect defects, motion steps or motion sequence can be used quite effectively. Motion step poka–yoke is also called block type and has wide applications. I recommend that people use this motion–step type more actively.

Implementing mistake–proof poke–yoke devices has the following advantages:

- Inspection feedback is done instantly
- Work methods that create defects are inhibited
- It carries out a 100 percent inspection

Because of these advantages, poka–yoke devices can effectively drive defects down to zero. Furthermore, although they have thus far been discussed in the context of self check, they can also be used with successive checks as well.

At company A, bottom covers of laundry washers were manufactured using five machine presses. In the second press, eight holes are made in each cover so that a motor can be attached. However, since the holes were small, about 3mm, punches often broke and covers without enough holes were created. To prevent this problem from happening a poka–yoke device was conceived for the third press which cut the bottom covers to size.

Eight pins were welded to the bottom of the cutting die. If even one hole was missing the cover would not go all the way to the bottom of the die. When this happened, a light–sensitive device would detect the abnormality, alert workers by sound, and shut down the whole production line, preventing the cover from moving on to the next process. The worker would immediately come and change the broken punch on the second press and restart the operation.

Until this device was introduced, as many as 50 to 100 defective products might have been created before a broken punch was noticed. This problem was eliminated by the new pins.

In this case, the eight pins welded at the bottom of the cutting die served as the mistake–proof functionality. They carried out

100 percent inspection and provided immediate feedback. This is an example of a control and contact type poka–yoke used for a successive check.

As shown in Table 2.2, different inspections have different applications. Choosing which inspection to use should be done based upon the following criteria:

- Visual inspection: successive check
- Physical inspection
- Inspection device is complicated and expensive: successive check
- Inspection device is simple and inexpensive: poka–yoke (self inspection, successive inspection)

Cost of inspection devices / Inspection Function	Cost	
	High	Low
Sensory inspection	Successive check	Successive check
Physical inspection	Successive check	Poka-yoke (Self inspection) (Successive check)

Table 2.2 Poka-Yoke and Continuous Inspections

Due to the introduction of an effective poka–yoke device and successive checks, the laundry department of company A achieved an impressive record that would have been impossible otherwise: zero in–process defects for three months straight.

H. Source Inspection
So far, I have recommended successive checks and self–inspections using poka–yoke. However, there is another very useful type of inspection called "source inspection." Source inspection prevents defects by controlling the conditions that influence quality at their source. There are two types of source inspections:

- Vertical source inspection: Traces problems back through the process flow to identify and control conditions that affect quality.

- Horizontal source inspection: Identifies and controls conditions within an operation that affect quality.

Company Y is a manufacturer of acid–proof porcelain. Many defects used to be created in the porcelain baking process. To correct this problem the company tried to change the baking temperature and time, but nothing seemed to eliminate the defects completely.

However, Mr. Kawakubo, the production chief, came up with a solution to the problem. He traced the problem through the process flow and found out that it stemmed from the very first process — the process where clay was mixed with water; apparently a mixing time of three days was too short. He ordered the mixing period to be extended to a full week and as a result, defects from baking dropped significantly. This is a very good example of a vertical source inspection.

The next example is that of a horizontal source inspection. Company H had a 6 percent defect rate in die casting. Although the company lowered their defect rate to 3 percent through QC activities, it would not go any lower.

The company then tried a better method of controlling the die casting process as follows:

- Strict control over the temperature of molten iron
- To keep the die temperature at a certain level they attached a thermometer to the die, which controlled temperature and the volume of the coolant
- Mold–releasing agent used to be applied every few shots, but the company developed a spray machine that sprayed the right amount of agent at correct intervals

These changes within the operation proved successful. A month later, the defect rate was at 2 percent. Two months later, it dropped even further to 1 percent.

Company A, the first manufacturer in the world to produce plastic tanks for washing machines, also attributes its success to a horizontal source inspection—improving conditions within an operation. The company researched how they could keep the die temperature uniform, and eventually they came up with the idea of using Freon to control the temperature of the cooling water. This modification allowed for the successful production of plastic tanks.

Company A also cut down defects by better controlling operational conditions. In one operation in which spot welding was required, the welding was checked by destructive testing—breaking welded parts randomly. However, the company questioned the effectiveness of such an inspection and, instead, introduced an electric current inspection device. If abnormalities are detected within the passing current, workers are alerted with a red light and an audible alarm. Any defective welds discovered in such a manner were rewelded and inspected again. Due to this fundamental improvement, defective welding was eliminated to zero.

In any situation it is important to look at the conditions that create defects and control them, instead of looking at the defects and wondering why. This way of thinking is the basis of all good inspections. In other words, source inspection is the most fundamental way of achieving a defect eliminating inspection.

The German style quality control mentioned earlier is an ideal example of source inspection. We should also remember that in some cases, poka–yoke devices can be used for source inspections quite effectively.

I. Promotion of IT System
When product models are changed, we tend to think that it is normal for the defects to increase, especially at the beginning.

However, IT Electronics was able to launch a new model that achieved an initial defect level of less than 1 percent. I heard the outline of their method to prevent defects from Mr. Yamagata, the company's department chief. So I talked about it, calling it the "IT System," at the IE courses I held.

During one of those courses, Mr. S, who happened to be attending from IT Electronics, stopped by my room at the hotel. While we were chatting he revealed that, "The first production line that implemented the IT system was actually mine."

"Really?"

"Actually, Mr. Yamagata talked us into it."

"Talked you into it, what do you mean?" I said.

"Well, he came to me and said, 'We're going to assemble the new model of televisions on your line, and I want you to know two things: one, make sure that the first 50 products are completely free of defects. Two, you can take as much time as you need for processing.'

"The production lot was 20,000. If he'd asked me to eliminate defects from all 20,000 products, I probably wouldn't have agreed. However, since it was only for the first 50 products, and processing time was not an issue, I decided to accept the task.

"Our factory had been doing successive checks for about five years by then. So we just enforced the rule more strictly — all the defects are sent back to the workers responsible and fixed before being sent to the next process.

"Again, we were able to carry it out without any difficulty since we didn't have to worry about processing time. The interesting thing is that, although we were able to spend as much time as we wanted for processing, it never became two or three times longer, it was about 20 percent more at most. Moreover, we were only originally aiming to eliminate defects of the first 50 products but by the end of the 20,000–piece lot, we found out that the overall defect rate was less that 1 percent, which was less than a tenth that of the previous model."

I was very impressed with the success of the system, as well as the tactic of Mr. Yamagata. If he had said that the defect rate of the whole 20,000 products had to be lower than 1 percent, the idea would not have been accepted. However, by assuring workers that they needed to focus only on the first 50 products, he overcame any psychological skepticism and ultimately achieved the goals for the implementation of the new television model.

Another important point to take note of here is that, when starting this "IT system," Mr. Yamagata asked cooperating factories to never make defects in the first 50 products. Furthermore, the incoming inspection was also made more strict for the first 50 products — 100 percent inspections as opposed to sampling.

This approach of IT Company works in other places as well. When I visited Company K, another electronics company, I asked the managing director, Mr. F, "How do you deal with defects associated with model changes?"

He said, "We first assemble our target number of products. Then if there are defects, we have our experienced workers fix them."

He told me that there was a production line that had just started working on a new model, so I went to the shop floor to take a look. There was a pile of products waiting to be fixed at the end of the production line.

Even with five experienced workers they could not keep up with the incoming flow of defects. A group leader said to me, "There's not much you can do when there's a model change," indicating that it was just assumed that the increase in defects was something to be expected.

I later talked with Mr. F about the example of IT Electronics and arranged to send three directors by airplane to visit the company the following day. I told Mr. F that the product quality should be the main concern, not the production volume after a model change.

Company K introduced IT Electronics' approach upon the launch of their next model. Since successive checks had already been introduced the year before and transition to the new approach went fairly smoothly.

When production of the new model started, their daily

production target was 100. On the first day, only 16 products were made. On the second day, it increased to 72, and by the third day 108 products were made. By the end of the first week, production surpassed the target by 20 percent.

As for in–process defect percentages, it was 24 percent on the first day, 5.5 percent on the second, and 2 percent on the third day. Products requiring repair at the end? Zero.

The following synopsis reveals how they achieved such results. In the production line of 20 people, the company assigned one instructor per five workers. On the first day, the instructors taught the new production method thoroughly. Moreover, if the line stopped as a result of successive checks, the instructor and the worker in charge studied the cause of the defect and changed the work method appropriately. Because of this intense scrutiny on quality and instruction, there was no time to make more than 16 products on the first day. However, the number of defects declined sharply the next day and by the third day, defects had fallen to one tenth the number produced using their conventional method. In addition, the production volume had more than reached its target by the third day. Previously, the production volume had never reached its target until the 15th day.

In general, when there is a model change people tend to excessively worry about a drop in production volume and therefore, give it top priority. However, we must realize that this thinking is flawed. When a new model is introduced the primary concern should be quality. In the end, focusing first on quality will actually increase productivity in the end.

We must remember that having appropriate poka–yoke devices and a successive check method are prerequisites for any successful IT systems.

J. Connection between QC Activities
Tasks commonly labeled as "QC activities" can actually be

categorized as follows:

1. Basic Concept
    a. Deming cycle

    b. Segregation inspection and feedback inspection

2. Management Method (based on inferential statistics)
    a. Analysis of the current situation: Causal chart, histogram

    b. Control method: Control charts, sampling inspections

    c. Measures: Experimental Design

The Deming cycle is akin to the idea used in the scientific method, and the segregation and feedback inspections were explained earlier. These terms helped me clarify my thoughts regarding the functions of inspections.

In any management method, sampling inspections, experimental design, and control charts are based on a foundation of inferential statistics and generally comprise the main focus of QC activities.

As mentioned earlier, around 1951, when I was working for Japan Management Association, Mr. H from N Electric, paid me a visit.

He said, "Do you know what quality control is?"

"It's carrying out effective inspections and eliminating defects, isn't it?"

"No, you have to use inferential statistics," he said and continued to lecture me about control charts, design of experiments, and sampling inspections for about an hour.

A particular part of his lecture really stuck with me. He said, "Even if you do a 100 percent inspection, there's no way to be completely thorough, it would take far too much time and trouble. It is much better to introduce a sampling inspection which has the backing of statistical science. Yes, from now on quality control without using inferential statistics is just nonsense."

After hearing this I became a believer of inferential statistics for a very long time. However, around 1965, when I heard Mr. Tokizane, the managing director at A Electric, say "Even a single television cannot be defective," the spell binding me to statistics was finally broken. I realized that sampling inspections are only a method of improving inspection operations, but by no means guarantee quality.

There is no denying that conventional QC activities, backed by inferential statistics, have made great contributions to quality control in Japan. However, it is very dangerous to blindly believe that quality control and required inferential statistics must go hand in hand.

Inferential statistics are a bit more effective in countries like the United States, where mass production is more common. However, in Japan where the market is smaller, German–style quality control is actually better. In order to shift from inspections that find defects to inspections that eliminate defects, Japan has to end its dependence on the use of inferential statistics.

The basic concept of QC activities—the Deming cycle and feedback inspection—is not wrong; however, the management methods based on inferential statistics are. Obsession with improving the efficiency of inspections using statistics took people's attention away from developing an actual means to eliminate defects. What really matters in quality control is assuring quality through practical means such as successive checks, self–checks, and source inspections, not by improving the efficiency of inspections.

Factories that carry out QC activities using inferential statistics sometimes say that their defect rates have been cut in half. However, in–process defects at those factories often stay around 3 to 6 percent. On the other hand, whenever they introduce successive checks, self–inspections (poka–yoke), or source inspections, their in–process defects drop to 0.1 percent. What does this tell us about statistical quality control?

2.2.4 Active and Passive Improvement of Transportation

When it comes to transportation it is important to understand that there are basically two types of improvements that can be made.

- Improvement of transportation — Improvement of layout
- Improvement of transportation operation — Using fork lifts, conveyors, etc.

A. Transportation Only Serves to Raise Costs

As mentioned earlier, transportation only serves to raise production costs, never product value. Yet, if we were to look at the breakdown of production hours at most factories, more than likely transportation along with processing would consume the largest portion, along with processing:

Processing: 45 percent

Inspection: 5 percent

Transportation: 45 percent

Delay: 5 percent

If you include transportation hidden within the motions of processing, it will probably surpass 90 percent. Therefore, improving transportation is an extremely important aspect of factory improvement.

It is often said that a country's standard of living greatly depends on the quantity and quality of natural resources and labor. Since Japan is scarce in natural resources, quantity and quality of labor becomes a major determining factor for the country's quality of living. Therefore, for those of us involved in manufacturing, wasting this precious labor on transportation should be considered a crime.

Granted, most people generally think that transportation is not desirable. However, not many people correctly understand that it is an abomination that should be pursued, identified, and eliminated. More often than not people just look at transportation as a necessary evil of production, assuming that not much can be done about it. They allow themselves to become satisfied with conveyors or fork lifts—in other words, improved means of transportation. However, these are passive transportation improvements.

The only way to eliminate transportation is through actively improving the layout. It should be pointed out that there are two aspects to layout change: improving machine layout in factories, and improving placement of parts and tools around workers.

B. Elements That Determine a Layout

Assume that there is one milling machine, M, and two lathes, L1 and L2. Product P flows from L1 to M and uses 80 percent of the capacity of M. Another product, Q, flows from L2 to M and uses 20 percent of the capacity of M. Now there is a plan to purchase and install a new machine. Since the new machine has priority over L1 and L2, one of them has to be moved. Which one should it be?

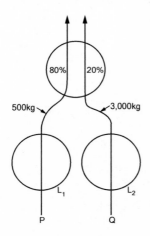

Figure 2.23 Conditions to Determine Layout

Eight out of ten people who are asked this question would say that L2 should be moved because L1 has a higher work load. But is this answer really correct? The correct answer is: "There is insufficient information to determine an answer to that question."

What would the answer be if the following additional information is given? The total weight of product P moved from L1 and M is 500 kilograms per month, whereas that of product Q is 3,000 kilograms per month. Put it another way, product P is small and light, yet its processing takes time, while product Q is large and heavy, yet its processing does not take much time. With this additional information, the correct answer to the proposed question is: L2 for product Q should be given priority and L1 for product P should be moved.

This example underscores the importance of determining machine layout based upon the magnitude of the transport difficulty and not by the magnitude of the machine work load.

Table 2.3 shows the factors to consider when determining the coefficient of transport difficulty.

Factors Affecting Transportation Difficulty	
1 Weight (W):	Greater weight means more difficult transportation.
2 Number of pieces (N):	Given the same weight, a greater number of pieces means greater transportation difficulty.
3 Volume (V):	Given the same weight and number of pieces, a larger volume means greater transportation difficulty.
4 Shape (F):	Given the same weight, volume, and number of pieces, the degree of transportation difficulty depends on shape, a rectangle being easier than sheets and slabs.
5 Balance (B):	Symmetry or asymmetry, localized concentration of mass, and other balance factors affect transportation difficulty.
6 Rigidity (S):	Whether an object is flexible or rigid or well-bundled or not affects the transportation difficulty.
7 State (C):	Transportation difficulties varies for gases, liquids, and solids. Even among solids, transportation difficulty differs for particulates, powders, and nodules. Even among liquids, transportation difficulty differs for slurries, suspensions, gelatins, etc.
8 Attentiveness (A):	Danger of scratching, denting, and safety-related precautions affect transportation difficulty.

Table 2.3 Factors Affecting Transportation Difficulty

C. Determining Layout Based on the Coefficient of Difficulty
The following is a procedural outline for determining machine layout based on the transportation difficulty coefficient.

1. Perform an ABC analysis of products

> In order to determine a machine layout based on product priority, conduct an ABC analysis over a given time frame as shown in Figure 2.24 (p. 78). In this example over a three month period, 10 out of 76 items took up 75 percent of the production volume. It was decided that the layout should be determined based on these 10 items.

2. Create a transportation flow analysis (Figure 2.25, p. 79)

> Create a transportation analysis chart by studying the process sequence of the selected items above.

3. Create a chart of transportation difficulty (Figure 2.26, Insert)

> Based on the monthly transportation weight and flow analysis of each item, calculate the total transportation volume between each machine.

4. Create transportation difficulty coefficient card (Figure 2.27, p. 80)

> For each machine, create a transportation difficulty coefficient card showing the "incoming" and "outgoing" weight.

5. Create trial layout plans (Figure 2.28, Insert)

> Create trial processing layouts based on the coefficients determined by the cards. If multiple machines compete for the same place, priority is given to higher coefficients. Make three trial plans this way.

6. Calculate optimal coefficient of trial plans

> If two machines are placed adjacent to each other, they are given O under the "layout continuity" section of the card, while the ones that are not are given an X. Calculate the optimal coefficient for each layout plan using the following equation: Optimal coefficient = Total O coefficients / Total coefficients.

Pick the plan with the highest optimal coefficient.

7. Make actual layout plans

Based on the selected tentative layout plan, draw a floor plan at a ratio of 1:50 that includes sketches of all machines. Again, if multiple machines vie for the same space because of the floor plan, the ones with higher transportation difficulty coefficients are first. Then, take the aspects related to operation and emergency into consideration next. Make three actual layout plans this way.

8. Calculate optimum coefficient of actual layout

For every actual layout plan, place the corresponding transportation difficulty coefficient cards on top and calculate optimal coefficients. Compare the optimal coefficient of each layout plan and select the plan with the highest value.

9. Draw transportation flows of the former and new layouts

Draw transportation flows of the new layout as in Figure 2.29. Make the length of the lines between machines correspond with the numerical size of the transportation difficulty coefficients. Problems can easily be spotted and improvement compared to the former layout can be visualized.

10. Comparison of optimal coefficients

Comparing the optimal coefficients of the former and new layouts quantifies the improvement. This technique has the following advantages:

- Any factory can find a machine layout that suits their particular plant and production needs
- The use of the optimal coefficient makes it possible to make an objective and quantitative judgment on which plan is the best
- Anyone can formulate an excellent layout plan

Because of these advantages this technique makes scientific layouts that minimize transportation within any factories reach.

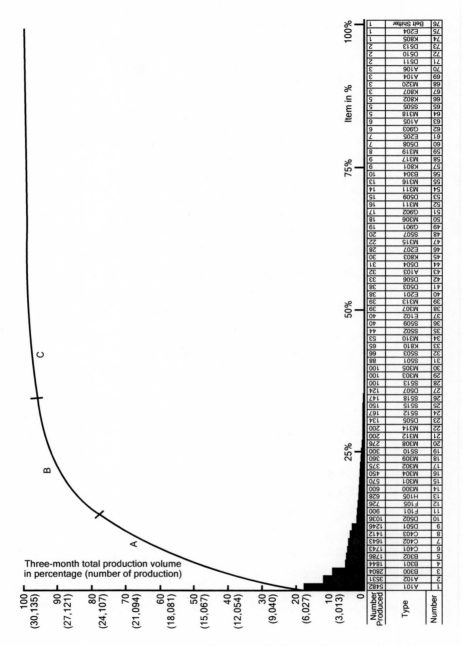

Figure 2.24 ABC Analysis of Production Volume

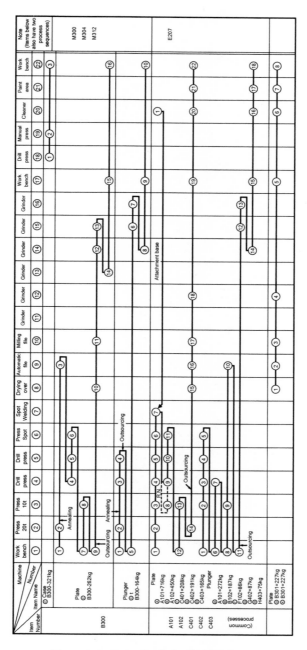

Figure 2.25 Route Analysis of Major Parts

Card No. 1

Receiving	Total 5326		Relation				
No.	Machine	Coefficient Former	Former	Tentative	Actual		
1	⑥	2607	O	O	O	Machine	
2	④	829	O	X	O	Work Bench	
3	②	781	O	O	O	No. 2	
4	⑨	683	X	X	X		
5	③	262	X	O	O		
6	⑤	164	O	X	O	Load	
7							

Sending	Total 8922		Relation		
No.	Machine	Coefficient Former	Former	Tentative	Actual
1	③	4303	X	O	O
2	②	2965	O	O	O
3	⑥	709	X	X	O
4	④	683	O	X	O
5	⑧	262	X	O	O
6					
7					

Card No. 2

Receiving	Total 4627		Relation				
No.	Machine	Coefficient Former	Former	Tentative	Actual		
1	①	2965	O	O	O	Machine	
2	③	1662	O	O	O	Press (20t)	
3							
4						No. 1	
5							
6						Load	
7							

Sending	Total 4627		Relation		
No.	Machine	Coefficient Former	Former	Tentative	Actual
1	③	1662	X	O	O
2	③	1085	O	O	O
3	①	781	O	O	O
4	⑨	565	X	O	X
5	④	534	O	X	X
6					
7					

Card No. 3

Receiving	Total 6842		Relation				
No.	Machine	Coefficient Former	Former	Tentative	Actual		
1	①	4304	X	O	O	Machine	
2	⑦	1454	X	X	O	Press (10t)	
3	②	1085	O	O	O		
4						No. 1	
5							
6							
7						Load	
8							

Sending	Total 7884		Relation		
No.	Machine	Coefficient Former	Former	Tentative	Actual
1	④	3028	X	O	O
2	②	1662	O	O	O
3	⑧	781	X	X	O
4	⑤	716	X	X	X
5	⑩	683	X	X	X
6	⑪	464	X	X	O
7	⑦	258	X	O	O
8	⑨	262	X	O	O

Card No. 4

Receiving	Total 4715		Relation				
No.	Machine	Coefficient Former	Former	Tentative	Actual		
1	③	3028	X	O	O	Machine	
2	①	683	O	X	O	Drill press	
3	②	534	O	X	X		
4	⑨	262	X	X	X	No. 1	
5	⑦	208	X	X	O		
6						Load	
7							

Sending	Total 4629		Relation		
No.	Machine	Coefficient Former	Former	Tentative	Actual
1	⑤	3800	O	O	O
2	①	829	O	X	O
3					
4					
5					
6					
7					

Card No. 5

Receiving	Total 4516		Relation				
No.	Machine	Coefficient Former	Former	Tentative	Actual		
1	④	3800	O	O	O	Machine	
2	③	716	X	O	O	Drill press	
3							
4						No. 1	
5							
6						Load	
7							

Sending	Total 3800		Relation		
No.	Machine	Coefficient Former	Former	Tentative	Actual
1	⑥	3636	O	O	O
2	①	164	O	X	O
3					

Card No. 6

Receiving	Total 3924		Relation				
No.	Machine	Coefficient Former	Former	Tentative	Actual		
1	⑤	2607	O	O	O	Machine	
2	③	288	X	O	O	Drill Press	
3							
4						No. 1	
5							
6						Load	
7							

Sending	Total 4269		Relation	
No.	Machine	Coefficient Former	Former	Tentative
1	①	2607	O	O
2	⑦	1662	X	O
3				
4				
5				
6				
7				

Card No. 7

Receiving	Total 1662		Relation				
No.	Machine	Coefficient Former	Former	Tentative	Actual		
1	⑥	1662	X	O	O	Machine	
2						Spot welder	
3							
4						No. 1	
5							
6						Load	
7							

Sending	Total 1662	
No.	Machine	
1	③	
2	④	
3		
4		
5		
6		
7		

Card No. 8

Receiving	Total 2705		Relation		
No.	Machine	Coefficient Former	Former	Tentative	Actual
1	②	1662			
2	③	781			
3	①	262			
4					
5					
6					
7					

Receiving	Total
No.	

Note:

1. As a general rule, totals of coefficients for receiving and sending should be equal.

2. Totals do not match if items are received from or sent out of the department, such as finishing area or outsourcing factories.

3. Totals will match if the cards are also created for the finishing area or outsourcing factories.

4. In this particular case, some totals no not match since receiving and sending between the finishing area and outsourcing factories are omitted.

Figure 2.27 Transport Difficulty Coefficient Card

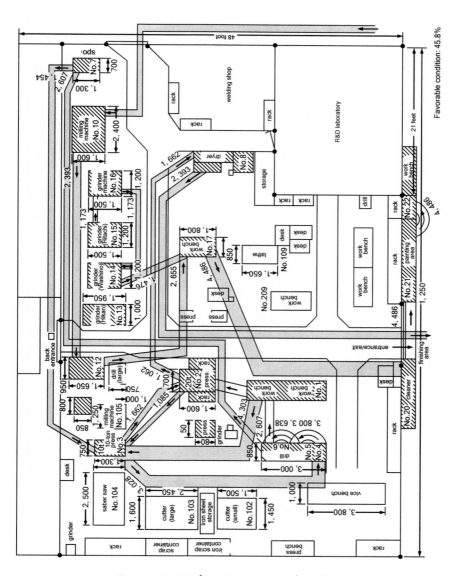

Figure 2.29a Machine Arrangement Flow Chart

81

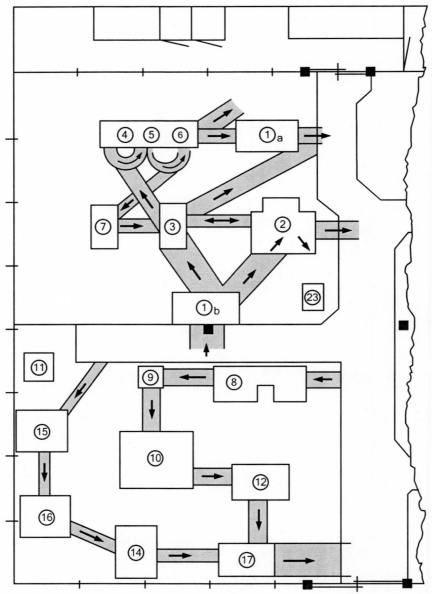

Note: Only pertinent machines are shown

Figure 2.29b Machine Arrangement Flow Chart

No.	Machine	Favorable Degree			Note
		Former	Tentative	Actual	
1	Work bench	8029	11180	13565	Add one or more
2	Press 20t	7027	8720	8155	work bench(s).
3	Press 10t	2747	11344	13262	
4	Drill press	5846	6828	8548	
5	Drill press	7600	8152	8316	
6	Drill press	6243	8193	8193	
7	Spot welder	0	1662	3324	
8	Drying oven	262	4579	4579	
9	Automatic file	0	5351	4786	
10	Milling Machine	262	5048	5310	
11	Grinder (2B)	0	781	0	
12	Grinder	0	5310	5048	
13	Grinder (Hikari)	0	0	0	The factory
14	Grinder (Washino)	2164	3337	1435	decided not to
15	Grinder (Hitachi)	1861	2123	1882	use this machine.
16	Grinder (Washino)	1173	2346	1173	
17	Work bench (deburring)	1476	9398	7141	
18	Drill press (new plant)	0	341	0	
19	Manual press	0	682	0	
20	Cleaner	4486	8972	8972	
21	Painting area	8972	8972	8972	
22	Work bench (for new plant)	4486	4872	4486	
Favorable degree total		62634	118146	117147	
Optimal coefficient		45.80%	86.50%	85.80%	

Note 1: Total of transport diffulty coefficient is 68309 x 2= 136,618 (Sum of receiving and sending).
Note 2: Lower numbers under "former (layout)" are the ones that needed layout improvement.

Table 2.4 Optimum Coefficient

D. When Transportation Cannot be Eliminated by Layout

When thinking about machine layout the goal is always to eliminate transportation. However, there are times when certain transportation is necessary. When a machine is part of multiple process sequences, (when different flows of multiple products merge at the machine), creating optimal conditions for every sequence can be very difficult.

If machines are inexpensive it is still possible to eliminate transportation by buying more machines. However, if machines are expensive, transportation may be unavoidable. This decision should not be a hasty one since a machine is only paid for once, whereas the cost of transportation has to be paid every time it happens.

In this sense, adopting better forms of transportation should be considered only after all the options of elimination are completely exhausted.

E. Layout Improvement and Transportation Improvement

Transportation is an activity that only serves to raise product cost—this premise is always true. However, as mentioned earlier, transportation is a direct result of the division of labor. In this sense, transportation could be considered to provide value to production as long as the benefits outweigh the cost of transportation. Conversely, this means that if the benefits of the division of labor does not outweigh the cost of transportation, it would be better to abandon the division of labor. After all, the fact that transportation raises product cost will never change. When introducing division of labor, a change in layout, or a new means of transportation, it is always important to weigh the benefits versus costs.

Layout and transportation improvements usually occur in four stages.

1. First stage: Improvement of the means of transportation is not even considered, let alone improvement of the layout.

2. Second stage: Only the means of transportation is improved, and improvement of layout is not considered.

3. Third stage: Layout is improved, but transportation still exists, although the means of transportation has been improved.

4. Fourth stage: Transportation is eliminated due to layout improvement.

Among those four stages, the third and fourth are considered as active transportation improvement; the second is considered passive. The first is out of the question.

When transportation has to occur and the means of doing so is being discussed, it is important to make decisions based on the nature of the transportation, rather than deciding things arbitrarily. The nature of transportation can be clarified by asking these questions:

- Is the transportation continuous or discrete?
- Is the transportation rout fixed or variable?
- Is it horizontal, vertical, or flexible?
- Is it powered or not powered?

Answers to these questions, along with the information presented in Table 2.5, help in figuring out appropriate means of transportation.

	Application of Transportation equipment																							
Power	Powered												Not powered											
Continuity	Individual transportation						Continuous transportation						Individual transportation						Continuous transportation					
Path	Fixed			Not fixed			Fixed			Not fixed			Fixed			Not fixed			Fixed			Not fixed		
Direction	Horizontal	Vertical	Arbitrary	Horizontal	Vertical	Arbitrary	Horizontal	Vertical	Arbitrary	Horizontal	Vertical	Arbitrary	Horizontal	Vertical	Arbitrary	Horizontal	Vertical	Arbitrary	Horizontal	Vertical	Arbitrary	Horizontal	Vertical	Arbitrary
Rail car													○											
Dump truck													○											
Monorail car													○											
Winch															□									
Chain block														△										
Manual hoist														△										
Jack														△										
Manual crane														△										
Powered rail car	○																							
Cableway	○		□																					
Crane			□																					
Pneumatic shipping			□																					
Rope shipping			□																					
Electric lift car						□																		
Elevator		△																						
Powered hoist		△																						
Wheelbarrow																○								
Carriage																○								
Push cart																○								
Manual lift car																○		□						
Electric cart				○																				
Fork lift truck						□																		
Chute																			○					
Roller conveyor																			○					
Turntable																			○					
Ball bearing conveyor																						○		
Goose-neck conveyor																						○		
Drop chute																				△				
Circular chute																				△				
Spiral chute																				△				
Automatic roller conveyor							○																	
Belt conveyor							○																	
Board conveyor							○																	
Powered turntable							○																	
Pull chain							○																	
Endless							○																	
Elevator conveyor							○																	
Trolley									□															
Endless cable									□															
Endless chain									□															
Bucket conveyor									□															
Screw conveyor									□															
Spiral feeder									□															
Suction pneumatic tube									□															
Pneumatic tube									□															
Magazine feeder								△																
Truck				○																				

Table 2.5 Transportation & Suitability Table

2.2.5 Active and Passive Improvement of Transportation

A. What are Delays?

A delay is a state in which time passes without the performance of processing, inspection, or transportation. A delay increases cost but never adds any direct value to the product.

Delays are phenomena that accompany processing, inspection, or transportation. But if you are not careful they happen everywhere and end up causing great loss in production. Managers are often not aware of the magnitude of the risk that delays have, or they think of delays as "unavoidable" or a "necessary evil" and just let them happen.

However, delays are a major problem and can have many negative production effects, such as: longer cycle times, an increase in stored materials and products, poor return on investment due to an increase in work–in–process materials, an increase in pallets, reduction in available storage space, and an increase in production cycle time due to storage activities.

Longer production cycle times are problematic, especially if the production cycle becomes longer than the lead time. This causes production operations to be rushed to meet delivery schedules leading to unnecessary strain and excess waste during production.

The method of production used can have a strong effect on incurred delays. In general, these methods can be reduced to the following types:

- Single–process method: The production quantity is large, such that a single product is produced by one process for more than 1 month.
- Common–process method: The production quality is not necessarily large, but multiple products are produced using a common process.
- Similar–process method: The production process for two or more products is not identical, but it is similar enough that the different products are produced using the same process. The machines not used are simply bypassed.

- Convergent–process method: There is no common or similar process; multiple products flow over different and intersecting processes.

With a convergent process, items emerging from one group of machines are passed to another group of machines. Because the flow is very complicated, a certain amount of delay is unavoidable. However, close observation of any convergent process will probably reveal that there is more delay than necessary. Indeed, what is believed to be a convergent process is actually made up of elements of common processes or similar processes. Such delays can be improved and fall within the category of process management improvement.

In reality, a pure convergent process is very rare. In most cases, processes that are believed to be convergent only appear as such because the process sequence for the upstream production is not well analyzed or designed and the spatial layout of the upstream machines is not optimal. Therefore, these two points should be checked. With a single process, production is continuous with products continuously passing from process to process. With convergent processes, production is intermittent with the flow of products stopping between each process.

Continuous production promises minimal delays, whereas frequent delays are expected with convergent processes. Delays within common processes and similar processes fall somewhere in between. In practice however, not enough effort is spent minimizing delays in all production modes, including single processes.

Issues regarding delay will be explained in detail in the following sections. For the sake of expedience, explanations will be limited to those occurring between two processes. This is because delays occurring between a greater number of processes can be considered a combination of delays occurring between two processes.

As discussed earlier, there are two types of delays: (1) process delays, in which an entire lot waits for the next process, and (2) lot delays, in which the remainder of a lot waits for one piece in the lot to be processed. The remainder of the lot may or may not be already processed.

B. Delivery Period and Production Cycle

One of the most important issues in production control, especially process control, is the relationship between delivery period (lead time) and production cycle time.

- Delivery period (D): This period begins when an order is received and ends when the order is delivered
- Production cycle time (P): This period begins when the first process starts and ends when the product is completed — including any subcontracting

If the lead time D is greater than production cycle P, (D = 15 days, P = 10 days, for example), it is not a problem. However, if P is greater than D (D = 15 days, P = 20 days, for example) an extension of the delivery deadline is inevitable. If the delivery deadline must be met, a tremendous amount of pressure is created. In most cases, the delay is still unavoidable.

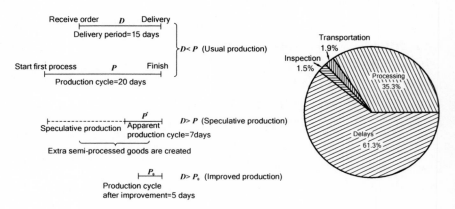

Figure 2.30 Order Period, Production Period, and Delays

Therefore, if such condition ($D<P$) is expected, the common practice is to start production early. This is called building to

forecast. Even if the actual production cycle is 10 days, this makes the apparent production cycle P shorter, such as 7 days.

This approach works as long as the forecast is correct. However, if it is not, problems occur. And even if the forecast is accurate, stock buildup of semi–processed goods is unavoidable.

For this reason, the best approach is to reduce the production cycle time. But first, we must recognize that delays account for a major part of the production cycle time and that delays can be significantly reduced if appropriate counter–measures are implemented.

C. Process Delays
(a) Production Cycle and Process Delay Period
Most people think that the production cycle is the sum of individual processing times. In most cases however, this is completely wrong. With most plants, the ratio of processing time to process delay time is between 1 to 4 and 2 to 3. This means that in order to shorten production cycle, it is more effective to cut down on process delay times rather than processing times.

(b) Characteristics of Process Delay
Different types of process delays have different characteristics. Delays necessitated by processes include:

- Process delays required for stabilizing a process
- Process delays not required for stabilizing a process

Process delays based on causal factors include:

- Process delays caused by surplus capacity
- Process delays cause by scheduling

The significance of process delay must be considered in light of the characteristics above. The word "surplus capacity" is an indication of the relationship between load and capacity. Surplus capacity is often confused with capacity. Capacity (measured in hours) is the ability to perform a task.

Load (also measured in hours) is the number of hours required to produce the number of products scheduled to meet demand (either build to order, or build to forecast).

Surplus capacity is calculated as follows:

Case A:

- Capacity: One machine capable of handling 176 hours worth of a work per month
- Load: 150 hours worth of work
- Surplus capacity:
- 176 – 150/176 = +14.8 percent

Case B:

- Capacity: Three machines capable of handling 528 hours worth of work per month
- Load: 500 hours worth of work
- Surplus capacity: 528 – 500/528 = +5.3 percent

In these examples, the capacity of the three machines in case B is greater than that of the single machine in case A, however surplus capacity is greater in case A.

A process delay is determined by any imbalance of *surplus* capacity, not capacity, of upstream and downstream processes. For example, if the surplus capacity of the next process is smaller than that of the preceding process, a process delay occurs. If the surplus capacity of the next process is larger than that of the preceding process, the next process will wait for the goods to arrive.

Again, attention is needed in distinguishing between surplus capacity and capacity, since they are often confused with one another.

D. Relationship Between Surplus Capacity and Capacity

As mentioned, surplus capacity is based on the relationship between load and capacity. In reality, load can change as defects and other production problems occur; in fact, the load can increase by an amount equivalent to the defect rate as more products need to be produced to offset those lost to defects. Similarly, capacity (the maximum amount of available production time) can also change due to machine breakdowns, worker absences, delays in supplied material, etc. However, we assume that production management has mechanisms in place (redundant machine capacity, surplus staffing capacity, and "just–in–case" inventory) to compensate for these phenomena, and they will not be addressed in the following discussion.

When we set up the production schedule (load), it is absolutely necessary to make sure that the surplus capacity of all processes is positive (+). If even one process has a negative (–) surplus capacity, the target production level cannot be achieved. If this happens to be the case, there are counter–measures we can take such as increasing available working hours by working overtime, using a two– or three–shift day, or hiring a subcontractor to make up the difference.

These measures work but they create timing gaps. Therefore, it is preferable if we can take measures that increase capacity without creating timing gaps, such as increasing capacity by decreasing delays.

When 300,000 pieces of part X are scheduled to be produced per month, each process should produce 300,000 pieces. It seems obvious that increasing production of only one process, to 500,000 pieces for example, would not make any sense. However, whether or not this solution is valid can only be truly understood by examining how the relationships between capacity and load come into play.

Assume that three stamping machines A, B, and C are used to produce part X. Press A blanks, press B punches, and press C forms.

The potential capacity of each machine is as follows (availability: 8 hours per day, 22 days per month):

Machine A: 80 cycles per minute ... 22 x 480 x 80= 844,800 cycles

Machine B: 60 cycles per minute ... 22 x 480 x 60 = 633,600 cycles

Machine C: 40 cycles per minute ... 22 x 480 x 4 = 422,400 cycles

Since load is the same for each machine, the surplus capacity of each machine differs:

Machine A

844,800 – 300,000/844,300 x 100 = +64.5 percent

Machine B

633,600 – 300,000/633,600 x 100 = + 52.7 percent

Machine C

422,400 – 300,000/422,400 x 100 = + 29.0 percent

Since all three presses above show positive (+) surplus capacity, this guarantees that the production of 300,000 pieces per month is possible. Also, since surplus capacity of each process is different, if the machines are used to their full capacity, an even greater amount of delays will occur between processes.

Just because machines have large capacity does not mean that capacity should be utilized. Only the required number of pieces, that match the scheduled load should be produced. Capacity that is necessary to handle the load is called required capacity.

If there is a gap between the machines potential capacity and required capacity, it is important to control the potential capacity to match the required capacity. This adjustment is crucial controlling process delays.

When 300,000 pieces of part X need to be produced, it would require Machine A to run for 62.5 hours, Machine B 93.8 hours, and Machine C to run for 125 hours. When there are large differences in cycle times for sequential machines or processes, as there are in this case, an intermittent production process, which causes many process delays, is often used. If the machines are part of a convergent process delays are unavoidable. In a convergent process a different combination of products will be run after part X. This means different process sequences with different excess capacities.

The problem is that intermittent production methods are also used with similar processes and common processes. Furthermore, intermittent production is used even for a single–process sequence, with the cause being the large difference in excess capacities of the machine in question. In these cases, use of intermittent production serves no purpose but to increase process delays.

If we try to eliminate process delays, synchronization is the only way. Synchronization is accomplished by satisfying the following two conditions:

- Leveling surplus capacity
- Coordinating start and end times

Even if a single–process sequence, common–process sequence, or similar–process sequence is changed to continuous production to eliminate process delays, reconciling the surplus capacity disparity, (the gap between potential and required capacity) becomes a major issue.

The easiest way to achieve synchronization is to reduce the surplus capacity to the required capacity level. One way to do this is to run the machine at a slower speed, but this may cause mechanical problems. In most cases this is done by stopping the machine once the required production level (load) is achieved. This method can pose numerous problems however, depending on the production period.

Consider the previous example of Machines A, B, and C that in sequence produce product X. The current production schedule calls for 300,000 units a month. To produce 300,000 units of part X, recall the Machine A has to run for 62.5 hours, Machine B for 83.3 hours, and Machine C for 125 hours.

Consider also that the 300,000 units required per month were produced in one continuous run, but not transported as a lot from one machine to the next until the entire lot was finished. If the machines were to be stopped when the required load was produced, the following delays would occur:

- Between Machines A and B—a maximum delay of 20.8 hours = lost opportunity of 100,000 pieces from Machine A
- Between Machines B and C—a maximum delay of 41.7 hours = lost opportunity of 150,000 pieces from Machine B

Consider the same example when the production is split between two runs of 150,000 pieces a month:

- Between Machines A and B—a maximum delay of 10.4 hours (per run) = lost opportunity of 50,000 pieces from Machine A
- Between Machines B and C—a maximum delay of 20.8 hours (per run) = lost opportunity of 50,000 pieces

As this shows, as the number of days of production decrease, the delays decrease. On the other hand, as the number of division increases the amount of time during which a machine stays idle decreases, and this makes it more difficult for the machine to be used for something else. If the number of division is lower, the machine is more likely to be used for some other job.

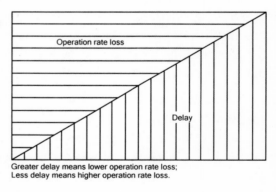

Greater delay means lower operation rate loss;
Less delay means higher operation rate loss.

Figure 2.31 Relation between Operation Rate & Delays

In other words, while a lower number of division improves the machine's operation rate, it brings about delays and problems such as the need for additional storage space and increased worker–hours.

One solution for these delays is to use inexpensive machines. Although this sacrifices machine operation rates it minimizes delays, storage space, and makes it easy to automate delay-related operations.

When we discuss division, what is at issue is not the number of production lots, but division of the lot being produced for transportation purposes. In other words, monthly production can be fixed at 300,000. What is necessary is frequent adjustment of the gap between the required capacity and the potential capacity of processes with high potential capacities. One method may be to stop the process after producing 100 pieces and start production once the delay approaches zero. The use of such a short run/stop cycle is what I mean by division. This method cuts back delays while sacrificing operation rate and is called the full work control method.

The same relationship can be seen in common–process sequence and similar–process sequence. In these cases however, how to deal with setup changeover becomes an important issue. Changeover can be completed quite fast—in a couple of minutes—if the SMED method is applied.

Furthermore, the best option is to attach two dies in a machine with high potential capacity in a way that can be replaced with a single step. For example, after part A is manufactured for two minutes, change the die immediately and switch to part B, and send parts A and B to their corresponding lines. If continuous production becomes possible in two lines this way, it could minimize delays without sacrificing machine operation rate.

To achieve this, development of a single–step setup (one-touch setup), an even more advanced form of SMED, is crucial. Single–step setup has already been successfully implemented in many factories.

I said earlier that when potential capacities are different, gaps in surplus capacity occur. In a case like this, if potential capacity can be averaged to match the highest capacity among the processes, tremendous improvement will result.

A thorough understanding of the following items explained thus far is very important for successfully implementing assembly-line process control and the non-stock production method:

- Averaging surplus capacity
- Averaging load
- Continuous and intermittent production method
- The relationship between potential capacity and required capacity
- The relationship between machine operation rate and delay compensation
- Common-process sequence and reduction of setup change over time
- Improvement of both operation rate and delays through one-step setup changeover

E. Process Delays Required for Process Stabilization

When we believe that a certain process delay is necessary, we must study it from two points of view: surplus capacity and schedule.

A process delay (sometimes called semi-processed goods) can stabilize a process flow in the following cases (Alphabet in parenthesis shows a type of flow curve shown later):

1. From the viewpoint of surplus capacity:

- The machine in the previous process is broken (Type A)
- Products do not arrive because a worker at a previous process is absent (Type A)
- Unexpected defects occur at a previous process (If defective rate is stable, production volume can be raised in advance to compensate for it—Type A)
- A subsequent process requires items immediately due to a change in the production plan (Type D)
- When setup time is long, the lot size is increased to im-

prove productivity (Type VE)

2. From the viewpoint of schedule:

- With anticipated production, a lead time is set to compensate for errors in demand forecast (Type D)
- When one machine provides items to several processes, certain items are produced in advance (Type OS)
- When lead time is permitted to compensate for scheduling uncertainty of receiving goods from subcontractors (Type A)

F. Unnecessary Process Delay

There are unnecessary process delays that occur in the following cases.

1. From the viewpoint of surplus capacity:

- When a machine in a subsequent process breaks down (Type B)
- When a worker is absent in the subsequent process (Type B)
- When a previous process uses overtime and two shifts while a subsequent process uses only a day shift because excess capacity is adequately balanced (Type VE)
- When there is a difference in the working hours of regular employees and part–time workers (Type VE)
- When overproduction occurs temporarily due to the large surplus capacity of the previous process, even though the working hours are the same (Type VE)

2. From the viewpoint of schedule:

- When more lead time was scheduled than required (Type D)

G. Flow Curve

Several other examples of process delays are best understood through the concept of a flow curve.

As shown in Figure 2.32, the y axis represents quantity, the x axis represents the day of the month. The amount of semi–processed goods at the beginning of the month is plotted along the y axis, the cumulative incoming line is drawn at the top, and the cumulative outgoing line (this also indicates the cumulative incoming line for the second process) is drawn at the bottom.

Date		1	3	4	5	6	7	8	10	11	12	Total
In	-	2	2/10	2/12	1/13	1/14	0/14	2/16	1/17	3/20	2/22	
Out	-	0	1/1	3/4	1/5	1/6	2/8	1/9	2/11	4/15	2/17	17
Remaining	6	8	9	8	8	8	6	7	6	5	5	5

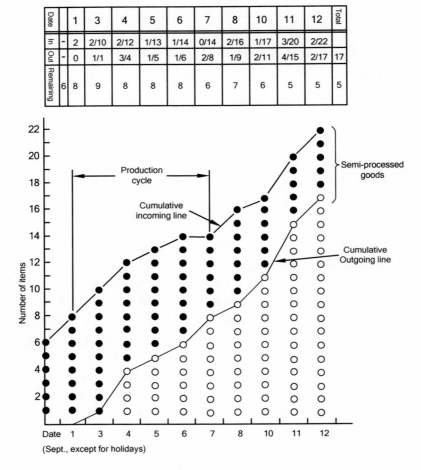

Figure 2.32 Cumulative Curve

The distance between the two lines indicate the following:

- Vertical distance between the two lines indicates the amount of semi–processed goods for each day
- Horizontal distance between the two lines indicates the

production cycle for the period – in this case, production cycle is defined as the sum of the process delay period and processing period

H. Delays and Flow Curve
Necessary Process Delays and Unnecessary Process Delays
A flow curve can be interpreted in the following ways:

- Line with large angle: large capacity
- Line with small angle: small capacity
- Horizontal line: no production

Take a look at the flow curve shown in Figure 2.33. The vertical distance between the cumulative incoming line and the cumulative outgoing line is used to draw a curve indicating fluctuations in the amount of delay. The standard deviation (c) of delay quantify fluctuation is determined. The value equal to 3σ is calculated. Assume that this value is 250 pieces (3σ= 250 pieces). If the mean value is 600 pieces, the difference between the mean and the 250 pieces (600–250=350 pieces) represents unnecessary stock.

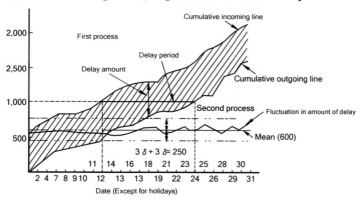

Figure 2.33 Inventory Volume Fluctuation Curve

Statistically this is because a delay quantity equal to 3σ will be sufficient to absorb variations 997.2 times out of 1,000. Moreover, because the exceptional 2.7 times (1000 – 997.3 = 2.7) occur with equal likelihood above the upper limit and below the lower limit, the probability that the lower limit is not reached (that is, the probability of the delay amount being equal to zero) is 1.35 (2.7/2) out of 1,000.

Therefore, if the two cumulative lines are close together because of a decrease in the incoming amount or an increase in the outgoing amount, the delay would be equal to zero and the next process would have to be stopped. However, even if such variations occurred, a delay quantity of 250 is sufficient to accommodate all situations except those that occur once in 1,000 times. For all practical purposes, this means there will not be a problem. Thus a value of 350 (600–250) indicates unnecessary delays.

Process Delays and the Shape of the Flow Curve
1. Unbalance Type (Type VE, VS)
In this case, there is imbalance between the incoming capacity and the outgoing capacity (production capacity of the second process).

Type VE
The incoming capacity is larger than the outgoing capacity. The production capacity of the second process is comparable to the load (Figure 2.34).

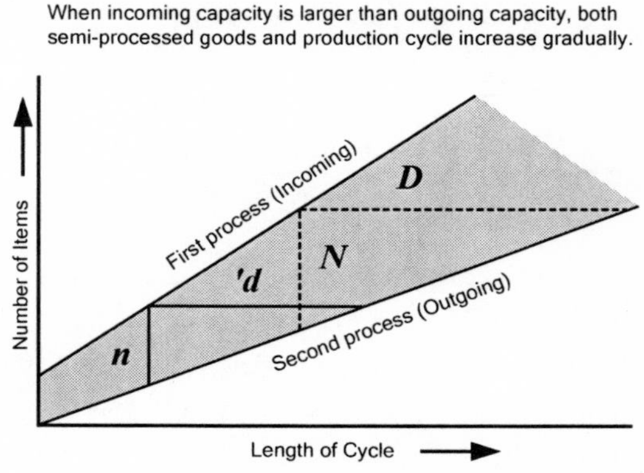

When incoming capacity is larger than outgoing capacity, both semi-processed goods and production cycle increase gradually.

Figure 2.34 Imbalance Type VE

In this pattern, process delays, or semi–processed goods, could increase infinitely. In reality however, infinite increase is not possible and incoming items have to stop at some point to regain a balance.

If 50,000 pieces a month is the production target, it is only natural that 50,000 pieces are produced at all the processes. However, people often get carried away by large surplus capacity, which is capacity of a machine if the load is the same, and produce at the machine's full capacity until this Type VE problem surfaces. By then, many process delays have accumulated between processes and production has to be halted abruptly.

In production, load should always stay the same throughout processes and machine capacity needs to adapt to it. In other words, as mentioned earlier, potential capacity and required capacity of machines must be adjusted properly. Although this requirement is very simple, those in charge of the shop floor often forget it and this problem emerges.

Type VS
The incoming capacity is smaller than the outgoing capacity. The production capacity of the second process is comparable to the load.

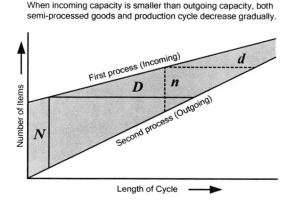

When incoming capacity is smaller than outgoing capacity, both semi-processed goods and production cycle decrease gradually.

Figure 2.35 Imbalance Type VS

In this particular case, process delays decreased gradually until they eventually hit zero. This method is not a problem until semi–processed goods (process delays) between the first and second process disappear. However, this cannot be used permanently. Shop floor managers need to pay attention to this pattern since there is often a misunderstanding that this type of problem will never occur so long as there is a large amount of semi–processed stock.

This condition can be addressed by increasing the capacity of the first process to match that of the second process. This can be done by taking measures such as increasing the number of machines, working overtime, and outsourcing.

2. Incoming Fluctuation Type A
The capacities of both first and second processes are well balanced and comparable to the load, but there are fluctuations in the capacity line of the first process.

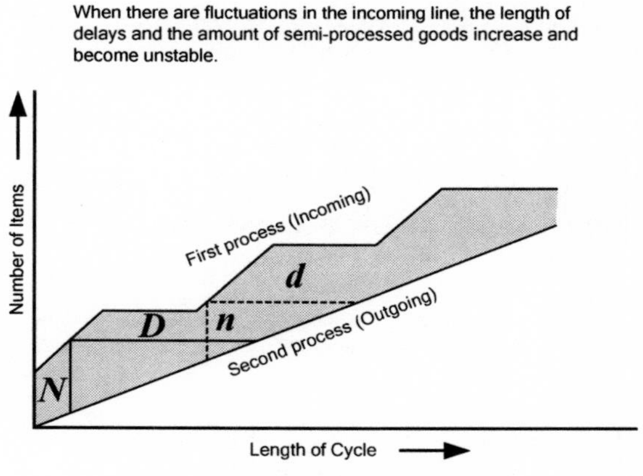

When there are fluctuations in the incoming line, the length of delays and the amount of semi-processed goods increase and become unstable.

Figure 2.36 Order Fluctuation Type A

Put differently, the first process produces at a high level for a certain period and then stops. However, both processes are balanced.

In this case the amount of process delays fluctuates, and a certain amount of delays are necessary in order to prevent shortage of products at the second process.

Among cases of process delays, this type falls under the following:

- The machine in the upstream process is broken
- Products do not arrive because a worker at an upstream process is absent
- Unexpected defects occur at an upstream process
- Larger lots are processed first to compensate for long setup times

A passive improvement of this process delay is to calculate the fluctuation of process delays and reduce it to match the value of 3σ.

An active improvement would be to eliminate process delays, as in the following examples:

- Take measures to prevent machine breakdown in the upstream process, and have a prepared backup plan in case of trouble
- Take appropriate measures to deal with worker absence
- Prevent defects as much as possible and supplement any losses quickly
- Implementing SMED, which will drastically cut back setup changeover time

3. Outgoing Fluctuation Type B

This type is the reverse pattern of type A, in that it has fluctuation in the capacity line of the second process. Overall, as seen in Figure 2.37, the capacities of the first and second processes are balanced and comparable to the load.

In this case, fluctuations will occur due to the following:

- Machine breakdown in the subsequent process, worker absence, fluctuation in defect rate
- When setup time is long, a larger lot is processed first
- Load is suddenly increased due to a change in the production schedule

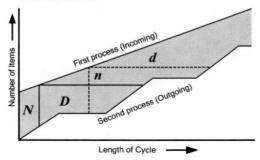

Figure 2.37 Delivery Fluctuation Type B

As in the previous case, the passive improvement is to reduce semi–processed goods to the minimum amount that can handle the variation in the quantity of process delays.

Active improvement includes:

- Taking measures to prevent machine breakdowns, worker absence, defects, or to minimize their impact
- Minimize setup time by implementing SMED
- Stop — or at least minimize changing the production schedule by drastically cutting back the production cycle

4. Incoming–Outgoing Fluctuation Type AB (Figure 2.38)

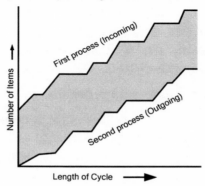

Figure 2.38 Order & Delivery Fluctuation Type AB

In this type of fluctuation the capacities of the first and second processes are balanced and comparable to the load, but each process has fluctuations in its capacity.

In general, the value of 3σ, a measure of the variation in the quantity of process delays, is a little larger than type A and type B, but the active and passive improvements of these types can also be applied in this case.

5. Parallel Type (Type O) (Figure 2.39)

In the parallel type of fluctuation, the capacities of the first and second processes are balanced, stable, and comparable to the load; the incoming and outgoing lines are parallel as well. The value of 3σ, a measure of the variation in the quantity of process delays, will be zero. This means the process delays can be zero. However, there are cases where process delays do exist because of the excessive lead time in scheduling, and it needs to be addressed. In this type, only active improvements which eliminate process delays exist, passive improvements do not.

Both incoming and outgoing capacities are the same and the amount of semi-processed goods differs. The production cycle becomes shorter if the semi-processed stock decreases.

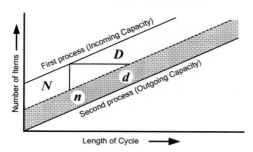

Figure 2.39 Parallel Type O

6. Step–Parallel Type (Type O) (Figure 2.40)

In the parallel type example shown above, production is continuous, in this type, production is intermittent.

Even though there is a break in straight lines in the chart,

105

as long as the two processes are balanced and parallel production is accomplished, 3σ becomes zero, which means process delays can be zero. Therefore, just as with the simple parallel type, active improvements which eliminate process delays are taken.

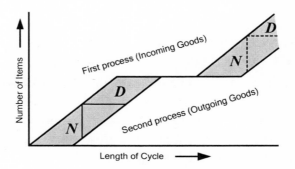

Ideal form of intermittent production. Incoming and outgoing goods are balanced, and they are also in harmony in terms of scheduling.

Figure 2.40 Two-Stage Parallel Type OS

Even though process delays can be eliminated this way, managers often maintain the illusion that they are necessary. We have to be careful not to fall into the same pattern of thinking.

7. Difference in Production Capacity and Process Delays
It is often heard on the shop floor that doubling production quantities also doubles process delays. If a conventional production method is used this is true, at least in theory. As explained so far however, the required amount of process delay and actual process delays change with the balance between upstream and downstream processes. They are not determined unilaterally by the production volume.

Take a look at the flow curve shown in Figure 2.41(a). The angle formed between line A and the x axis is twice that of line B. However, because the capacity lines of the first and the second processes are parallel, the length of the line indicating the process delay remains constant for each day. This means that 3σ is zero and no process delay is required. In other words, the process delay can remain unchanged and be equal to zero even if production capacity is doubled.

In this way, process delays are directly affected by the balance between the first and the second processes, and the fluctuation in the production curve of these processes, but it is not directly affected by a doubling of production.

Even when production capacity is doubled, it is possible to reduce process delays greatly by balancing the upstream and downstream processes and reducing fluctuations in the production capacity of each process. The ideal shape is for the incoming and outgoing lines is to be parallel and as close to each other as possible, as in Figure 2.41 (b).

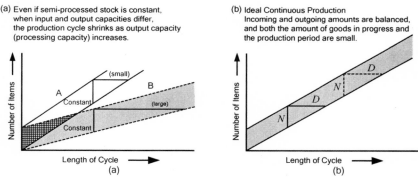

(a) Even if semi-processed stock is constant, when input and output capacities differ, the production cycle shrinks as output capacity (processing capacity) increases.

(b) Ideal Continuous Production
Incoming and outgoing amounts are balanced, and both the amount of goods in progress and the production period are small.

Figure 2.41 Production Ability & Process Delays

Process Delays and Cushioning Effects

Process delays can be utilized in two ways: to accommodate changes in production schedules and machine breakdowns, or the occurrence of defects.

- Quantitative cushion: An amount of product in excess of what is required for production—is produced to be used in case of emergency
- Scheduling cushion: The required amount is produced ahead of the time required by production to meet emergency needs if necessary, using the extra time

Of the two cushions, a quantitative cushion can compensate for both quantitative and scheduling needs. However, if production is altered by a model change, for example, any surplus must be scrapped. Therefore, it is better to use a quantitative cushion for items that are on a tight schedule and are repeatedly produced.

Although the risk of wasted inventory is low with a scheduling cushion, there is the risk of having to catch up in a limited amount of time. Therefore, a scheduling cushion is used for individual production, when production only begins after an order is received.

Generally, quantitative cushions are used more often. However, using scheduling cushions strategically is quite effective in reducing process delays.

I. Improvement of Process Delays
Although many ways of improving process delays have been discussed, they can all be categorized as either active or passive improvements.

(a) Active Improvement
Synchronization is the only and absolute method to bring process delays down to zero. There are three ways to synchronization:

- Balance out the surplus capacities of upstream and downstream processes — this can sometimes mean balancing out the required capacities
- Synchronize timing
- Eliminate variation factors which require process delays

(b) Passive Improvement
Passive improvement is the reduction of process delays to the minimum amount that can accommodate variation factors such as machine breakdowns, defects, and changes in production

schedules. In general, the term "process management improvement" means the reduction of process delays in this manner.

J. Lot Delays
(a) Lot Delays and Production Cycle
As mentioned earlier, lot delay is the state in which an entire lot, except for the one piece being processed, is waiting either processed or unprocessed.

Since process delays occur between processes they are conspicuous. Lot delays on the other hand, are hidden within production time and can easily escape attention.

As shown in Figure 2.42, in "lot operation," production cycle

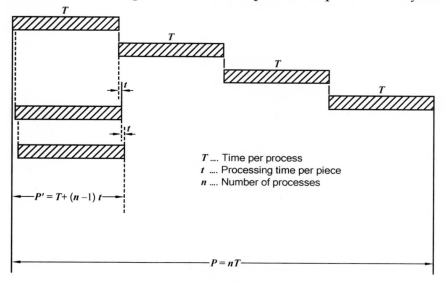

Figure 2.42 Lot Delays & Production Period

P can be defined as $P = nT$, where time per process is T and the number of processes is n.

If continuous operation is used — when passing the item to the next process immediately after the previous process is finished — the production cycle is defined as $P = T + (n-1)t$, where t is the processing time per piece.

If T is 5 hours, t is 1 minute, and n is 4, the production cycle of the two operations can be compared as below:

$$P = T + (n-1)\ t/nT = 5 \text{ hr} + (4-1) \times 1 \text{ min.}/4 \times 5 \text{ hr}$$

Since the term $(n-1)t$ is much smaller than T in general, the relationship above can be approximated as follows:

$$T = 1/n = 1/4$$

By cutting down the lot size to one and making the production continuous, the production cycle of a four–process production is reduced to one–fourth, and that of a ten–process production is reduced to one–tenth. Dramatic reduction becomes possible.

Along with the reduction of process delays, the relationship between delivery period and production cycle can also be improved, which makes process control that much easier.

(b) Lot Delays and Setup Time
As discussed so far, cutting down the lot size can reduce pro-

Setup time	Principal Operation Time per Item	Lot size	Apparent Operation Time	Ratio
4 hours	1 min.	100	$1 \text{ min.} + \dfrac{4 \times 60 \text{ min.}}{100} = 3.4 \text{ min.}$	100%
4 hours	1 min.	1,000	$1 \text{ min.} + \dfrac{4 \times 60 \text{ min.}}{1,000} = 1.24 \text{ min.}$	36%

Table 2.6 Setup Time & Lot Size

duction cycle dramatically. However, there is a persistent belief among plant managers that reducing the lot size can spread out setup time over a large number of pieces and reduce labor per piece. Therefore, lot delays, the by-product of large lot production, are often not considered to be a problem. In one sense this notion is true. Take a look at Table 2.6 (p. 110).

110

In this case, setup time is four hours. Just by increasing the lot size, apparent processing time is reduced by as much as 64 percent. For this, large lot tends to be welcomed, especially in press operations or plastic molding operations. However, this rationale is mistaken for two reasons.

First, the percentage of time used for setup goes down in terms of processing lot, but what really matters in shortening the production cycle is transportation lot, not processing lot. Therefore, even when processing lot size is 1,000 pieces the production cycle can be shortened by just reducing the transportation lot to one. The downside of using a small transportation lot is that it will increase the frequency of transportation, but this can be effectively remedied by layout improvement.

Second, the dramatic reduction in setup time made possible with the use of SMED setups, will completely invalidate the myth that large lot production is beneficial because setup time is long. SMED can cut down the setup time to merely a few minutes. There are many successful examples of SMED which serve as a proof of its effectiveness. (SMED is explained in Chapter Four.)

In summary, when it comes to active improvement of lot delays there is only one option: reducing the transportation lot size to one. It is the most effective way to minimize the production cycle. Passive improvement is to reduce the lot size as close to one as possible.

It should also be mentioned that various patterns of flow curves, discussed earlier, apply to lot delays in the same way.

2.2.6 Process Improvement and Flow Operation
A. Three Aspects of Process Improvement
There are three aspects to process improvement as shown in Table 2.7 on the following page.

		Active Improvement	Passive Improvement	
		(α) Process Improvement	(β) Process Improvement	(θ) Operational Improvement
Processing		In order to minimize processing, consider the processing from the standpoint of VE (value engineering). This includes considering ways to eliminate processes or casting methods that do not create burrs in the first place.	Merge or split processes so that division of labor can be used.	Improve methods of operation, such as cutting which only produces a lot of scraps.
Inspection		• Conduct inspections which eliminate defects. (Source inspection, self inspection, poka-yoke) • Conduct successive checks to minimize defects. • Conduct total inspections.	Conduct QC activities.	• Automate inspection. • Conduct random inspection.
Transportation		Improve layouts to eliminate transportation.	Improve layouts to minimize transportation.	• Use better methods of transportation, such as conveyors, fork lifts. • Eliminate incidental transportation, such as placing and removing items from shelves, by using fork lifts, etc.
Delays	Process Delay	• Eliminate process delays through synchronization. (Adjusting the balance and timing of surplus capacities.) • Prevent the factors which change surplus capacities, such as machine breakdowns.	• Adjust the gap between potential and required capacities effectively, in order to minimize process delays. • Reduce process delays by carrying out process control effectively.	Minimize process-delay-related operations through better organization and the use of machines.
	Lot Delay	Eliminate lot delays by reducing the size of transportation lot to just one.	Reduce the transportation lot.	• Minimize lot-delay-related operations through better organization and the use of machines. • Minimize lot delays by introducing SMED.

Table 2.7 Three Aspects of Process Improvement

B. What is Flow Operation?

Discussions about flow operation are often focused only on results, such as process–order machine layout or synchronization. However, I believe that the discussion on how to achieve these results is what is really necessary. Flow operation, which I advocate, can be achieved by satisfying the following conditions.

(a) Streamlining Processing

When streamlining processing, α, or β–type improvement in Table 2.7 (p. 112) should be considered first.

When division of labor is considered, the first thing to think about is the division of labor in terms of quality. That is, classifying the difficulty of operation and the skill level of workers into A, B, and C, and match them. Next comes synchronization — balancing out cycle times of each process. As a rule, division of labor in quality should always be given priority over synchronization. Efforts should be made to minimize processing time before anything else.

(b) Streamlining Inspection

Consider implementing α, or β–type improvements as shown in Table 2.7, such as inspections that minimize, or better yet, eliminate defects and 100 percent inspections.

(c) Streamlining Transportation

To improve layout in order to eliminate transportation, process-sequence layout should be used. If there are complicated process sequences to consider, using my method of transportation difficulty coefficient would make it possible to choose the most effective process–sequence layout.

(d) Streamlining Delays

Streamlining Process Delays

In order to eliminate process delays, carry out synchronization by averaging surplus capacities among processes, and adjust timing accordingly. As mentioned before, when averaging surplus capacities and adjusting potential and necessary capacities, balancing out process delays and the machine operation rates become important issues.

Streamlining Lot Delays

The basic measures are to adopt α–type improvements as shown in Table 2.7, and eliminate lot delays. If appropriate, β–type can also be used.

To realize flow operation means satisfying the following conditions:

1. Make processing more efficient through methods like division of labor.

2. Improve inspections to eliminate defects.

3. Improve layout to eliminate transportation.

4. Carry out synchronization and adjust timing to eliminate process delays.

5. Reduce transportation lot to one to eliminate lot delays.

Note that the word "conveyor" is not mentioned here at all. There is a common misconception among manufacturers that a flow operation is equivalent to a conveyor operation. This is completely false. Even if goods are passed from hand to hand without using a single conveyor, as long as the above conditions are satisfied, it is a true flow operation. Conveyors are generally used because they facilitate transportation and promote synchronization between processes.

Another common misconception among manufacturers is that flow operations are only used for assembly operations such as for cars and television. Again, this is not true. A flow operation can be used for various types of production as long as the five conditions above are met. For example, it can be used just as effectively for operations such as machining or manual operation. If flow operation is understood and applied correctly it is the ideal form of production.

Since delays only serve to raise cost, I am always reminded of a Japanese adage: "The only thing you should save is money, and the only place you shouldn't move things to is a pawn shop," seems to have an aspect of truth.

When I visited Company F in the United States, I was told that because their inventory is so large the company had to invest in automation and computer management of their storage. I replied, "Stock never produces profit; the production cycle needs to be shortened. Setup time should also be shortened by using the SMED setup. After all, the only thing you should stock pile is money. " At this, people nodded and laughed.

C. Abolishing Conveyors

Recently in the European markets, conveyors have been criticized, and even discontinued in some cases; I believe this to be a mistake. If anything should be discontinued, it is the division of labor, not the use of conveyors. Denying conveyors, which facilitate transportation, is simply wrong. The difficulty with the division of labor is that it could be inhumane since excessive division leads to monotony; the accompanying synchronization makes workers feel that they are forced to work. However, if these problems are addressed, the division of labor is an excellent method of production.

Naturally, respecting the comfort of workers is important, but it should not be forgotten that a high standard of living can only be supported by high productivity, and also contributes to more comfortable lifestyles. Striking a balance between humanity and productivity is a challenging, yet very important issue.

When I went to West Germany, I heard that the management and the labor union at one company agreed on two things: to make the takt time longer, and operations with a takt time shorter than 1.5 minutes are not allowed. Paying more respect to human nature is an issue that should be discussed more in Japan as well.

2.3 Active and Passive Improvement of Operations
2.3.1 Operation Functions
Operations can be classified as in Figure 2.43.

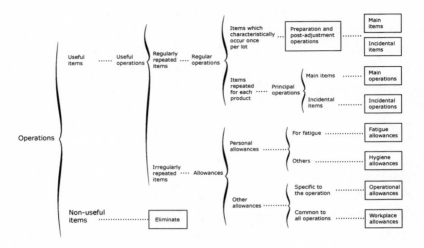

Figure 2.43 Content of Operations

A. Preparation, Post–Adjustment Operations (Setup)

This refers to the operations which occur only once before the principal operation, such as the preparation of technical drawings, materials, jigs, machines and so on. Getting properly dressed for work is sometimes included in this category.

B. Principal Operations

This is the center of all operations.

Processing: Cutting, molding, casting, etc.

Inspection: Inspecting with eyes or equipment

Transportation: Moving things

Delay: Things stay on shelves or in storage

C. Incidental Operations

These are the operations which support principal operations.

- Processing: Attaching and removing things, operating switches, etc.

116

- Inspection: Grabbing and placing items or equipment.
- Transportation: Placing and removing items from transportation equipment, etc. Incidental operations take up a large portion of transportation operations, so palettes and fork lifts were invented to address these issues.
- Delay: Placing and removing things from shelves or storage.

D. Fatigue Allowances
These allowances are designed to accommodate recovery from physical or mental fatigue.

E. Personal Hygiene Allowances
These allowances are used mainly to satisfy physiological needs such as thirst, lavatory needs, wiping off sweat, and so on.

F. Operational Allowances
These allowances handle operations that are usually unique to a specific operation and occur irregularly, such as fixing machine breakdowns, lubricating, removing cutting scrap, etc.

G. Workplace Allowances
These allowances are for troubles that happen irregularly and are common for each operation such as material delays and machine breakdowns.

At factories, production is now done by machines and humans. Table 2.8 on the following page shows their individual contributions to each aspect of operation. As shown, mechanization is being pushed forward these days and most principal operations are done by machines. Humans tend to take care of incidental operations. Therefore, if the number of workers needs to be reduced, improving incidental operations, preparation, and post–adjustment operations is the most effective way.

	(A)	(B)	(C)	(D)	(E)	(F)	(G)
	Preparation, Post-adjustment	Principal operations	Incidental operations	Fatigue allowances	Personal-hygiene allowances	Operational allowances	Workplace allowances
Human	◎	○	◎	◎	◎	◎	◎
Machine	◎	◎	○	✕	✕	△	◎
◎ Involved greatly		○ Involved moderately		△ Involved a little		✕ Not Involved at all	

Table 2.8 People, Machine, & Operation

2.3.2 Setup Improvement
The best way to improve preparation and post–adjustment is to do large–volume production, so that setup operations are not necessary. In Japan however, markets do not call for large–volume production. In fact, low–volume mixed model production is what many Japanese factories have to live with.

In some instances factories try to increase the lot size in order to reduce the effect of long setup times, and they end up overlooking major downsides — the increase in delays and production cycles, and a decrease in their return on investment.

If SMED (Single Minute Exchange of Die) is used, setup time that used to take two hours can be dramatically reduced to only six minutes. This system should be taken up more actively.

2.3.3 Improvement of Principal Operations
Principal operation are divided into two types: main operations and incidental operations.

A. Improvement of Main Operations
Improvement should be considered from two aspects: improving the methods related to processing, inspection, transportation, and delays, and by introducing automation.

B. Improvement of Incidental Operations
Improvement should be considered from two aspects: improv-

118

ing the methods related to operations such as attaching and re-moving, loading and unloading stock, switch–panel operations, and also by introducing automation.

2.3.4 Improvement of Allowances

A. Improvement of Fatigue & Personal Hygiene Allowances

These allowances are for people. There are two types of im-provement: improving the work itself so that workers will not get tired, and giving them appropriate fatigue allowances.

There are also two aspects to personal hygiene allowances: improving the work environment to lower their necessity, and giving appropriate allowances along with preparing proper fa-cilities.

B. Improvement of Operational & Workplace Allowances

Again, there are two aspects to their improvement: fixing the causes which would require these allowances, and giving ap-propriate allowances.

2.3.5 Development of Pre–Automation

One of the ways to improve principal and incidental operations, as well as each allowance, is introducing pre–automation. This will be discussed further in section 4.2, Development of Pre–Automation.

2.4. Improvement of Processes and Operations

2.4.1 Production Activity and Methods of Analysis (Figure 2.44)

The front side of production activities are considered to be processes, while the back side is considered to be operations.

The method to analyze the current situation of processes is called process analysis. Analysis of operations can be categorized into the following:

- Principal operation analysis: Study of principal opera-tions.

- Time study: Analysis of principal operations in terms of time.
- Motion study: Analysis of principal operations in terms of motion
- Operation analysis: Study of all operations including principal operations
- Continuous operation analysis: A method that analyzes all the operations continuously
- Work sampling, Snap reading… Methods that analyze operation selectively.

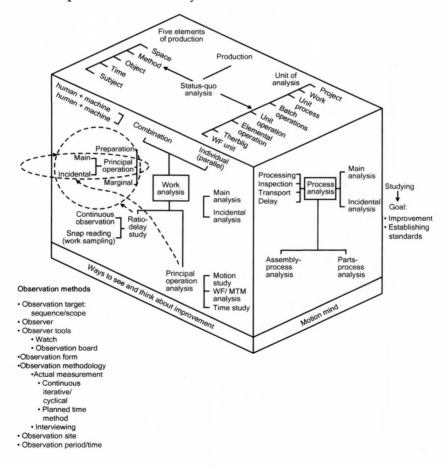

Figure 2.44 Analysis of Process & Operation

2.4.2 Improvement of Processes and Operations

Processing and transportation each take up about 45 percent of worker–hours in actual production. Therefore, improvement of transportation is quite effective in reducing hours. Processing is the only aspect of a process that contributes to raising product value. Other aspects of processes, namely inspection, transportation, and delays, only drive up the cost.

Among processing operations only principal operations raise product value. However, only about 30 percent of worker–hours are actually used to this end. This means that a mere 13.5 percent (45 percent x 30 percent = 13.5 percent) of worker–hours truly contribute to production.

In operations, incidental operations take up the largest portion followed by preparation and post–adjustment (setup operations). Therefore, improving these aspects leads to significant reduction in operation hours. It is important to understand these point in order to reduce labor–hours.

CHAPTER TWO SUMMARY

Plant improvement must be carried out based on a solid understanding of the structure of production. The reader also needs to understand that there are always two types of improvement for process or operations: active and passive. Lastly, one–piece–flow operation is quantitatively the most efficient form of production and should be widely introduced. When introducing one–piece–flow operation, the balance between efficiency and human nature needs to be taken into consideration.

III FUNDAMENTAL APPROACHES TO PROCESS IMPROVEMENT

The topic of process improvement was touched on in the previous chapter. In this chapter it is explained further with actual examples from shop floors across the globe.

3.1 Improvement of Processing

Active improvement of processing includes improvement of specific techniques and improvement from the perspective of VE (value engineering). Passive improvement includes improvement from the perspective of IE (Industrial Engineering) such as the division of labor and the convergence of process sequences.

3.1.1 Vacuum Molding

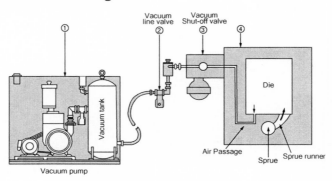

Figure 3.1 Vacuum Die–casting

A. Stepping Closer to Vacuum Die–Casting

In 1974, I visited with the die–casting associations and factories of Germany and Switzerland to speak about SMED. During my time there I had a chance to observe what is called "vacuum die-casting" at two different companies: Daimler–Benz in Germany, and Bühler in Switzerland.

In standard non–vacuum die–casting, a removable die is set to a fixed die. After that, molten metal is injected into the die under high pressure then cooled down to solidify. The problem with this method is that burrs (which need to be removed with a trimming press) and pinholes are likely to form in the process.

Pinholes form because trapped air remains inside the die once it is closed. In theory, it is possible to force only the air out from a vent by using high pressure, while keeping all the molten metal inside. In reality this is almost impossible. As long as there air remains in the die, the phenomenon of pinholes simply cannot be avoided.

What happens if the die is then vacuumed? Since air is the

124

source of the problem, naturally burrs and pinholes would disappear along with air. This method is called vacuum die–casting, and I witnessed many successful cases of it while I was in Europe. This was a truly efficient form of casting, so after coming back to Japan, I suggested that die–casting companies introduce this vacuum method. The replies I received went along these lines, "We've already sent people to see vacuum casting and know that it's a preferred method. However, our prototype didn't work well because calculating the timing of vacuum and injection was incredibly difficult. We also considered paying for the know-how, but it was too expensive for us." At this, I had to give up my idea.

In 1976, I had another chance to tour Europe. At Thurner Corporation in Germany, I was told that the company's defect rate of turn tables dropped from 20 percent to 5 percent by introducing vacuum die–casting. In Switzerland, I heard more about the technique at Bühler corporation, and I was reminded once again of its necessity in Japan.

When I went back, I heard that company M purchased Bühler's vacuum die–casting machine. I went over to their factory immediately to see the machine's performance. To my surprise, not even a single burr was produced in the castings, it clearly spoke of the power of vacuum casting.

While I was there, I thought the application of this technique should not be limited to die–casting. There were no reasons it would not work for other areas such as plastic molding, rubber extrusion, and metal stamping.

Soon after this visit, I went to plastic company D, and asked the workers to conduct an experiment on vacuum molding. The company makes protective covers for television cathode–ray tubes. There were springs at the edge of each cover that were used to attach it to the tube and it was crucial that they had enough strength. However, the springs tended to be weak because of their location. We tried vacuum casting of the covers, and the result was — their strength jumped up remarkably! With the conventional non–vacuum method, plastic tended to be less dense at the edges, and therefore more brittle. The vacuum method created a cover that was strong all the way to the edges.

B. Key Points of Vacuum Molding

The vacuum method can be used for production methods such as plastic injection and powder compressing just as effectively as for die–casting. The following are the key points to keep in mind when implementing this technique.

(a) Removal of Air

To create a vacuum, the air pressure must be zero. If we assume that the air pressure is one atmosphere otherwise, the difference may not seem to be significant. However, we need to remember that the pressure of the trapped air can climb up to 100 atmospheres by compression and become very problematic. Although measures such as air vents are commonly used, it is clear that the best measure is to eliminate air altogether. It is similar to an air raid siren, for example—shooting down a bomber itself is more effective than running away or hiding in shelters.

(b) Types of Air to Remove

The following three types of air need to be expelled during casting:

1. αair — The air which exists inside the material. When "bulk specific gravity" of a material is discussed, it means that the material is porous and includes air.
2. βgas — The gas which is created through chemical reaction when metal or plastic is melted, or the steam created when water evaporates.
3. θair — The air which exists inside the die, sprue, or sprue runner.

In vacuum die–casting, θair is what is removed. However, when granular or powdery material, such as plastic or rubber, is used, removal of αair and βgas also need to be considered.

There are types of plastic molding machines that are labeled "vacuum molding machines." When using these machines, we need to know that they have the ability to remove αair and βgas, but not necessarily θ air.

There is also a type of a vacuum molding machine in which a heated material board is placed on top of a mold with numerous vacuum holes. The material is sucked against the mold from underneath by the power created by the vacuum. This type of machine is different from the type of vacuum molding being discussed here.

(c) Balance of Molding "$t : t'$ "
The balance of the following t and t' is important in molding.

- t — solidifying time: Affected by material, temperature of the molten material, and the cooling conditions
- t' — injection time: Affected by variable factors such as material, temperature of the molten material, cooling conditions, injection pressure, distance from the sprue, thickness, the number and angle of bends in the sprue runner, and the existence of air

In general, t' has to be less than half of t ($t' < t/2$).

There are two types of injection:

1. Direct injection: Molten material fills the mold from the sprue opening to the opposite end of the die cavity (resin, rubber, etc.).

2. Reverse injection: Molten material fills the die either from the farthest point of the sprue, or the lowest point (die-casting, metal casting, etc.).

Injection type is an important factor to consider when deciding the location of vacuum outlets.

(d) Shape of the Product
- Simple shape: A shape which allows the molten mate-

rial to move smoothly in one direction; the degree of vacuum does not have to be high

- Elaborate shape: A shape in which materials merge or air pockets tend to form due to narrow areas; the degree of vacuum needs to be high

(e) Placement of Vacuum Outlet

When deciding the placement of the vacuum outlet, balance between the following aspects must be taken into careful consideration:

- Placement based on product quality
- Opposing end of the sprue — To expel air at the end
- Merging area — To expel air left at the merging section
- Air pocket area — To expel air from air pockets
- Placement based on the ease of operation

If the outlet is placed at a parting line, removal of flash and processing of the castings becomes very easy.

(f) Setting Vacuum Outlets

Setting the outlet appropriately is crucial in vacuum molding.

Critical slit: This is the biggest size slit that expels air, while at the same time prevents the escape of resin (2/100–3/100mm). The size changes depending on type, temperature and pressure of the material.

Vacuum outlet: Rectangular-shaped slits at the mouth of an outlet are very effective. Covering the outlet mouth with critical slits is not advisable since the slit size would change when the die is sucked against it.

Multi–slits: Makes it possible to expel air even if a portion of holes are plugged.

Outlet pipe: Air is sucked through multi–slits and goes through outlet pipes. These pipes do not have to be narrow, they should be designed to remove air swiftly and from several places .

Push–out pins: It is very effective to use push–out pin areas (used to extract the casting), as vacuum outlets — these parts are located at the ends of the dies, otherwise air pockets tend to form. The size of these outlets can be as small as critical slits.

If there are places where air pockets always form due to design, it is effective to place push–out pin shaped outlets because the pins are fixed and air is expelled from their surroundings.

Valve and critical slits: It is efficient to use a valve to withdraw the majority of air, and critical slits to withdraw the rest.

Step–by–Step Flow Check: The path of molten material inside the die can be identified by making several products with the varying amount of material injected: 20, 40, 60, 80, and 100 percent. By doing this the areas where material reaches last, where it merges, and air spots can be elucidated.

Along with this step–by–step injection, using the following constant speed coefficient (the speed at which materials reach certain points) is also effective in discovering the material flow.

Constant velocity coefficient S

$S = f\alpha(t \times 1/l \times 1/n \times c \times \theta \times R)$

t = thickness

l = distance from the sprue

c = existence of bends

n = number of bends

α = overall correction factor

θ = correction factor based on the angle of bends

R = correction factor based on the R for the bends

Lines based on the constant speed coefficients can be drawn at certain time intervals after injection. Lines similar to the constant–pressure lines on meteorological charts are created, and the progression of the molten material can be shown on paper. This will help choose the best location for the sprue and the vacuum vents; this also makes it possible to control the location where the material merges in the die.

(g) The Number and Location of Vacuum Outlets

Vacuum outlets need to be considered from the perspectives of quantity and quality.

- Quantity: The larger the number of vacuum outlets and the size of their cross–section areas, the faster it is to vacuum the die cavity—in some cases, using valves makes vacuuming more efficient
- Quality: The number and placement of outlets needs to be decided taking the end areas of the die, merging area, and air pockets into account, so that the molten material can be pulled in and packed to every corner of the die

(h) Vacuuming Methods

It is best for vacuum pressure to be higher than 750mm. Vacuum gauges show 760mm as the absolute vacuum where an atmospheric pressure is zero. Therefore, more than 750mm means the remaining air shown on the mercury gauge is less than 10mm.

- Direct method: The die and the pump are directly connected—takes a long time to vacuum the die cavity

Die ➝ Pump

- Indirect method: There is a tank between the die and the pump; air in the die cavity can be moved to the tank in a short amount of time, usually 1 to 1.5 seconds—air in the tank can be vacuumed during off-line setup

C. Combined Method

Assume that the volume of the tank is 100 times that of the die cavity in the following example:

- After the die is closed, open up valves 1 and 2 at once—the air in the die cavity immediately travels to the tank.

Once meters 1 and 2 show the same pressure, close valve 2, the degree of vacuum becomes 1/101 atmospheres.

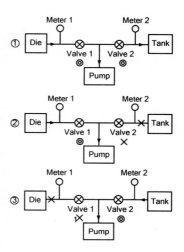

- Suck in the remaining air in the die cavity using the pump. Once done, close valve 1.
- Connect the pump to the tank and then open valve 2. Vacuum the air in the tank during off–line setup.

This combined method is the most effective in achieving the highest level of vacuum.

(a) Timing of Injection

There are two types of injection timings:

- Step type: Injection is done after the die is vacuumed completely. Die–casting is generally conducted in this method because the dies need to be airtight; for this purpose, insertion of molten metal is sometimes halted midway, or hard dies are used.
- Parallel type: Injection and vacuuming are done at the same time.

This method is often used in plastic molding. In general, vacuuming stops when injection is completed.

(b) Volume of Vacuum Tanks

It is desirable for the volume of a vacuum tank to be more than 100 times that of the die. The volume of the die includes the following: die, suction pipe, and push–out pins. Big vacuum tanks do not mean that vacuum pumps also need to have large capacities; it means that vacuuming needs to start early, an hour prior to the injection, instead of 30 minutes, for example.

131

(c) Vacuum Pump

If there are places where the material merges or air pockets form, the vacuum pressure should be higher than 750mm.

> Venturi type: A type of vacuum pump which extracts air in die cavities by sending high–pressure air through a narrow pipe attached to the die. Although this method can only achieve vacuum lower than 600mm, the equipment is uncomplicated and reasonably priced. Therefore, it is suitable for simple dies in which materials flow only in one direction.
>
> Pump type: There are water seal vacuum pumps (degree of vacuum = 700mm) and oil seal vacuum pumps (degree of vacuum = 760mm). Proper pumps need to be selected depending on the usage. Since it takes a long time to create a vacuum one should pay attention to the diameter of the vacuum pipes, if they are too small the process takes too long.

(d) Achieving Airtightness

An insufficient seal is the most likely cause when vacuum castings fail. If the die is not completely airtight, vacuuming has an extremely adverse effect—bringing air in from outside, instead of removing it. Because of this, achieving airtightness is paramount in successful vacuum casting.

It should also be understood that airtightness is required only when the die is closed. There are companies hesitant about introducing vacuum casting because they believe that an airtight condition has to be maintained at all times; which is technically more challenging.

The following points need to be considered to accomplish airtightness:

- Parental Die: Vacuum outlets are usually placed in the stationary die. The outlet and the joints to the vacuum pump need to be sealed with o–rings—making the die surface smooth (using tapered joints also helps seal air in).

- Side Core: Use the above methods: o–rings, polishing, and tapered joints — to seal the place where a side core is attached. Covering the joints to increase air–tightness is also effective.
- Push–out Pin: When the die blocks are clamped together, covering each push–out–pin area is effective in making the die airtight. If the inside of these covers can be evacuated, it is even better — using o–rings and gaskets for the covers is also recommendable (using o–rings for each push–out pin is not effective).
- When creating airtightness, it is better to do it with pressure–bonded parts instead of moving parts, with respect to the resulting effects on future maintenance.

In summary, success of vacuum casting hinges on the conditions of the following three areas — vacuum pressure, airtightness, and vacuum outlets. As mentioned earlier, if the die is not completely sealed, a vacuum method can bring about adverse effects.

D. Applications and Advantages of Vacuum Casting

The discussion so far has focused on die–casting and plastic molding. However, applications of vacuum casting are much broader.

For example, a vacuum method is used during the vulcanized molding of o–rings, as a result, pin holes in the finished products almost disappeared. Great success of the vacuum method is also reported with the extrusion of rubber and the production of clay for ceramics. However, when the material is viscous or thick like clay, it needs to be pushed through slits once to make it flakier, and to remove more air from the material.

When vacuum molding is used for powdery material, pinholes also disappeared completely and the molding time was cut in half. Using the conventional method air needed to be extracted by compression a few times during the molding process, a ritual that was negated with the introduction of vacuum molding.

Furthermore, if the air behind the material is vacuumed out when deep drawing is conducted with a machine press, the drawing condition greatly improves. When this technique was used for plastic molding, for example, injection time was shortened from 12 seconds to 2 seconds, the shot cycle was shortened by 30 to 80 percent, and weld lines disappeared.

In this way, vacuum molding has various advantages. The most common advantages are listed on Figure 3.2.

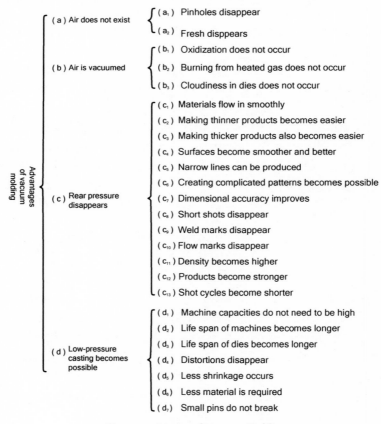

Figure 3.2 Merits of Vacuum Molding

(E) What Vacuum Molding Teaches Us

The existence of air in molding dies has always been a concern. In the past, air escapes and air vents were invented to address the problem of air. These approaches were far too passive. We recognized air as a nuisance, but did not register it as something that needed to be (or even could be) eliminated actively.

Since air surrounds us on Earth, we often become oblivious to it. Perhaps this lack of awareness may is why we never exerted greater efforts to understand how air relates to our work.

There is a lesson to be learned from vacuum molding: even with operational methods we approve of, there will always be revolutionary alternatives if we only bother to think deeper. Indeed, there are many things that we are not conscious of and take for granted. We need to call these things to our attention and reconsider whether or not they are the best methods.

3.1.2 Division of Labor in Quantity and Quality

Many people have the misunderstanding that the division of labor simply means dividing the work; this is not true. There are two different types of division of labor: quantitative and qualitative division of labor.

> Quantitative division of labor: A large task is divided among multiple workers. The same operations are performed in parallel.
>
> Qualitative division of labor: A task is divided based on difficulty; for example, A, B, and C level. Workers are then separated based on their skill level, and matched correspondingly with a task suitable for that skill level, as in Aa, Bb, Cc.

The only advantage of quantitative division of labor is that it can shorten production time, whereas qualitative division of labor can truly boost productivity.

There is a canning factory I consult for in Karatsu, Kyushu. Whenever I visited the factory, I asked the plant manager, Mr. Kitahara, what kind of problems they usually encounter. He said, "The quality and quantity of our labor isn't stable, so our efficiency rate is low and our defect rate is high. It's a constant headache."

In general, only those in management positions are full–time workers at canning factories because their production varies greatly depending what is in season. It can be shellfish, fish, or mandarin oranges that are canned, and most factory workers are hired on a daily basis. At this particular factory, a company bus goes to the corporate housing area of a nearby mining operation every morning, and those who can work that day come to work and get paid on their way back. Therefore, most workers are temporarily employed, leading to the plant manager's concern about the stability of labor quality and quantity.

During this visit, canning of mandarin oranges was in full swing. First, oranges are spread out on a conveyor belt approximately one–meter wide. 50 workers, standing on both sides of the belt, cut a small niche into the peel of each orange close to its stem using a wooden tool. Starting from that niche, the oranges are peeled and placed back on the conveyor belt.

I asked the plant manager, "You told me that workers are hired on the daily basis, but aren't there people who come here every day?"

"Of course, there are even people who have been coming here for years," said the manager.

"Is that so? Then, could you choose the ten most skilled workers among those who come here every day? "

"Ten most skilled workers? What for?"

"You'll see. I'd like to do a little experiment," I said. The following is what I did: I asked the ten skilled hands to concentrate on making a cut near the stem. The remaining 40 workers concentrated on peeling.

Thirty minutes later, the result was in: the work efficiency improved by 10 percent, and the defect rate dropped by 90 percent.

Until then, the most common cause of defects was cuts in oranges made by the wooden tools. Since the task of pulling the skin and cutting it lightly demanded precision, those who are not used to the work often damaged the oranges by cutting them too deep.

In other words, there were two operations with two different levels of difficulty. Making light cuts into the skins was more difficult and, as such, an A–level job. Peeling, on the other hand, was easier; a B–level job. I assigned workers to the jobs that corresponded with their skill level — A–level workers to A–level jobs, B–level workers to B–level jobs. This was qualitative division of labor.

In this case, the 10 percent increase in efficiency was helpful, but what really helped lower the production cost was the 90–percent decline in the defect rate. The plant manager, Mr. Kitahara, told me after the experiment, "I didn't realize that division of labor could be used for relatively simple tasks like these. Now I know that qualitative division of labor is extremely important."

3.1.3 Consolidation of Process Sequences
If there are multiple types of products that share the same process sequences, consolidating their production lines is easy.

The challenge arises when low volume — mixed model production is carried out. Not many plants try to consolidate and organize their complicated process sequences. We should know that as long as there are some common processes, consolidation is possible, and doing so will lead to efficient processing.

When isolating common processes from different process sequences, using non–interference numbers is very useful.

SUMMARY
In many cases, process improvement is accomplished through the improvement of techniques specific to each process. When thinking about technical improvement, however, it is important to remember the difference between active and passive im-

provement. Considering improvement from the perspective of VE (Value Engineering) is also meaningful.

3.2. Inspection Improvement

Active inspection improvement involves modifying inspections so that they do not merely find defects but eliminate them altogether. To achieve this, source inspection, self inspection, and successive inspection must all be adopted. Above all, inspections should be 100 percent inspections; poka–yoke devices help implement these measures. Passive improvement includes mechanization of inspection methods and using sampling inspections.

3.2.1 Inspections that Eliminate Defects

As mentioned before, the following are the inspections that can eliminate defects

- Source inspection: Tight management of processing conditions that determine the quality of products. If abnormal conditions are detected, correct them before defects are actually created.
- Self inspection: An inspection capacity is built into each operation so that all the defects that occur in an operation can be detected during that operation.
- Successive inspection: The worker at the next operation immediately checks all products from the previous operation, immediate action is taken when a defect is found. This could be viewed as passive improvement, but it is active since it prevents defects from recurring and reduces the defect rate dramatically.
- 100 percent inspection: Even though sampling inspection has the backing of statistics, it is only a method for improving inspection operations, not a method for guaranteeing quality. Reducing the complexity of inspection procedures to the level of sampling inspection can make a 100 percent inspection possible.

3.2.2 Poka–yoke and Quality Control

The basic concept of quality control should always be to take action before defects are created, not after — and carry out 100 percent inspection that guarantees quality. In order to carry out 100 percent inspections as efficiently as sampling inspections, as well as eliminate defects, using poka–yoke devices is the best approach.

Poka–yoke Inspection Methods
(a) Poka–yoke Correction Types
There are two ways in which poka–yoke can be used to correct mistakes:

- Control type: When the poka–yoke is activated it shuts down the process by stopping the machine or conveyor, or locking up the clamps, so that the problem can be corrected. This is the strongest corrective device as it simply makes it impossible to create defects.

- Warning type: When the poka–yoke is activated it alerts the worker by a buzzer or lamp, but will allow defective processing to continue if workers do not respond to the warning. Therefore, it should be used only when defects do not lead to serious problems (it should also be noted that blinking lights and sound are more effective in attracting worker attention than light).

(b) Poka–yoke Detection Types
In addition to understanding that poke–yoke is effective, we also need to understand how to set it up. The following are the most common types of poka–yoke. In the past, only the contact method had been used. However, application of poka–yoke was limited, and in the spirit of improvement, other methods were conceived later.

- Contact method: This identifies defects by detecting whether or not contact is made between the device and some feature of the product's shape or dimension.

- Fixed–number method: This identifies defects by determining whether or not a set number of movements/actions have been made.
- Motion–step method: This identifies defects by determining whether the established steps or motions of a procedure are followed.

Detection method / Regulating function / Setting function / Types of inspection	Physical method						Sensory method
	Control type			Warning type			
	Contact	Fixed-value	Motion-step	Contact	Fixed-value	Motion-step	
Source inspection	◎	◎	◎	○	○	○	○
Self inspection	◎	◎	◎	○	○	○	○
Successive inspection	◎	◎	◎	○	○	○	◎

Table 3.1 Poka-yoke Classifications

140

Examples of Poka–yoke

The following are actual shop floor applications of each method.

(a) Contact Method

1. Attaching Hose Brackets (Kanto Auto Works) (Figure 3.3)

Problem: Brackets for flexible hoses are sometimes attached upside down.

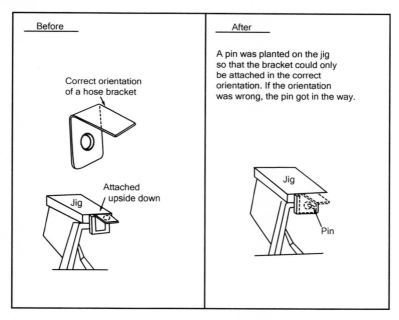

Figure 3.3 Preventing Mistakes in Bracket Installation

Result: Mistakes disappeared.

Cost: 100 yen

2. Attaching Fuel Tank Support (Kanto Auto Works)

Problem: Fuel tank supports were sometimes attached upside down.

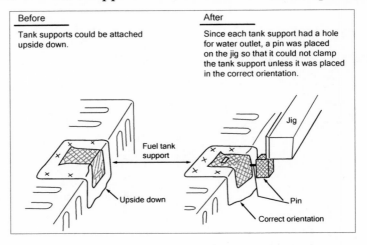

Figure 3.4 Preventing Mistakes in Fuel Tank Installation

Result: Mistakes disappeared.

3. Poka–yoke for Attaching Defroster Nozzle Supports (Kanto Auto Works)

Problem: Defroster nozzle supports were sometimes welded backwards with a multi–spot welder.

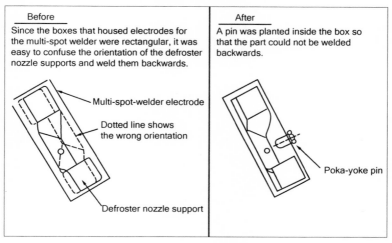

Figure 3.5 Preventing Mistakes in Nozzle Installation

Result: Mistakes disappeared.

Cost: 200 yen

4. Poka–yoke for Attaching Brake–Wire Clamps (Kanto Auto Works)

Problem: Clamps for right–side brake wires are different from left–side wires. Although appropriate jigs had to be used to hold the clamps, the jigs could accommodate both right and left clamps, making it possible for them to sometimes be attached backwards.

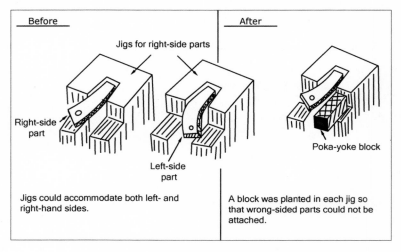

Figure 3.6 Preventing Mistakes in Clamp Installation

Result: Mistakes in attachment disappeared.

Cost: 300 yen

5. Poka–yoke for Burr Detection (Taiho Kogyo)

Problem: Burrs often remained inside engine brackets, making the parts unusable.

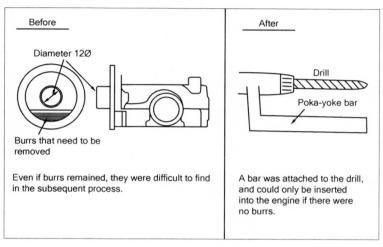

Figure 3.7 Burr Detection Machine

Result: It became impossible to forget deburring.

Cost: 500 yen

6. Poka–yoke for Body Rocker Spec Difference (Kanto Auto Works)

Problem: Rocker panels for deluxe–model cars had holes, whereas the ones for standard models did not. Even so, they were sometimes confused and attached to the wrong models.

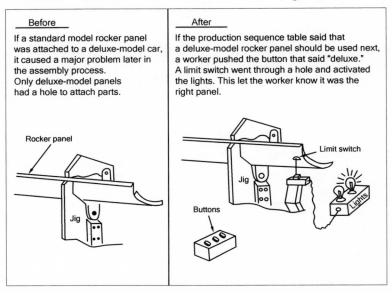

Before

If a standard model rocker panel was attached to a deluxe-model car, it caused a major problem later in the assembly process. Only deluxe-model panels had a hole to attach parts.

After

If the production sequence table said that a deluxe-model rocker panel should be used next, a worker pushed the button that said "deluxe." A limit switch went through a hole and activated the lights. This let the worker know it was the right panel.

Figure 3.8 Body Rocker Panel Specification Difference

Result: Mistakes dues to this specification difference dropped to zero.

Cost: 5000 yen

7. Poka–yoke to Prevent Hook Mix–Up (Arakawa Auto Works)

Problem: When attaching hooks, right and left parts were sometimes mixed up.

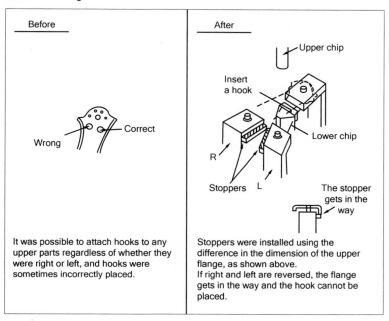

Before	After
Wrong / Correct	Upper chip, Insert a hook, Lower chip, R, Stoppers L, The stopper gets in the way
It was possible to attach hooks to any upper parts regardless of whether they were right or left, and hooks were sometimes incorrectly placed.	Stoppers were installed using the difference in the dimension of the upper flange, as shown above. If right and left are reversed, the flange gets in the way and the hook cannot be placed.

Figure 3.9 Prevention of Reverse Installation

Result: Complaints from this issue were eliminated.

Cost: 400 yen

8. Poka–yoke for Attaching Plate Releasers (Arakawa Auto Works)

Problem: Parts called "plate releasers" were sometimes attached upside down.

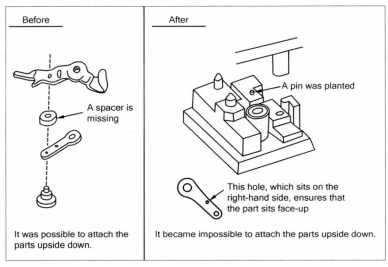

Before

After

A spacer is missing

A pin was planted

This hole, which sits on the right-hand side, ensures that the part sits face-up

It was possible to attach the parts upside down.

It became impossible to attach the parts upside down.

Figure 3.10 Prevention of Reverse Installation

Result: Reverse attachment was eliminated.

Cost: 200 yen

9. Poka–yoke for Spacer Attachment (Arakawa Auto Works)

Problem: Spot welding was done without using spacers, even though they should have been used.

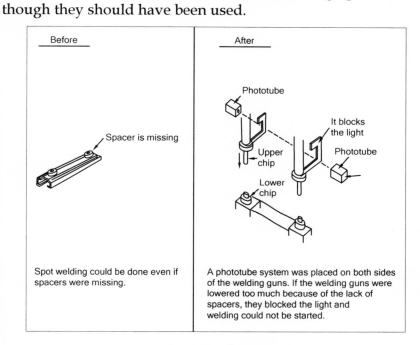

Figure 3.11 Prevention of Spacer Omission

Result: Complaints from this issue were eliminated.

Cost: 32,000 yen

10. Poka–yoke for Cutting Operation (Taiho Kogyo)

Problem: Due to abnormalities in the material forwarding mechanism, short materials were sometimes created.

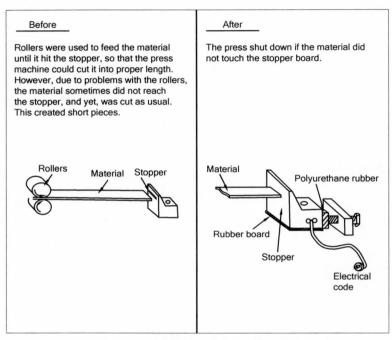

Before	After
Rollers were used to feed the material until it hit the stopper, so that the press machine could cut it into proper length. However, due to problems with the rollers, the material sometimes did not reach the stopper, and yet, was cut as usual. This created short pieces.	The press shut down if the material did not touch the stopper board.

Figure 3.12 Prevention of Unequal Cutting

Cost: 108,000 yen

11. Poka–yoke for Detecting Groove–less Bearings (Taiho Kogyo)

Problem: Bearings were supposed to have grooves, but the ones without the grooves proceeded to the subsequent process unnoticed.

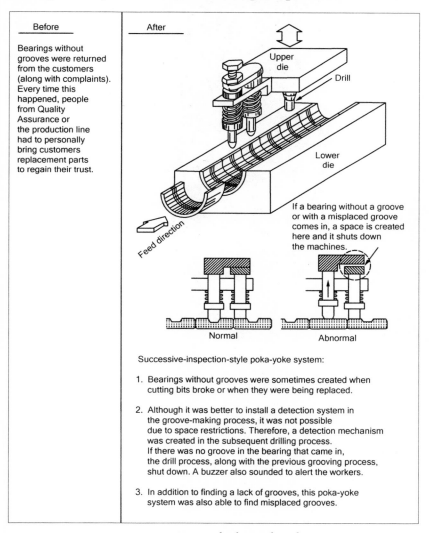

Before

Bearings without grooves were returned from the customers (along with complaints). Every time this happened, people from Quality Assurance or the production line had to personally bring customers replacement parts to regain their trust.

After

Upper die

Drill

Lower die

If a bearing without a groove or with a misplaced groove comes in, a space is created here and it shuts down the machines.

Feed direction

Normal

Abnormal

Successive-inspection-style poka-yoke system:

1. Bearings without grooves were sometimes created when cutting bits broke or when they were being replaced.

2. Although it was better to install a detection system in the groove-making process, it was not possible due to space restrictions. Therefore, a detection mechanism was created in the subsequent drilling process. If there was no groove in the bearing that came in, the drill process, along with the previous grooving process, shut down. A buzzer also sounded to alert the workers.

3. In addition to finding a lack of grooves, this poka-yoke system was also able to find misplaced grooves.

Figure 3.13 Groove Checking Poka-yoke

151

Figure 3.14 Groove Checking Poka-yoke

Result: Products without grooves were eliminated. Misplaced grooves could also be detected.

Cost: 5,000 yen

12. Poka–yoke for Drilling (Taiho Kogyo)

Problem: Holes were supposed to be created in products using drills. However, when problems such as drill breakdown occurred, products without holes were produced and sent to the subsequent process.

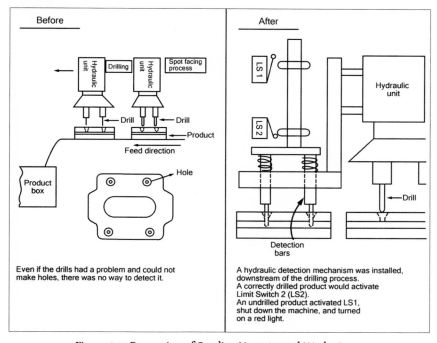

Even if the drills had a problem and could not make holes, there was no way to detect it.

A hydraulic detection mechanism was installed, downstream of the drilling process.
A correctly drilled product would activate Limit Switch 2 (LS2).
An undrilled product activated LS1, shut down the machine, and turned on a red light.

Figure 3.15 Prevention of Sending Unprocessed Work pieces

Result: Unprocessed goods were eliminated.

Cost: Since discarded materials were used, unit cost is zero.

13. Poka–yoke for Center–Pillar Assembly (Kanto Auto Works)

Problem: Mix–up of outer, inner, and right and left sided parts sometimes occurred in the assembly process.

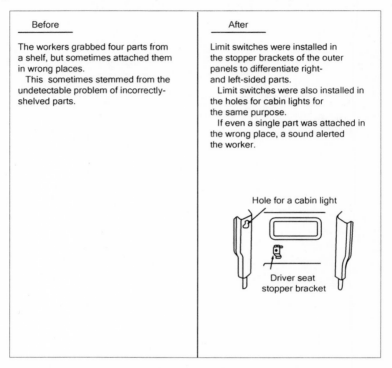

Before	After
The workers grabbed four parts from a shelf, but sometimes attached them in wrong places. This sometimes stemmed from the undetectable problem of incorrectly-shelved parts.	Limit switches were installed in the stopper brackets of the outer panels to differentiate right- and left-sided parts. Limit switches were also installed in the holes for cabin lights for the same purpose. If even a single part was attached in the wrong place, a sound alerted the worker.

Hole for a cabin light

Driver seat stopper bracket

Figure 3.16 Prevention of Reverse Installation

Result: Assembly mistakes were eliminated.

Cost: 5,000 yen

14. Poka–yoke for Lowering a Pin (Taiho Kogyo)

Problem: Spot welding of the roof and body rocker was done automatically while on the conveyor. However, if a certain pin was not lowered in the previous process, the car would end up going through the subsequent process without being welded.

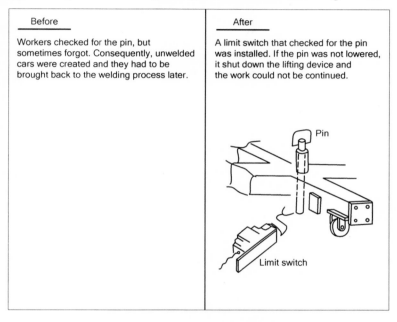

Before	After
Workers checked for the pin, but sometimes forgot. Consequently, unwelded cars were created and they had to be brought back to the welding process later.	A limit switch that checked for the pin was installed. If the pin was not lowered, it shut down the lifting device and the work could not be continued.

Figure 3.17 Prevention of Welding Omission

Result: The welding process was never skipped again.

Cost: 5,000 yen

15. Poka–yoke for Closing Rear Doors (Kanto Auto Works)

Problem: The rear door of each car was supposed to be closed by the workers when the cars came out of the painting process. If this was forgotten, the rear door might hit things and get damaged.

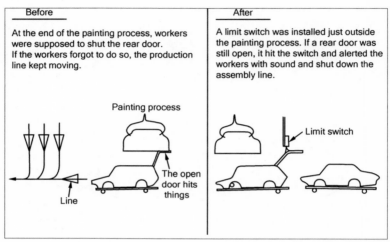

Before	After
At the end of the painting process, workers were supposed to shut the rear door. If the workers forgot to do so, the production line kept moving.	A limit switch was installed just outside the painting process. If a rear door was still open, it hit the switch and alerted the workers with sound and shut down the assembly line.

Figure 3.18 Prevention of Forgetting to Close Doors

Result: Rear–door damage dropped to zero.

Cost: 100,000 yen

16. Poka–yoke for Defective Cam Bushings (Taiho Kogyo)

Problem: When there are abnormalities in machines or with material feeding, short cam bushing were created. Since sampling inspections were used at the factory, as opposed to 100 percent inspections, defects were often found by the customers.

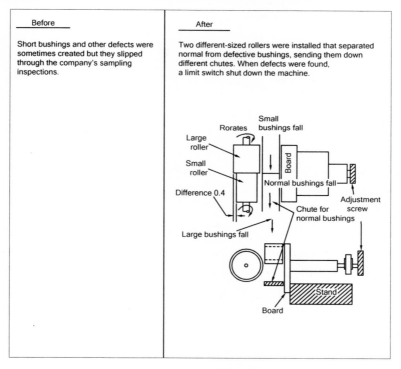

Before	After
Short bushings and other defects were sometimes created but they slipped through the company's sampling inspections.	Two different-sized rollers were installed that separated normal from defective bushings, sending them down different chutes. When defects were found, a limit switch shut down the machine.

Figure 3.19 Prevention of Unequal Lengths

Result: Short bushings and other defects were eliminated.

Cost: 50,000 yen

157

17. Poka–yoke for Attaching Price Tags (Taiho Kogyo)

Problem: Prices tags were sometimes forgotten.

Figure 3.20 Prevention of Price Tag Omission

Before

The worker in charge was solely responsible for remembering the tags.

After

A conduction chain was installed after the tag–attaching process. If a price tag was missing, electrical current passed through the chain and sounded an alarm to alert the worker.

Result: The tags were never forgotten again.

Cost: 108,000 yen

(b) Fixed Number Method

This method identifies defects by determining whether a given number of movements are made. There are control type and warning type versions of this method.

1. Poka–yoke for Bolting Down Propeller Shafts (Central Motor)

Problem: All four bolts used for propeller shafts need to be tightened to a specified torque. At times, workers forgot to tighten them uniformly and sometimes, forgot to tighten some bolts altogether.

Figure 3.21 Prevention of Bolt
Omission (a)

Figure 3.22 Prevention of Bolt
Omission (b)

Before
Since the torque was so variable, the group leader started sample inspections. In doing so, bolts that were not tightened were sometimes spotted.

After
Torque wrenches with built–in limit switches started to be used. When the torque reached a pre–determined level, green lights would light–up on the board that corresponded with each bolt. If all four bolts were not tightened, a buzzer went off. If the bolts were not tightened within 30 seconds of the buzzer, the line was shut down.

Result: Bolts that were not tightened at all, or tightened with inappropriate torque, disappeared.

Cost: 150,000 yen

2. Poka–yoke for Bolting Down Drive Plates (Central Motor)

Problem: Six bolts were used for drive plates. Sometimes bolts were not fastened at all, or fastened with insufficient torque.

Figure 3.23 Prevention of Drive Plate Omission (a)

Figure 3.24 Prevention of Drive Plate Omission (b)

Before

Impact wrenches were used. Although sampling inspections were done, certain parts were not visible after the transmission was attached.

After

The workers were given ratchet torque wrenches with micro–switches. Unless all six bolts are tightened at the pre–determined torque, a stopper would not release the engine and it could not be sent to the subsequent process. A red light also alerted the worker in charge.

Result: Bolts that were not tightened at all, or tightened with inappropriate torque, disappeared. Sampling inspections became unnecessary.

Cost: 80,000 yen

3. Poka-yoke for Spot Welding (Central Motor)

Problem: Since there were many parts that needed to be attached to radiators, such as nuts, cramps, and brackets, the workers occasionally missed a few spot welds.

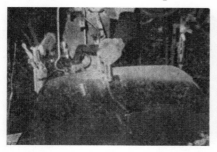

Figure 3.25 Prevention of Welding
Omission (a)

Figure 3.26 Prevention of Welding
Omission (b)

Before

At the end of the welding process, each worker counted the number of welded spots and tried to make sure that all were accounted for.

After

Using a small electrical current, after each spot weld was completed, a light corresponding to the weld would be activated on a board. When the last light on the board came on, a buzzer notified the worker.

Result: Defects dropped to zero and counting became unnecessary.

Cost: 35,000 yen

4. Poka–yoke for Torque Check (Kanto Auto Works)

Problem: After upper control arms were attached to the car frames, their torque was supposed to be checked. However, this inspection was sometimes forgotten.

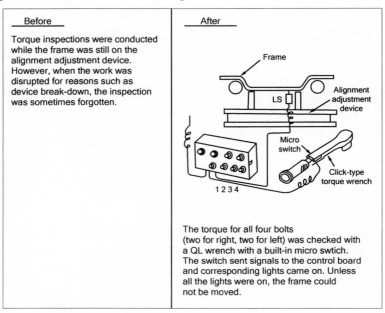

Before	After
Torque inspections were conducted while the frame was still on the alignment adjustment device. However, when the work was disrupted for reasons such as device break-down, the inspection was sometimes forgotten.	The torque for all four bolts (two for right, two for left) was checked with a QL wrench with a built-in micro swtich. The switch sent signals to the control board and corresponding lights came on. Unless all the lights were on, the frame could not be moved.

Figure 3.27 Prevention of Wrench Use Omission (a)

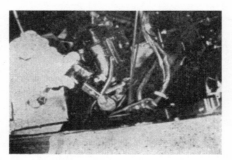

Figure 3.28 Prevention of Bolt
Omission (b)

Result: Torque inspections were never forgotten again.

Cost: 70,000 yen

5. Poka-yoke for Nut Welding (Kanto Auto Works)

Problem: Six nuts were supposed to be welded for each product, but even if less than six were welded, it sometimes went unnoticed.

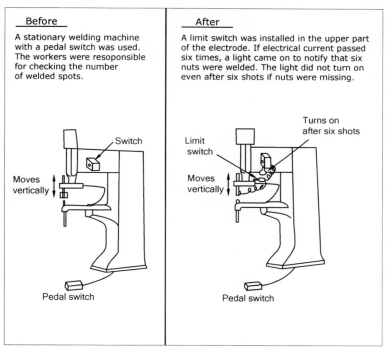

Figure 3.29 Prevention of Welding Omission

Result: The problem of missing nuts was eliminated.

Cost: 7,000 yen

6. Poka–yoke for "Ratchet" Counting (Arakawa Auto Works)

Problem: In each box, workers were supposed to put 90 pieces of a product called "Ratchet," but the number sometimes varied.

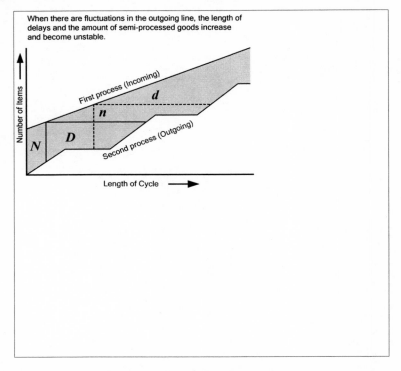

Figure 3.30 Prevention of Ratchet Number Inconsistency

Result: Counting mistakes disappeared.

Cost: 1,000 yen

7. Poka–yoke for Leak Inspection (Matsushita Electric Industrial, Laundry Machine Department, Shizuoka factory)

Problem: When problems arose at the production line, leak inspections were sometimes forgotten.

Figure 3.31 Prevention of
Inspection Omission

Before
Whether or not the inspection was carried out depended entirely on the workers' memory.

After
Every time the inspection was conducted, each worker pushed a switch. If the inspection was not done in order or omitted, a light on the inspection board did not turn on. Furthermore, if the light did not turn on after a certain time, the production line shut down.

Result: The inspection was never forgotten.

Cost: 80,000 yen

(c) Motion–Step Type

This poka–yoke checks whether the established steps or motions of a procedure are followed. Again, control type and warning type methods are used. This method is quite versatile and has a broad range of applications.

1. Poka–yoke for Handle–Cover Welding (Arakawa Shatai Kogyo)

Problem: Drilling and spot welding of parts called "reinforced uppers" used for rear seats were supposed to be done in the same process. However, spot welding was sometimes forgotten.

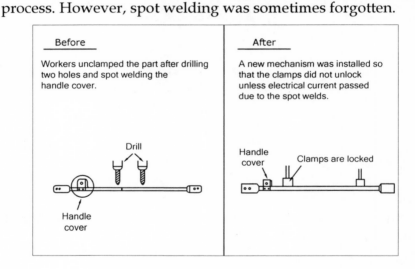

Figure 3.32 Prevention of Installation Omission

Result: Welding was never forgotten.

Cost: 2,200 yen

2. Poka–yoke for Bracket Stop Handles (Arakawa Shatai Kogyo)

Problem: Parts called "bracket stop handles," would sometimes continue downstream without being attached.

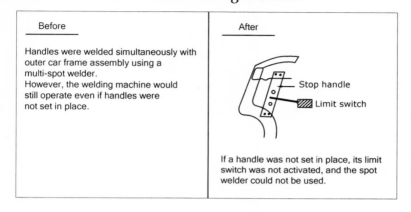

Before	After
Handles were welded simultaneously with outer car frame assembly using a multi-spot welder. However, the welding machine would still operate even if handles were not set in place.	Stop handle Limit switch If a handle was not set in place, its limit switch was not activated, and the spot welder could not be used.

Figure 3.33 Prevention of Installation Omission

Result: Stop handles were never forgotten.

Cost: 2,200 yen

3. Poka–yoke for Attaching Spacers (Arakawa Shatai Kogyo)

Problem: When pieces necessary for seat reclining functionality are assembled, spacers were often forgotten.

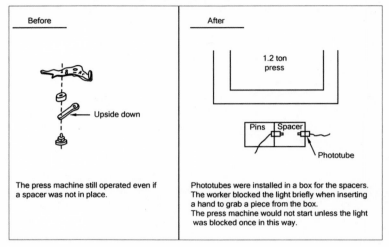

Figure 3.34 Prevention of Spacer Omission

Result: Spacers were never forgotten again.

Cost: 24,500 yen

4. Poka–yoke for Detecting Flat Tires (Central Motor)

Problem: Flat tires or tires with insufficient air pressure were sometimes attached. The production line had to shut down every time this problem was detected.

Figure 3.35 Flat Tire Detection Device (a)

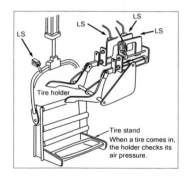

Figure 3.36 Flat Tire Detection Device (b)

Before
Before attaching tires, the worker checked their pressure.

After
In the tire attaching machine, a device to inspect air pressure was installed. If the pressure was not enough, a buzzer sounded to alert the workers.

Result: The production line was never shut down again due to this defect.

Cost: 180,000 yen

5. Poka–yoke for Erasing Production Sequence Table (Central Motor)

Problem: Multiple models of rear axle shafts are assembled based on a production sequence table. After assembling each model, the workers were supposed to remove the sequence table from the work bench. However, this step was sometimes forgotten and wrong shafts were assembled as a result. This caused problems in a later process.

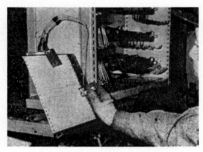

Figure 3.37 Assembly Order Management Device

Before
The workers removed items from the sequence table line by line.

After
The workers used a stamp with a built–in micro switch to erase appropriate items on the table. If they forgot, the stopper holding the shafts would not release and they could not be sent to the subsequent process.

Result: It became impossible to assemble shafts based upon previously used sequence tables.

Cost: 20,000 yen

6. Poka–yoke to Prevent Screws from Falling into Motors (Matsushita Electric, Laundry Machine Department)

Problem: When suspension systems were being attached, screws sometimes fell into the motor.

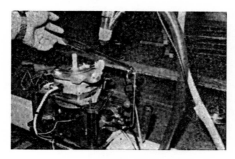

Figure 3.38 Screw Blocking Device

Before

The workers had to be careful not to let the screws fall, but the mistake could not be eliminated. Once a screw was in the motor, it was difficult to remove.

After

A lid was placed over the opening in the engine to block the screws. Unless the lid was in place, the driver would not turn on.

Result: Screws never fell into the motors again.

Cost: 5,000 yen

7. Poka–yoke to Prevent Short Circuits (Matsushita Electric, Laundry Machine Department, Mikuni factory)

Problem: When the brake wheel was attached with bolts between the motor and the drying tub of laundry machines, the bolts sometimes ruptured the insulation bushing, resulting in a short circuit.

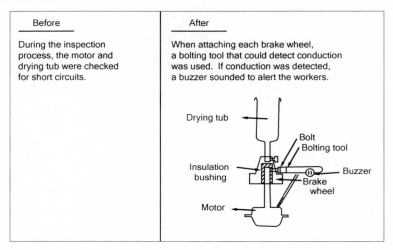

Before	After
During the inspection process, the motor and drying tub were checked for short circuits.	When attaching each brake wheel, a bolting tool that could detect conduction was used. If conduction was detected, a buzzer sounded to alert the workers.

Figure 3.39a Short Circuit Detection Device

Figure 3.39b Short Circuit Detection Device

Result: Products with short circuits never proceeded to the final process.

Cost: 10,000 yen

172

8. Poka–yoke for Attaching Compression Packing (Matsushita Electric, Laundry Machine Department, Shizuoka factory)

Problem: Compression packing needed to be fitted under the tub of each laundry machine; however, it was sometimes forgotten.

Figure 3.40 Washing Machine Parts Detection Device

Before
The workers tried not to forget the procedure.

After
When the tub of the laundry machine rolled in on a conveyor, it hit a limit switch installed in a stopper. This triggered a poka-yoke clamp to come down. The clamp had a large cartoon label that said, "Did you remember the compression packing?" When the worker reached into a box to grab compression packing, a photo tube installed in the box sensed the movement of their hand and raised the clamp.

Result: Compression packing was never forgotten again.

Cost: 10,000 yen

9. Poka-yoke for Assembling Rear Upper Cowls (Kanto Auto Works)

Problem: There were two types of rear upper cowls: ones with holes for mirrors and ones without. They were often mixed up and wrong parts were attached.

Before	After
After checking a job card, workers were supposed to choose an appropriate type of part.	There was a corresponding job card for products with holes and without. One kind of job card was given a notch. Depending on whether or not there was a notch on the job card, a limit switch was activated and modified the assembly mount in a way that made it impossible to attach wrong parts. Furthermore, if wrong parts were set in place, a light and buzzer alerted the worker. 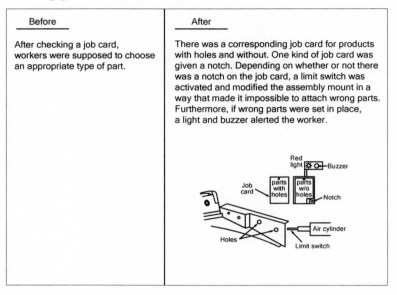

Figure 3.41 Installation Omission Device

Result: Part mix-up was eliminated.

Cost: 15,000 yen

10. Poka–yoke for Inserting Cotter Pins to Ball Joints (Kanto Auto Works)

Problem: Although lower ball joints are critical parts, their cotter pins were sometimes forgotten.

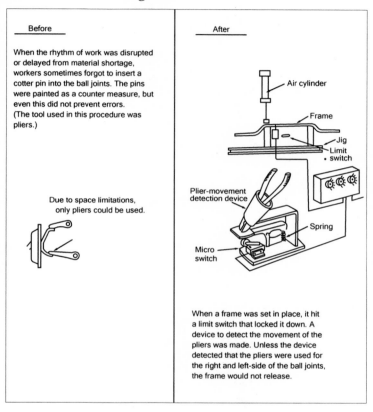

Figure 3.42 Installation Omission Device

Result: Cotter pins were never forgotten again.

Cost: 20,000 yen

11. Poka–yoke for Filling Differentials with Oil (Kanto Auto Works)

Problem: During the assembly process, oil was supposed to be filled in differentials, but this was sometimes forgotten.

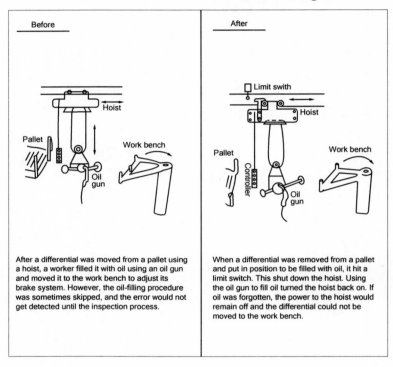

Before

After

After a differential was moved from a pallet using a hoist, a worker filled it with oil using an oil gun and moved it to the work bench to adjust its brake system. However, the oil-filling procedure was sometimes skipped, and the error would not get detected until the inspection process.

When a differential was removed from a pallet and put in position to be filled with oil, it hit a limit switch. This shut down the hoist. Using the oil gun to fill oil turned the hoist back on. If oil was forgotten, the power to the hoist would remain off and the differential could not be moved to the work bench.

Figure 3.43 Prevention of Oil Omission

Result: Oil–filling was never forgotten again.

Cost: 6,800 yen

12. Poka–yoke for Body Number Punching (Kanto Auto Works)

Problem: On top of each radiator support, a body number was punched. However, the workers sometimes made various errors such as punching the air, punching twice, or forgetting to punch.

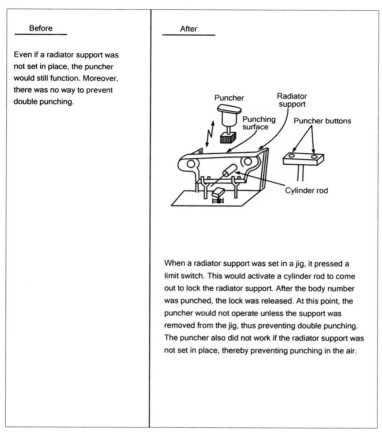

Before

Even if a radiator support was not set in place, the puncher would still function. Moreover, there was no way to prevent double punching.

After

When a radiator support was set in a jig, it pressed a limit switch. This would activate a cylinder rod to come out to lock the radiator support. After the body number was punched, the lock was released. At this point, the puncher would not operate unless the support was removed from the jig, thus preventing double punching. The puncher also did not work if the radiator support was not set in place, thereby preventing punching in the air.

Figure 3.44 Prevention of Stamping Mistake

Result: Punching mistakes were eliminated.

Cost: 25,000 yen

13. Poka–yoke for Drilling Board Sets (Arakawa Auto Works)

Problem: Drilling of board sets was sometimes forgotten.

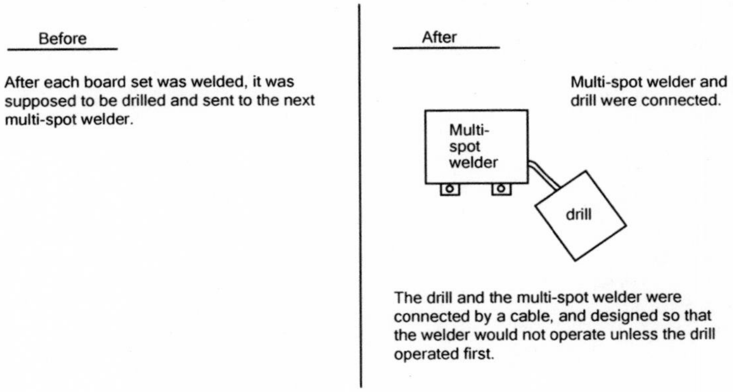

Before

After each board set was welded, it was supposed to be drilled and sent to the next multi-spot welder.

After

Multi-spot welder and drill were connected.

Multi-spot welder

drill

The drill and the multi-spot welder were connected by a cable, and designed so that the welder would not operate unless the drill operated first.

Figure 3.45 Prevention of Drilling Omission

Result: Drilling was never forgotten again.

Cost: 1750 yen

14. Poka–yoke for Tightening Water Feed Valves (Matsushita Electric, Laundry Machine Department, Shizuoka factory)

Problem: Water feed valves used for laundry machines needed to be tightened with two screws. Sometimes, one of them was forgotten.

Figure 3.46 Prevention of Process Omission

Before
Two types of pneumatic screwdrivers, A and B, were supposed to be used to fasten water feed valves, but the workers often forgot to use Screwdriver B.

After
When Screwdriver A was used, a ring slid across a bar above the worker and stopped at a certain point. When Screwdriver B was used, the ring slid to an opposite direction and hit a limit switch. If both screwdrivers were not used within a certain period of time, a buzzer sounded to alert the worker.

Result: Screws were never forgotten again.

Cost: 3,000 yen

15. Poka–yoke for Tightening Laundry Machine Bearings (Matsushita Electric, Laundry Machine Department, Shizuoka factory)

Problem: Laundry machine bearings were supposed to be tightened twice — first with an automatic torque wrench, followed by a manual torque wrench — so that they could withstand constant vibration. However, the second tightening was sometimes forgotten.

Figure 3.47 Prevention of Tightening Omission

Before
There was no way to confirm that the second tightening was done.

After
Manual torque wrenches with built–in ink were used. Since tightening left a mark on a nut, anyone could easily check if the second tightening was done.

Result: The second tightening was never forgotten again.

Cost: 500 yen

16. Poka–yoke for Injecting Adhesive (Matsushita Electric, Stereo department, Audio player factory)

Problem: Adhesive bond was supposed to be injected inside the tone arms of record players, but it was sometimes forgotten.

Before
The workers were solely responsible for remembering whether or not the adhesive was injected.

After
(a) Set the tone arm in place.
(b) Inject adhesive
        Tighten screws
Remove the tone arm

Figure 3.48 (a)
Set the tone arm in a jig and clamp it down.

Figure 3.48a Glue Detection Device

Figure 3.48 (b)
Inject adhesive using a syringe.

Figure 3.48 (c)
Tighten two screws and remove the tone arm. If the button to inject adhesive was not pressed by this point, the clamp would not release the tone arm.

Figure 3.48b

Result: Adhesive injection was never forgotten again.

Cost: 5,000 yen

Figure 3.48c

17. Poka–yoke for Tightening Nuts (Matsushita Electric, Stereo department, Audio player factory)

Problem: A nut on tone arms was supposed to be tightened using a torque driver, but the tightening was sometimes forgotten.

Before
The workers were supposed to remember on their own to tighten.

After
Clamp down a tone arm

Make adjustments (place a nut)

Tighten the nut

Release the clamp

Figure 3.49(a)
Set a tone arm in a jig and clamp down the arm's base.

Figure 3.49a Nut Torque Detection

Figure 3.49(b)
Make necessary adjustments of the tone arm, place a nut by hand, and tighten it with a torque driver.

Figure 3.49b

Figure 3.49(c)
The clamp released the tone arm when the torque driver was put back in a driver stand.

Result: Tightening was never forgotten again.

Cost: 2,000 yen

Figure 3.49c

18. Poka–yoke for Affixing Stickers (Matsushita Electric)

Problem: Products without appropriate stickers were sometimes found in the inspection process.

Before	After
The workers were solely responsible for remembering the stickers.	Tape with stickers was rolled out of a labeling machine. Bending the tape at a sharp angle caused half of a sticker to peel off and stick out. A phototube was installed to detect when a sticker was exposed as such. If the worker did not remove the sticker within 20 seconds, the takt time for this process, a buzzer sounded and the conveyor was shut down.

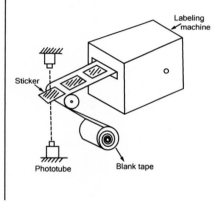

Figure 3.50 Labeling device

Result: Stickers were never forgotten again.

Cost: 15,000 yen

19. Poka–yoke for Undercoat Painting (Arakawa Auto Works)

Problem: At this plant some cars required undercoating, while others did not. However, painting errors such as undercoating a car that did not require it and vice versa, had been happening, and unnecessarily painted cars had to be discarded.

Figure 3.51 Preventing Painting
Mistakes

Figure 3.52 Preventing Painting
Mistakes

Figure 3.53 Preventing Painting
Mistakes

Before
Based on a production sequence table, if undercoating was required, worker A hung two S–shaped hooks on the car body. After the washing and drying process, worker B was supposed to double–check the requirement of painting based on the sequence table. If no undercoating was required, worker B was supposed to remove one of the hooks. Worker C undercoated the car only if there were two hooks left. However, errors seemed to be unavoidable, resulting in a loss of about 300,000 yen every month.

After
A sliding frame was set in each production sequence table to eliminate the risk of reading wrong lines.
If necessary worker A was instructed to hang an S–shaped

184

hook immediately after looking at the sequence table to eliminate memorization errors.

On the production sequence table, workers made note of when their work was completed.

The production sequence table was modified with new instructions for double checking the need for undercoating. After the washing and drying process, worker B double–checked the production table as instructed, and hung a rectangular tab at the end of the S–shaped hook that worker A hung if a car required undercoating. In this manner, neither forgetfulness on the part of worker B, nor a mistake made on the part of worker A, would result in unnecessary undercoating.

Moreover, the spray gun that worker C used could only be released by taking the tab and inserting it in a detection device. The device also had a built–in timer, allowing it to spray only one car at a time.

The spray gun locked automatically when placed back into its holster.

- Figure 3.51 Poka–yoke for Undercoat Painting (Production Sequence Table) — Worker A takes out an S–shaped hook immediately based on the production sequence table.

- Figure 3.52 Poka–yoke for Undercoat Painting (S–shaped hook and rectangular tab) After the washing and drying process, worker B hangs the tab at the end of the hook.

- Figure 3.53 Poka–yoke for Undercoat Painting (Rectangular tab and detection device) Worker C unlocks the spray gun by inserting the rectangular tab into the detection device.

Result: Painting errors were eliminated, saving the company 4,000,000 yen a year.

Cost: 30,000 yen

20. Poka–yoke for Shutting Coolant Valve (Taiho Kogyo)

Problem: Tap water was used as a coolant at the company lab, but the water valve was frequently left open.

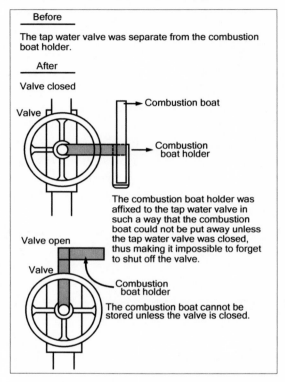

Figure 3.54 Valve Tightening Device

Result: The valve was always shut after use.

Cost: 1,000 yen

Application of Poka–yoke

As long as poka–yoke devices are appropriately designed, not only can they find defects, but they can eliminate them altogether. Thus, the use of poka–yoke is truest form of quality control.

As we have learned so far, poka–yoke can be inexpensively installed, and used very effectively to perform 100 percent inspections.

As explained earlier, there are two types of poka–yoke feedback, "control type" and "warning type" that either stop the work, or alert the workers if abnormalities are detected. The control type is a stronger corrective device, so the introduction of this poka–yoke type should be considered first.

There are also three different ways in which poka–yoke devices detect abnormalities: contact type, fixed–value type, and motion–step type. It should be noted that motion–step has the widest range of application and can be used regardless of the types of products or operations.

Furthermore, poka–yoke can be used for any of the inspection types mentioned earlier: source, self, and successive inspections. If it is used for source and successive inspections, it can eliminate defects. If it is used for successive inspections only, and defects cannot be fixed, a small amount of defects may be unavoidable.

Although poka–yoke devices excel in eliminating defects, they have one downside: they cannot be used for visual inspections in which human senses are required to detect abnormalities. However, if visual inspections are used on the shop floor, we should still make an effort to turn it into more of an objective physical inspection, by quantifying the degrees of abnormalities.

One way to avoid visual inspections is to detect the causes of defects at their source by carrying out a source inspection. Poka–yoke could be used this way. For example, it is often considered that a visual inspection has to be used to check paint color. However, conditions that affect the color can be controlled at the source. In this case, in order to stabilize the amount of paint sprayed, the appropriate range of paint in the tank can be determined and checked. The air pressure to spray the paint can also be inspected and maintained at a certain level. Effort should always be made to turn visual inspections into physical inspections this way.

It should also be added here that poka–yoke is a quite effective method to realize "pre–automation" discussed later in the book.

SUMMARY

The most effective inspection improvement is a 100 percent inspection that eliminates defects. The most effective way to achieve this is to use poka–yoke.

3.3 Transportation Improvement
The most effective, active improvement of transportation is one that reduces transportation to zero. This can only be achieved through layout improvement. Passive improvement of transportation involves changing the layout, or using conveyors and forklifts, in a way that reduces transportation.

3.3.1 Selection of Layout Types
These various layout types, except for the non–controlled irregular layout, are discussed below.

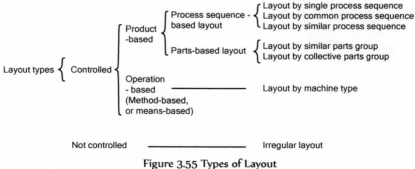

Figure 3.55 Types of Layout

A. Product–based and Method–based

Process is the flow in which materials transform into products. It is natural that the product–based layout minimizes transportation. However, operation–based layout is convenient in terms of work management. It is necessary to take into account the pros and cons of both of these layout types.

B. Operation–based Layout

An operation–based layout is equivalent to machine–type layout in that the same types of machines are placed together. This type of layout is often used in the following cases:

- Worker skill level is insufficient and assistance from the foreman is required
- The capacity of the same types of machines needs to be leveled — otherwise, the operation rate of the machines becomes too low and the number of machines increases unnecessarily
- When production is high diversity, mixed model and operational convenience is more important

This layout type, however, comes with disadvantages in terms of process, such as the increase in transportation and the difficulty of process management.

C. Product–based Layout

A product–based layout, which can be subdivided into a parts–based layout and a process–sequenced–based layout, is appropriate in the following cases:

- Workers' have sufficient skills and do not require much technical assistance from the foreman
- The operation is simplified, standardized, mechanized, and the skill level of workers' does not need to be high
- The capacity of the same type of machines does not need to be leveled
- It is more important to reduce transportation and carry

out better process management, even if the operation rate has to be sacrificed a little

(a) Collective Parts–Group Layout and Similar Parts–Group Layout

When the production is high diversity and high volume, a parts–based layout is often used. A parts–based layout can be further divided into two, depending on the criteria of division.

- Collective–parts–group layout

Machines are divided depending on which section of the product they are used for. For example, machines required for engine–related parts are grouped together, machines required for transmission related parts are grouped together, etc.

- Similar–parts–group layout

Machines are divided depending on the type of parts they handle. For example, machines that handle gears are grouped together, machines that handle shafts are grouped together, etc.

Within each group, the layout of the machines can be random, based on the machine–type, or based on the process sequence.

(b) Single–Process Sequence, Common–Process Sequence, and Similar–Process Sequence Layout

When the loss from transportation needs to be minimized and process management needs to be more convenient, a process–sequence layout should be used. However, in order to realize this:

- Worker's skill level must be high
- Operations must be simplified, standardized, and mechanized
- It must be possible to lower machine operation rates to a certain degree

There are three types of process–sequence layouts and the appropriate type should be chosen depending on the nature of production.

A single-process sequence layout, which is based on the process sequence of a single type of product, is appropriate in the following case:

> Production is extremely low in diversity and high in volume.
>
> Worker skill level is high, and the operation is highly simplified, standardized, and mechanized. Machine operation rates can be lowered to a certain degree.

A common-process sequence layout is appropriate under the following circumstances:

> The diversity and volume of production is average.
>
> Worker skill level is average, and the operation is moderately simplified, standardized, and mechanized — the operation rate of machines cannot be lowered much.
>
> There are common processes among different types of products.

A similar-process sequence layout, which heavily emphasizes processes, is used under the following circumstances:

> The production is high in diversity and low in volume.
>
> Worker skill level is average, and the operation is moderately simplified, standardized, and mechanized. The operation rate of machines cannot be lowered much.
>
> The loss from transportation needs to be minimized.
>
> A machine layout that makes process management easier is desirable.

(c) Selection of Layout Types

As explained so far, machine layout is decided after going through several decision-making processes.

First, whether the layout should be controlled or non-controlled is decided. Second, when the diversity and volume of production is high, whether or not a parts-based layout should be used is decided. Lastly, either a machine-type layout or a process-sequence layout is chosen depending on whether process or operation is given more priority.

If a process–sequence layout is chosen, the type of process–sequence layout should be intrinsically decided. A single–process sequence layout is appropriate if orders are large enough to produce a single product continuously for at least one month.

If orders are not large enough for a single product to be produced continuously for a month, and yet many products share identical processes, a common–process sequence layout should be used. However, if product orders are not large enough to match machine capacity, the combination of a common–process sequence and a similar–process sequence can be used. For example, 80 percent of the time, the line can be used for a common–process sequence, and the rest of the time for a similar–process sequence.

If the process sequences of multiple products do not have much in common, a similar process–sequence layout is used.

After deciding to use a process–sequence layout, an appropriate layout type is decided based on the nature of production — the production volume and the similarity of process sequences. In other words, the best layout is decided based upon the objective nature of production — not the subjective opinion or taste of people. There is no place for voices such as, "Based on my experience, machines should be laid out this way."

Once a layout has been selected, one should consider the following:

> How low are machine operation rates allowed to be? (This is irrespective of worker operation rates.)
>
> How many machines should each worker operate?
>
> How much should machines be automated?
>
> Machine maintenance.
>
> Safety of operations and other issues such as the handling of heat, noise, and dangerous materials.

Again, the consideration of these items should have no bearing on our layout choice, which is based on the intrinsic nature of our production. Rather, these items serve only to fine-tune the layout type that has already been chosen.

3.3.2 Transportation is a Crime

Mr. Hori, the president of a company that made dies for plastic molding, attended one of the IE courses I held. He came to talk with me after the first day of lecture.

He said, "You told us today that transportation is a crime. Of course, I never thought that transportation was good, but I always seemed to think that production wasn't possible without it. What you said really made me think."

His comment was based on the following comment of mine: "In production activities, there are two types of work — one that adds value to products, and one that doesn't. Among the four aspects of processes; namely processing, inspection, transportation, and delays, processing is the only activity that adds value, the rest only raise costs. Transportation is especially wasteful, taking up around 45 percent of worker hours.

"A nation's quality of living is greatly affected by two things: one, the amount of natural resources available, and two, the level of labor productivity. Unfortunately, the natural resources of our country, Japan, are scarce. This means that in order to raise the standard of living, raising the labor productivity of our nation is crucial. Therefore, wasting precious labor on cost-raising transportation is a crime for anyone involved in the manufacturing industry."

He said, "I recognize that transportation doesn't add value. However, my factory does a typical low volume — mixed model production, and I just can't see how transportation could be eliminated. The variety of processes is too diverse."

I said, "Why don't you try an ABC analysis of your three main products, and study their process sequences. There are many people in the world, but the majority of them can be divided into four groups, if you use blood type as a separation criterion — Type A, B, AB, and O. If you were to check the 'blood type' of your process sequences, you might find there are really only a few different types. "

The following day, Mr. Hori came to me again. "It looks like the majority of our products have only about four 'blood types' as you said. I'm going to tackle this transportation issue when I go back."

About a month later, I visited his factory. Mr. Hori told me that right after he came back from my course, he studied the process sequences at the shop floor and discovered that 95 percent of production can be done in only four types of process sequences. He said, "A machine–type layout was used before — lathes are placed together in one area, milling machines are placed together in another, for example — but we changed it to a process–sequence layout instead.

"It wasn't easy since the floor space is limited here, but I talked with the workers many times until they were convinced about the benefit of the new layout. So, one Saturday, we stopped production altogether and everyone helped change the layout. We also installed metal bridges between machines so that products can slide on them.

"The first sign of improvement was the drop in the use of cold compresses. The workers used to lift products that weighed 30 to 50 kilograms and often hurt their backs, so the company had compresses at the ready. But after the rearrangement, they weren't needed.

"We also used to use lift cars to transport products. When there weren't enough cars, delays happened. The machines were idled during transportation as well. These problems disappeared and the production increased by 50 percent without increasing the number of workers.

"Furthermore, we started the multi–machine type operation

that you spoke of. For example, we installed a limit switch in the cutting machine so that it stops automatically. Now, while the machine is cutting, the worker can operate other machines. Each worker is able to handle double the workload this way.

"Delays between each process decreased, and because floor space is used so efficiently now, there's more of it. Best of all, now that the production cycle has been halved, we never miss delivery deadlines. Our fund turnover also improved, making fund management much easier.

"Until I heard your lecture, I'd always thought of transportation as an inconvenient, but inescapable part of production. Now that my perspective has changed, I can't help but notice transportation. I'm surprised at how much that awareness can change people."

As Mr. Hori said, it is important to clearly perceive transportation as a crime. Aren't we forgetting the fundamental improvement—namely the elimination of transportation, by using band–aid measures such as conveyors or forklifts? It is time to ask this question and view transportation in a different light.

SUMMARY

Among the four phenomena of processes, transportation takes up just as many worker hours as processing itself; however, it does nothing but raise costs. Therefore, we have to start by clearly recognizing it as waste. The best improvement is to eliminate transportation through layout changes, and the best layout should be chosen systematically.

In the following section, improvement of delays is discussed. Layout improvement is also crucial for decreasing delays. Furthermore, because it is necessary to decrease the transportation lot to one to minimize delays, transportation is likewise reduced by such an improvement.

3.4 Delay Improvement

The balance between the delivery period (D) and the production cycle (P) must be dealt with on a daily basis. If the two are not in balance, expedited work or delivery delays occur. In cases like these, people want to react by extending the delivery period (D), instead of shortening the production cycle (P), assuming that the latter is simply impossible.

Another common misunderstanding is thinking that processing time makes up the majority of production cycle. In fact, it is delay time that makes up the majority of production cycle.

There are two types of delays: process delay and lot delay. Process delays can be eliminated through synchronization and lot delays can be eliminated by decreasing the transportation lot to just one, even though this increases transportation. Therefore, improvement of layout is extremely important. The so called "flow production" makes these improvements possible.

Actively improving delays means to eliminate both process delays and lot delays; in other words, implementing a one–piece flow production. Passively improving is to minimize delays by improving process management.

Delays are already discussed in chapter two, so one–piece flow production is explained in this chapter.

3.4.1 Basic Concept of One–Piece Flow

A. Two Aspects of Process Management Improvement

There are two types of process management improvement — active and passive. In general, passive measures are the ones most often discussed, not active measures.

Process management should be considered from two perspectives: schedule management and surplus–capacity management. In terms of schedule management, balancing the delivery period and the production cycle is very important. (Figure 3.56)

Delivery period (D): This period begins when an order is

received and ends when the order is delivered.

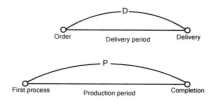

Figure 3.56 Relation between D & P

Production cycle (*P*): This period begins when the first process starts and ends when the product is finished (subcontracting is also included in this time period).

D<P: If *D* is less than *P*, expedited production happens often and delivery deadlines are missed. Schedule management becomes difficult.

D>P: If *D* is greater than *P*, product delivery deadlines can be met. However, if *D* and *P* are close, deadlines may still be missed if schedules are not properly managed.

When the delivery period is close to, or shorter than, the production period, people often try to compensate with passive measures. But the effectiveness of doing so is nothing compared to reducing the production cycle through active measures. Using active measures can reduce *P* by up to 80 or 90 percent, thus solving the very root of the problem. However, such measures are only possible so long as one–piece flow production is realized.

There are also active and passive improvement measures in the other aspect of process management, surplus–capacity management. Passive measures in this case would be trying to adjust and control surplus capacities without making any changes to the current capacity of machines. On the other hand, active measures would be realizing one–piece flow production and raising machine capacities anywhere from 50 to 100 percent. The successful implementation of many factories is testament to the supreme effectiveness of active improvement measures.

Of course, there will always be factories where switching 100 percent of production to a flow system is simply impossible. However, even in these cases a 70 to 90 percent conversion is always possible. I have seen many companies that pay no interest in switching to a one–piece flow production system, mainly due to the ignorance of the nature of their own production. I would like to encourage readers, using the following examples as a reference, to review their own production and start taking up active improvement measures.

B. Structure of Production

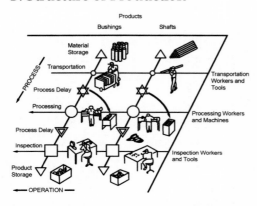

Figure 3.57 The Structure of Production

As we have already seen, production consists of a network of processes and operations (Figure 3.57). Processes are made up of four phenomena: processing, inspection, transportation, and delay. Correspondingly, there are processing operations, inspection operations, transportation operations, and delay operations.

Operations can be further divided into three as follows (Figure 3.58):

1. Preparation, post–adjustment operations (Setup operations).

2. Principal operations (Main operations, incidental operations).

3. Allowances.

The first among these three, setup operations, may have the least impact on one–piece flow production. However, reducing setup time by using SMED will certainly make it easier to accommodate expedited production and raise production capacity. When a flow production system is introduced it is desirable to make times even, but this may be difficult if different machines are placed in series. However, if setup time is less than 10 minutes, the difference in setup times will not lead to major losses.

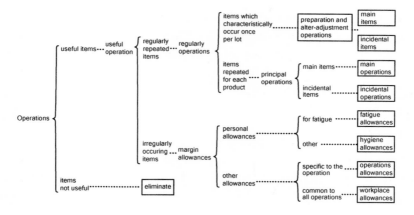

Figure 3.58 Content of Operations

Second, I would like to talk about principal operations and the one–piece flow production system. Principal operations, which constitute 70 percent of worker hours, can be further divided into main and incidental operations, which correspondingly make up 30 and 40 percent of worker hours. In this case, grinding itself is the main operation, while mounting and dismounting work pieces to and from the machine can be considered incidental operations. Incidental operations, namely attaching and detaching work pieces, and switch panel operations, take up as much as 40 percent of worker hours because these operations are done manually. If they could be automated, a significant reduction in worker hours would result.

Automatically dismounting work pieces usually does not pose much of a problem, but mounting work pieces poses a challenge in the case of batch production. Work pieces are often thrown together randomly in boxes, making correct orientation of each piece and mounting it to a machine technically difficult. This, however, can

Operation \ Process	Processing	Inspection	Transportation	Delay
Setup operations	○	□	△	×
Main operations	◎	▣	▲	×
incidental operations	○	□	△	×
Fatigue allowances	◎	▣	▲	×
hygiene allowances	◎	▣	▲	×
Operations allowances	◎	▣	▲	×
Workplaces allowances	◎	▣	▲	×
Elimination	◎	▣	▲	×

Figure 3.59 Process & Operation Improvement

199

be solved easily by using a one–piece flow system. Since only one piece is sent at a time, its orientation and position can be easily adjusted between processes. In other words, a flow operation makes it easier to automate work piece attachment and switch panel operations. Successful automation can reduce incidental operations anywhere from 60 to 80 percent, and help increase production capacity. This will correspondingly result in an 80 to 90 percent reduction in worker hours.

Third, the one–piece flow production system also has a positive influence on allowances. Introduction of flow system intrinsically encourages better machine maintenance since a single break–down will halt the entire production line. Operational allowances that accommodate machine break–downs are usually irrelevant once a flow system is in place.

In this way, one–piece flow systems prompt fundamental reform of both processes and operations. But only those who rise to the challenges associated with these reforms will reap the tremendous benefits of one–piece flow production.

(a) Low Volume, Mixed Model Production and ABC Analysis
Even from those who understand the benefits of one–piece flow production, I often hear, "Our factory can't possibly use flow production since our production is mixed model and low volume." This type of resignation usually comes from not understanding the nature of their production.

Figure 3.60 is an example of an ABC analysis graph from S Electric Company, a plant that produces solenoids. This graph was drawn to display the cumulative items produced, with the biggest production items plotted first. In this graph, the near vertical segment is labeled A, the near–horizontal segment is leveled C, and the segment in–between is labeled B.

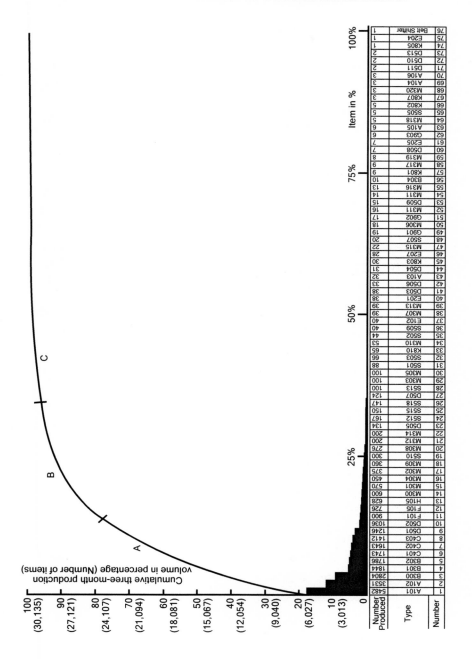

Figure 3.60 ABC Analysis at S Electronics

201

An analysis based on this type of classification is called an ABC analysis. The classification helps select important products that should be targeted for one–piece flow production, or any other improvements. In most factories, the top 30 percent of products account for as much as 70 percent of the production volume. In the case of S Electric, 10 out of 76 items accounted for 75 percent of the production volume, resulting in a decision to designate these items for flow production.

In another factory, an ABC analysis revealed that 20 out of 150 items accounted for as much as 70 percent of their production volume. After introducing one–piece flow production for these 20 items, the company experienced a 70 percent increase in production capacity, an 80 percent reduction in the production cycle, and zero delivery delays.

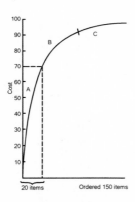

Figure 3.61 ABC Analysis at Z Company

At Company Z, a kitchen sink manufacture, delivery delay was a chronic problem. When I visited their factory, I had a conversation with the foreman.

I asked, "What do you think is causing the delivery delay?"

The foreman said, "The mixed model and low–volume nature of our production."

"How many types of parts do you produce here?"

"About 1,200 types."

Upon my request, the company conducted an ABC analysis of their production and found out that 350 types of items accounted for 80 percent of their production volume. The company did a further analysis on the parts classified as A, based on their width and thickness, instead of length. This additional analysis revealed that only 86 types of items accounted for the A segment. Following this conclusion, the manufacturer introduced a new production method—the wooden materials used for these 86 items were cut in the proper dimensions and finished with a plane in advance. When they were actually used, only the length needed to be adjusted. After this improvement, the company was able to decrease the production cycle, reduce the amount semi-processed goods by 60 percent, and solve its chronic problem of delivery delays.

These examples show that one–piece flow production is not only for mass production, but can be used even if production is high in diversity and low in volume. At most factories using an ABC analysis will often reveal that 30 percent of products account for as much as 70 percent of the production volume. This means that vast majority of companies can reap the benefits of flow production.

(b) Variables and Invariables
In addition to the ABC analysis, there is another method that makes initiating one–piece flow production easy for low–volume, mixed model production—separating invariable aspects of production from the rest. Many companies tend to think that because of the number and types of their orders, as well as delivery deadlines that are not fixed, flow production cannot be used at their factories. In reality, there is almost always an aspect of invariability in what people may think is totally variable.

At one lighting equipment factory I was told that the plant had low efficiency and high defect problems. When I inquired about the cause, the foreman's answer was typical: "Because our production is high in diversity and low in volume," adding that there were 600 types of manufactured items. I said, "Aren't there items that are produced every month at a steady volume?" This question prompted them to conduct a study. When the study was completed, it became clear that as much as 30 percent of items were actually produced every month at a nearly constant volume. The company decided to dedicate three out of eleven production lines for these invariable items; in these three lines, flow production was used. In addition, the same amount and the same type of products were sent in the same order every month.

As a result, the company's target efficiency rate was achieved and the defect rate plummeted by 80 percent, in spite of the fact that only part–time workers handled these lines.

A similar result was achieved at a gear manufacturer. The company had a build–to–order, and low volume, mixed model production style. However, careful study on orders revealed that an order from one auto maker came monthly at almost the same volume. So the manufacturer made a flow–production line specifically for this stable order, and assigned one foreman and two workers there. As a result, the company's delivery delays became zero, production tripled, and the defects were cut by 80 percent.

A careful study of production often uncovers more invariable aspects than expected. These examples are testaments that even if production is low volume, mixed model the invariable parts of production can be separated for more efficient flow production.

When I explain the benefit of finding invariables in production, I sometimes use this analogy. If there are a few good young boys in a large group of delinquents, the good boys may end up assimilating with the rest. Is it not better to separate the two and take care of each group properly?

(c) Is Low Operation Rate Better?
If people are asked, "Which do you think is better—Machine A with high operating rate or Machine B with low operating rate?" Almost everyone will probably answer that Machine A is better, but is this really true?

G Woodworking plant manufactured legs for televisions using lot operation, with machines laid out according to their types. I proposed an improved flow arrangement using two lines, each dedicated to a particular style of TV (Figure 3.62). I asked the plant manager to automate a number of machines including grinders, routers, planers, and saws. I also recommended the automation of handling operations such as turning the products over and around and transporting them from one process to the next.

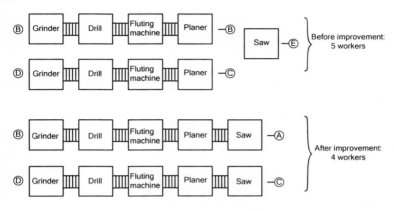

Figure 3.62 Flow Production at G Woodworking

When I visited again the following month, the plant had organized the machines into two lines. However, there was only one saw for the cutting process and the machine was operating independently — not connected to the either of the lines. The machine handled parts for each line alternately, creating work–in–process in the interim.

I asked the plant manager why the plant did not buy one more saw and install the machines in both lines. He told me, "The machine's operation rate is already not very high — 80 percent now. If we install two machines, it'll drop to 40 percent. That would be wasteful."

After that, I went to the company's president to talk about the company's decision to not buy an extra saw. I facetiously asked him, "Do you not like to make profits?"

"Of course, I like to make profits!"

"Then, how much does a saw cost?"

"Probably about 400,000 yen."

"You have two workers in each line of A, B, and C, D, plus another worker, E, for the saw — five in total. If you add one more

FUNDAMENTAL PRINCIPLES OF LEAN MANUFACTURING

saw so that there's one saw for each line, you can eliminate the need for Worker E. If a 400,000–yen investment can eliminate the need for one worker, isn't that worth sacrificing operation rate?"

"You're right," he said, and decided to purchase another saw immediately.

Executives and managers often pursue nothing more than short–sighted gains in machine operation rates and lose sight of what is more important—profits. It is deplorable that so many in management positions maintain this nearsighted view.

At a machinery factory of Automaker Y, 700 workers operate as many as 3,500 machines. In other words, each worker operates five machines on average. Although the machine operation rates are low, the factory is financially successful.

When we think about whether or not additional machines should be purchased, we need to keep in mind that machines are paid for only once. Conversely, workers are paid indefinitely. If the machine price is extremely high, the machine operation rate can be given priority over other factors. However, in the end, making profits is the ultimate purpose of production.

It should also be mentioned that if a drastic reduction in setup time is possible through a one–step setup changeover, a single machine can be used for multiple lines without negative outcomes.

C. Key Points in Realizing One–Piece Flow Production
Conduct an ABC analysis and select major products that need to be manufactured in flow production. Using flow production for the products that are manufactured regularly is also effective.

Switch machine layouts to process–sequence layouts.

Reconsider the following key points:

- Transportation between processes
- Orientation and dimension control and centering for the subsequent process

- Loading
- Cutting
- Unloading
- Safety devices for emergencies

Below is the simple explanation of each point.

> Only one piece is sent to a subsequent process at a time, therefore, automation of transportation becomes just as important as layout improvement. It is preferable to use improvement methods such as conveyors.

> Success of one–piece flow production often hinges on successful orientation, dimension control, and the centering of work pieces for the subsequent processes.

> Loading of work pieces can be done manually, however, automated loading using devices such as air cylinders, magnetic devices, and limit switches, is better.

> Although manual cutting does not hinder a one–piece flow operation, it is still better to automate cutting.

> Although it is easy to automate the unloading, the method of unloading should still be chosen carefully, since some methods — such as blowing air, may make it difficult to control the orientation for the subsequent process.

> The use of emergency safety devices are not necessarily needed in flow production. However, the devices are highly recommended in order to realize unattended operation in the future.

Among these points, the first (transportation between process) and second (orientation, dimension control, and centering for the subsequent process) are the most important points to consider.

(d) Optimize Line Balance

In flow production, as long as profits are realized, the operation rate of machines can be lowered. Therefore, if a process creating a bottleneck uses an inexpensive machine, one more machine should be added — even if it means operation rates will suffer.

Ideally, if the surplus capacities of all the machines in the line are properly balanced, a drop in operation rates will not occur. Thus, leveling the surplus capacities of machines in the same line, or creating "line balance," is essential. As a matter of fact, I have seen several cases where flow production failed simply because machine surplus capacities were not balanced out thoroughly.

(e) Cushion Stock

After introducing one–piece one–piece flow production, it is sometimes necessary to retain a certain amount of inventory, or "cushion stock," in the warehouse for use when machines halt for reasons for maintenance or blade replacement. If cushion stock is used, it is important to think about effective means of moving the stock to and from the warehouse.

However, when a machine breaks down for unknown reasons it is also important to stop the entire line until the cause can be found and fixed. This will prevent the same problem from happening again.

Ways to minimize cushion stock by reducing the frequency and duration of blade replacements should be researched. Frequency can be reduced by improving the blade material, duration by using SMED. H Industry succeeded in shortening its blade replacement time from 40 minutes to 3 minutes in this manner. A computer–operated machine that automatically replaces blades is the most effective method.

(f) Leveling Setup Time

When introducing flow production, leveling setup times also becomes an important issue. In general, if setup time varies from machine to machine, such as 2 hours for Machine A and 40 minutes for Machine B, the machine with the shorter setup time has to be adjusted to the machine with the longer setup time. Such time loss is often avoided by doing set–up changeovers outside of regular work hours. These are passive improvement measures.

Instead, active improvements, such as SMED should be implemented. If setup can be done in three to five minutes, the loss from machine setup time variance will be a negligible one or two minutes. Procedures of introducing flow production, along with its merits, are summarized in the diagram below. (Figure 3.63)

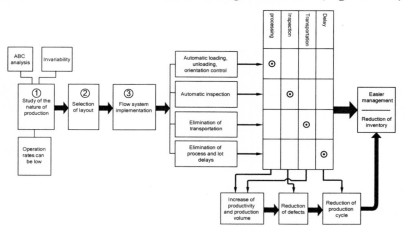

Figure 3.63 Order of Flow Production

E. Merits and Demerits of One–Piece Flow Production
Flow production has many merits, as well as a few demerits.

Merits
(a) Reduction of Production Cycle
Flow production can eliminate process and lot delays, as well as realize a drastic reduction in the production cycle. It also improves the relationship between delivery time (D) and production cycle (P), contributing to better schedule management.

(b) Increase of Production Volume and Productivity
The extra worker hours that result from the elimination or reduction of transportation can be used instead for actual processing. This naturally increases production volume. Automation of loading, unloading, and attitude control of work pieces helps raise the machine operation rates, leading to increased productivity.

209

(c) Reduction of Defects

The one–piece flow created by one–piece flow production makes it easy to conduct feedback inspections that provide immediate feedback on defects. In other words, defect–eliminating inspections are a result of one-piece flow.

(d) Effective Use of Floor Space

Flow production requires the effective use of floor space to reduce transportation paths and the distance between machines, resulting in drastic delay reductions. The space efficiency rate — the indicator of effective floor use, can be raised from 60 percent to 80 percent. This can lead to a 30 percent increase in productivity without increasing floor space.

(e) Easier Management

If there are 60 machines on the shop floor that do not use one–piece flow production, naturally, 60 separate units have to be managed. However, if flow production is introduced and 10 lines with six machines each are created, each line becomes a single unit, thus drastically reducing managerial requirements.

Overall scheduling and controlling becomes easy since there are one sixth the units to consider in this case. This merit, along with the increase in productivity, reduction of production cycle and defects, make process management significantly easier. Many plants have already proved these advantages to be true.

Demerits

(a) Broader Impact of Machine Breakdown

One machine breakdown can influence the entire production line. This can be minimized by preventing problems through maintenance.

(b) Broader Impact of Worker Absence

The absence of a single worker could potentially shut down the line. This can be minimized by using the following measures:

- Reduce unscheduled absences through better labor management
- Reduce the absence rate by lowering work intensity
- Reduce the workforce itself through automation
- Have spare workers

There are a few other minor demerits, but over all, the benefits of one-piece flow far outweigh the demerits. Moreover, one-piece flow production is a prerequisite for the next stage of improvement "pre-automation."

3.4.2 Examples of One-Piece Flow Production
A. Flow Production of Bolts
(December, 1972, Saga Tekkosho, Fujisawa plant, Maeyama Osamu)

(a) Outline of Bolt Production Process

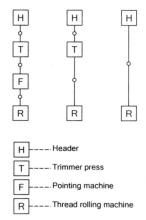

H ----- Header
T ----- Trimmer press
F ----- Pointing machine
R ----- Thread rolling machine

Figure 3.64 Bolt Production Process

Figure 3.65 Wire Material

The following summarizes a basic bolt manufacturing process:

1. Material

A bundle of hot-rolled wire, weighing from 360 to 1,000

211

kilograms, is used (Figure 3.65). Several raw material types are used ranging from low–carbon steel and alloy, to non–iron metal; their plasticity changes depending on the shape. Before the next process, heat treatments such as process annealing and spheroidizing annealing, are done.

2. Wire drawing

Heat–treated wire is pickled to remove scales, and then is wire–drawn into proper dimension through dies.

3. Cold pressing

A machine called a "header," cuts material to the proper length and forms the head into a cylindrical shape.

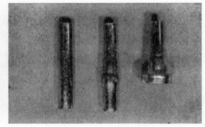

Figure 3.66 Header

Figure 3.67 Press

4. Trimming

A "trimmer" press cuts the head into a hexagon (Figure 3.67).

5. Finish

Depending on the purpose, pointing or deburring is done.

6. Roll threading

A thread rolling machine makes threads on bolts (Figure 3.68).

Figure 3.68 Threader

(b) Reason Behind Improvement

Around 1959, bolts were made only at Saga's main factory head-quarters. Although a significant increase of production volume was required, floor space at the main plant was restricted and could not meet the demand. The president happened to know a management consultant, Mr. Shigeo Shingo, and asked him to come to the plant for consulting.

The machines in the plant were arranged according to their type. Thus, all header machines were placed together. Naturally, lot production was used and pieces that went through the header process were placed temporarily in nearby storage, and then transported to the subsequent process. This storage of semi-processed goods consumed about 30 percent of the factory's floor space, and the placement of each group of machines was not ideal. Research concluded that by the time the wire rod became a finished product, the total transportation distance was a much as 700 meters. Furthermore, it was pointed out that the task of scooping up pieces into the hoppers of trimmers and thread roll-ing machines was quite tedious and time–consuming.

After executives held discussions about these downsides the company decided to introduce a belt conveyor line in which machines would be rearranged according to the process sequence, and connected with conveyors for automatic transportation.

In June of 1960, based on several research studies conducted after the decision, three conveyor belt lines began operation in an experimental plant built on Saga property. The company carried out further research, improved the lines, and gained confidence in the new system. Finally, during the New Year holiday of 1960/61, hundreds of machines in the main plant were re-arranged and the workers were given two extra days-off. At the first of the year, one-piece flow production of their new belt conveyor lines was successfully launched.

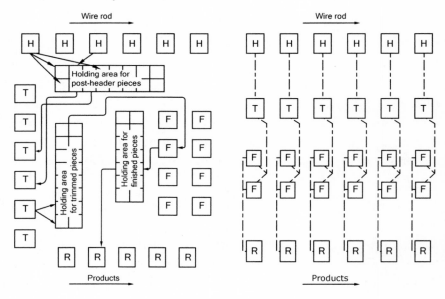

Figure 3.69 Machine Arrangement *vs.* Process Order Arrangement

Due to this success, Fujisawa plant, which started its operation in November 1961, was able to initiate production using a one-piece flow production system. The system was further improved thereafter.

After the introduction of one-piece flow production, the amount of semi-processed goods plummeted, and the production volume increased without expanding floor space. Workers were also spared the exhausting duty of scooping up pieces into hoppers, also contributing to the productivity increase.

(c) Course of Improvement

Back in 1960, no factory in Japan had yet introduced one–piece flow production for bolts, making our company the first to tackle this challenge. Indeed, we faced and overcame many challenges, the most significant of which are discussed below.

1. Creating Atmosphere

Since one–piece flow production was not used in the screw industry at all back in 1960, the workers naturally felt uneasy about a new, unknown system.

The company assigned well–qualified people to be in charge of the three experimental lines. They exchanged various opinions based on their experience and improved the lines.

Even if flow production was superior to the conventional style of production, there were numerous inconveniences on the path to its implementation. Those in charge faced, pursued, and solved these problems one at a time. In turn, these challenges made the workers more passionate and confident about the new system, and worked favorably in the end.

The three experimental lines were also tangible examples of the new system, and just by seeing them, the workers developed an interest in the system, which in turn, led to an understanding. Having the workers understanding turned out to be a huge advantage later. When the company made the decision to switch the main factory to the new flow system, all workers supported it unanimously.

By the time machine layout was changed during the New Year's holiday of 1961, the change went smoothly since the employees knew in advance the benefits of the system. Their involvement and understanding played an important role in the successful outcome.

2. Establishing Line Balance

As mentioned, bolt production is made up of several processes. The company first looked into the capacity of each machine to establish an overall balance. A study discovered that pointing machines had a lower capacity than other machines, so two pointing machines were installed in each line. The pointing machines also required frequent blade replacement. Therefore, existing feed hoppers were used to store cushion inventory for the pointing process.

3. Development of Continuous Washing System

In the past, bolts needed to be washed before the thread rolling process in order to remove lubricant from the previous processes. Washing was done in batches by immersing a significant amount of bolts into a cleaning agent, then dried. Since this cut into the flow of production the company fabricated a rotary washer (Figure 3.70). This machine was able to automatically take in one bolt at a time for washing and send it out for drying. The invention enabled bolts to flow from the first to the last process.

Figure 3.70 Continuous Washing Machine

4. Installing Bucket Conveyor System

In the new flow system, only one piece is sent to a machine at a time, so carrying pieces automatically was a must. At first, bolts were carried on conveyors with dividers. This was problematic as the bolts would sometimes rolled off. This required the conveyor be kept at a low angle, making the distance between machines unnecessarily long. The company tried several different models of conveyors to address the problem. In the end, a "bucket" conveyor system was taken up since it could handle the sharp angle. The problem of pieces falling from the conveyors was also addressed by the "butterfly–style board" fabricated in–house.

Figure 3.71 Bucket Conveyor

5. Separation of Scraps

In some machining processes considerable amounts of scrap are created. To prevent scraps from getting on conveyors, an in–house separation device was installed between machine and conveyor as necessary.

6. Rotary Feeder

Before bolts entered each machine, they needed to be orientated a certain way. Some machines had a feeder to fix orientation inside their hopper, however there were some that did not. Therefore, a new "rotary–style feeder" (Figure 3.72) was developed, and it performed better than the conventional feeders.

Figure 3.72 Rotary Feeder

7. From Machine-type Assignment to Line-by-Line Assignment

In the past, workers only operated the machines that they specialized in. For example, trimmer technicians were trained so that they could handle their specialized machines as efficiently as possible. When one-piece flow production was first introduced, the workers still operated one type of machine, regardless of the lines. However, it soon became clear that workers tending only one line made more sense in terms of quality and production. Therefore, the factory decided to place two workers per line instead, and they were responsible for all the machines in the line. Later, a single worker was able to tend each line due to further experience and improvement.

8. I-line and N-line

The flow production lines were formed in a straight, 'I' shaped line with two workers on each line. Through further improvements it became possible for one person to tend each line. After "one-man line" was realized, the machine arrangement was changed to an N-shape to make it easier for one person to control all the machines.

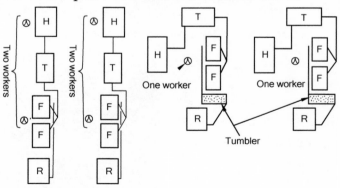

Figure 3.73 I–Type Line & N–Type Line

9. Material-Shortage Signals

Signals to alert material shortage due to abnormalities, such as machine or conveyor problems, were installed so that workers would notice and take swift, appropriate action, even with a one-person-per-line setup.

Figure 3.74 Material Shortage Signal

Figure 3.75 Belt Conveyor Line

(d) Merits and Demerits of One-Piece Flow Production
The merits and demerits of the one-piece flow production system at our company can be summarized as follows.

Merits
1. Reduction of Production Cycle
The production cycle was shortened significantly. For example: for a 20,000-piece lot, the conventional system required 15 days to manufacture a product, whereas the new system required only one day. (Figure 3.76) This eliminated the problem of missing delivery deadlines.

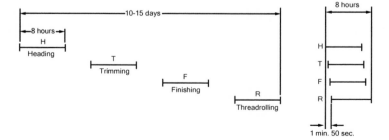

Figure 3.76 Process Time Comparison

219

2. Reduction of Semi–Processed Goods

Since the majority of semi–processed goods disappeared, their storage became unnecessary. The company was able to add more production lines in the same floor space. After the flow system was introduced, the floor space necessary for each machine was reduced from 16m2 to 13m2.

3. Easier Process Management

Since each production line had five machines, the number of units to be managed was reduced to one fifth, making schedule planning and control much easier. This, in combination with the production–cycle reduction, made process control much easier.

4. Reduction of Transportation

Since transportation between processes was done by conveyors, transportation worker hours became zero. This also eliminated the need for transportation equipment.

5. Increase in Operation Rate

Because the task of transportation and scooping parts into hoppers disappeared, the time spent for these tasks could be used for monitoring and adjusting machines, machine operation rates greatly improved (Figure 3.77).

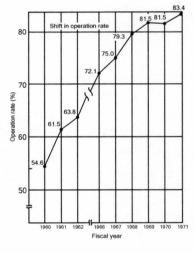

Figure 3.77 Shift in Operation Rate

6. Better Machine Maintenance

Because workers had more time for maintenance, machine breakdown rate declined.

7. Better Quality

Under conventional batch production, defects were found only after a large number of defects were already created. Under the new flow system, each item was sent to the subsequent process, making it easier to spot abnormalities much sooner. Moreover, defect–detection devices were installed between each process, providing immediate feedback and allowing appropriate measures to be taken. This led to better quality control and reduced the defect rate.

8. Multiple–Machine Operation

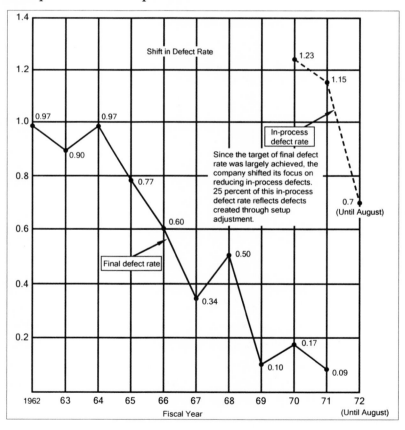

Figure 3.78 Shift in Detention Rate

Since the task of transportation and scooping up semi–processed goods became unnecessary, it became possible for each worker to operate multiple machines. This contributed greatly to raising productivity (Figure 3.79).

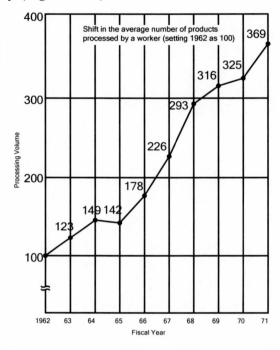

Figure 3.79 Shift in Production

Demerits
1. Machine Increase

If the capacity of a machine in a production line is not level with other machines, the capacity of a turret, for example, was only 80 percent of other machines, one more machine has to be added. Although the number of machines increased after one-piece flow production was introduced, the turrets cost about 500,000 yen and it was possible to pay them off in a year or less, taking the benefits of one-piece flow production into account. Increasing the number of machines naturally decreases the operation rates of certain machines. This may seem to contradict one of the merits mentioned before — increased operation rates. However, overall operation rates still increased even if that of the added machines went down.

2. Loss from Uneven Setup Time

Because the setup times of headers, machine presses, and thread rolling machines were different, the entire line had to wait until the last one was set up. To minimize this loss, setup changeovers were often done outside of regular work hours. However, not everything could be done during overtime hours and loss resulted. After making efforts to use the Single Minute Exchange of Die system, the company successfully reduced setup time. Also, the turret machine's blade needed to be replaced more often than other machines, and this carried with it the possibility of stopping the entire line. This was solved by installing a feeder hopper in the subsequent process that could hold about 30–minutes worth of items. The hoppers served as a cushion and enabled changing blades without stopping the entire line. The turrets' capacity, of course, is calculated including this down time for blade replacement.

3. Increase of Downtime Due to Machine Breakdown

If even one machine broke down, it affected the entire line. This led to complete machine maintenance as well as better stock of spare parts. When minor machine breakdowns happened, feed hoppers provided cushion inventory and prevented the entire line from stopping.

4. Time and Cost of Rearrangements

Time and cost of rearrangement was unavoidable. The cost of rearrangement was about 100,000 yen per machine. There was also a temporary drop in productivity, as expected. In spite of these demerits, the merits of the flow system completely overwhelmed any negative side effects from adopting it.

(e) Future Plans

Although the company only converted its bolt production to a flow system, they made further improvement plans for the future.

Figure 3.80 Developing Pre-Automation

- Introducing flow production to all processes including wire-drawing, heat treatment, and plating
- Realize unattended operation by installing devices to detect machine abnormalities and defects, eventually developing into pre-automation
- Realize single–minute setup time and use the flow system even for low–volume, high–diversity production

By implementing these improvements, the company realized high–quality, low–cost production even during economically difficult times.

B. One–Piece Flow Production of Engine Bearings
(1972, December, Taiho Kogyo, Hosoya plant, Kawakado Tamotsu, Nakao Chihiro)

Our company specialized in bearings, such as car engine bearings and thrust washers. Our engine bearings were expected to withstand the harsh conditions of engines that were steadily becoming lighter and more powerful. We made an effort to improve our production technology and develop bearings in various materials, and as a result, we believed that the quality and performance of our products stood at the top of the industry.

In the past, using a flow production system for engine bearings was considered impossible because of the high precision manufacturing required. The following report shows how we disproved this notion with the generous guidance from Mr. Shigeo Shingo from the Institute of Management Improvement.

(a) Process Outline

In engine bearing production, sintered and cast bimetal strips go through various processes (such as pressing and broaching) and develop into final products as shown in Figure 3.81.

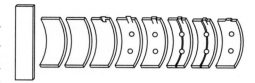

Figure 3.81 Engine Bearing Production

First, press operations were done in a machine that could handle cutting, as well as preparatory and final casting. Second, material width was adjusted, its surface planed, and grooved as necessary. Third, a tooth was made with a press, along with holes if necessary. Fourth, height and thickness was adjusted using a broaching machine. Finally, overlay was applied as necessary, anti–corrosion treatment was done, and the product was completed.

Lot production was used in the past. At first, a large volume of raw materials were produced at once using a big machine press. Then, multiple types of products were made using these items. This method had the following problems:

1. A huge volume of work–in–process goods was created.
2. Progress of production could be unclear.
3. Although there were piles of semi–processed items, a shortage of final products sometimes happened, inconveniencing our customers.
4. In order to prevent product shortage, excessive product inventory was created.
5. Since production follow–up was not sufficient, expedited production sometimes had to happen.
6. The amount of work–in–process could be more than that of final products.

The Japanese auto industry, in the face of trade and capital liberalization, was pressuring auto parts makers like ourselves to start high–volume production, reduce costs, raise quality, handle frequent model changes, and establish a full–line policy and daily–order system. In order to meet these demands, amidst labor shortages and increased labor–costs, we needed a revolutionary means of process improvement.

(b) Stages of Process Improvement
First Stage
Back in 1966, only batch production was used for bearings. There were a litany of problems with this method: early exhaustion of funds for energy costs, sub–material costs, wages, excessive inventory, wasteful use of warehouse and floor space, high transportation costs, and an unsafe work environment.

In order to address these issues, we decided to move ahead with process improvement using the following ideas:

- Eliminate waste completely
- All activities that do not add value are considered waste
- Discontinue work that requires practice — after eliminating wasteful work, automate what is left while minimizing spending
- Cut back on workers and give more valuable, higher–level work to each
- Automate simple processes that are functionally important and enhance credibility

(The word *automate* is used to mean that the work is not only mechanized, but the machines also have the ability to make judgments.)

At first, an improvement team was formed with three technical workers and two setup workers. In order to change from batch production to one-piece flow production, the time for each process needed to be the same and transportation between processes had to at least be improved, if not eliminated.

Bushings that the company made before were circular, and they could be rolled to the subsequent process. Engine bearings, however, are semi–circular and obviously do not roll. Therefore, the improvement team had to conceive a completely new transportation method. The team members brought together ideas

226

and tried out everything they could. They had neither money nor confidence, so they fabricated experimental transportation devices using the ends of steel plates and scrap metal. Every time they tried a new device, a new problem cropped up, but through trial and error they improved and tried again.

At first, either conveyors or chutes were used between processes. Things moved, but further improvement was necessary. Since the machines were not designed with one–piece flow production in mind, pieces did not come out in any regular orientation. Therefore, their orientation had to be manually fixed before loading them in a subsequent machine. If only a large volume of work pieces could have been transported automatically, the workers could have worked on different tasks instead.

The team members mixed features of different types of conveyors through trial and error and succeeded in making a conveyor that could transport, align, and stack (Figure 3.82). By adjusting the machine press takt time with subsequent processes, the team finally succeeded in starting flow production using small lots.

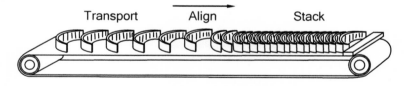

Figure 3.82 Multiple Function Conveyor

In the past, a large–scale press produced several types of parts, which were then sent to different processes according to type, after being stored. In other words, the process setup had one starting point and several ending points. After the improvements, several production lines complete with relevant machines were made. As a result, process management became much easier and this led to a significant inventory reduction and established a strict observation of delivery deadlines.

When improvement efforts finally got to this point, the team celebrated over a few beers. They felt as if they were coming out of a long tunnel with their destination in sight. During their trial and error stage, some in the company talked behind their back saying that the team was confusing their job as their hobby, but overcoming obstacles and disproving the rumors helped them build confidence.

Due to this success less worker hours were required. This also meant that an equivalent number of workers had to be withdrawn from the production lines. There was opposition to this from the shop floor, but the team convinced the workers and chose creative workers from the production lines. They were educated by the team about industrial engineering, welding techniques, and electricity, and joined the improvement work. When they made some successful improvement they went back to their original line and implemented it. Due to this system, the shortage of technical workers was alleviated and a creative mood spread across the shop floor. When the devices the improvement team worked on were brought to the shop floor, they were sometimes sent back immediately because the shop floor workers had even better ideas. This positive mood spurred on the factory's improvement trend.

Second Stage

At first, the team succeeded in aligning products on the conveyor, but they still had to be manually placed at the mouth of the subsequent process. In their next stage of improvement, the team connected each process completely using conveyors or chutes, so that products could be sent into subsequent processes smoothly. Figure 3.83, 84, and 85 are a few of the transportation devices created for that purpose.

Although this further improvement connected every process, there was still a problem. When trouble happened, such as a blade braking off, for example, the line kept moving while sending unprocessed goods to the following process. To prevent this, workers had to stand and watch the machines. Because this was wasteful, everyone above honcho level got together once a week to talk about ways to decrease worker hours. They tried out new ideas immediately on the shop floor and eventually succeeded in installing a poka–yoke successive–check device between each process as in Figure 3.85. This enabled just a few workers to oversee each line.

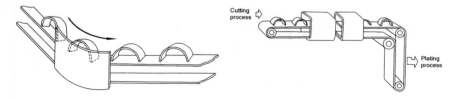

Figure 3.83 Divertible Conveyor   Figure 3.84 Long Distance Conveyor

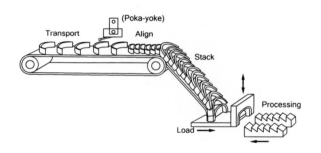

Figure 3.85 Multi-Function Conveyor

Due to these improvements, our Hoysoya plant, which specializes in engine bearings, was able to produce thousands of different engine bearings at levels of about five million per month. At the factory, ten mass–production lines, a few medium–volume production lines, and a few high diversity, low–production lines were created to accommodate varying demand, design, and processing difficulty.

Figure 3.86 shows the process sequence and machine layout, Figure 3.87 shows part of our production lines. Since the machines were laid out according to process sequence and conveyors were used in between, the factory succeeded in eliminating boxes from its shop floor. The conveyors and chutes connecting the machines could control the amount of stacked pieces (in–process inventory) and run automatically. Due to this in–line stock, the entire line did not have to be stopped when adjusting dimension or changing dies.

Uncoiling   Pressing   Chamfering/   Making teeth/   Finishing outer surface   Finishing inner surface
               Grooving   Drilling oil holes

Figure 3.86 Engine Bearing Process

Figure 3.87 Machine Layout

(c) Result of Process Improvement and Future Plans

The outcome of process improvement is summarized below.

- Reduction of work–in–process inventory. Compared to the previous lot production, the amount of work–in–process inventory was reduced by 99.5 percent.
- Process control became more precise. The company was able to meet demands for a daily–order system. Expedited production due to product shortage never happened again.
- Transportation boxes became unnecessary.
- Damage from transportation was eliminated.
- Each process had a light that would alert the workers of

abnormalities. These lights helped in preventing machine problems and keeping the operation rates from dropping.

- The shop floor was expected to be neat and dust be kept at a minimum. After improvement, the factory became more organized, as a result, the workers became more active and responsive to trouble.

All the machines added for improvement were all fabricated in house, minimizing cost. Each one eliminated the need for one worker and, on average, cost only around 400,000 yen.

As a result of all its efforts, compared to 1967, Hosoya plant's productivity per person was quadruple, and its investment efficiency was double that of other factories. Consequently, starting from 1965, in a seven year period, the company was able to triple its sales volume without increasing the number of employees. Its growth was more phenomenal after the Hosoya plant opened in 1968. Figure 3.88 shows how much process improvement contributed to management.

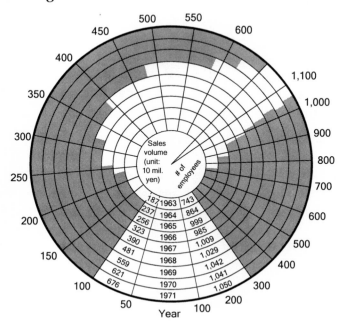

Figure 3.88 Sales Volume & Employees

Although one–piece flow production was finally realized at our company, improvement never really ends — it only advances. There were still two problems with the new system. One was the short time the production lines could run unattended. In the new lines there were devices that checked the product quality and stopped troubled machines and alerted workers in case of abnormalities. However, the longest they could run unattended was only one hour. Moreover, we still needed to reduce setup changeover times significantly to better accommodate the daily–order system. The Hosoya plant was working hard on these issues.

To address these problems we needed to work on various things: machine maintenance; raising precision and durability of blades, tools, and dies; modularized machine parts that tend to degrade; and reducing setup and repair time.

Touting the motto, "Be afraid of the status quo" we wanted to keep moving forward, however slow, and continue innovating and making better products. We hope our case study helps other people in their pursuit of one–piece flow production.

3.4.3 One–Piece Flow Production and Line Balance

When introducing flow production, the following needs to be considered to keep the machines in balance:

- The surplus capacity of machines should always be positive. If even one process is negative, it can create a bottleneck and stop of the flow of products.
- If the capacity of all machines is positive, a basic condition of flow production is satisfied. However, if the gap between required capacity and available capacity is too big, it will lead to low operation rates. Therefore, appropriate decisions that take into account the merits of flow production (along with the corresponding demerits incurred from low operation rates) need to be made.
- The issue of low operation rates should be considered differently depending on if it is applied to workers or

machines. In the case of machines, the depreciation period is extended. In case of workers, the cost is continuous. For this reason, it is often better to introduce flow production and keep the worker operation rates high while keeping machine operation rates low.

A. Case Study — D Press Industry

When I suggested introducing the flow system to D Press Industry's press operation, the shop floor immediately opposed it saying, "It's impossible because our machine capacities are not level." I was told that each machine had the following capacity:

Blanking machine	90 times/min.
Press (punching)	60 times/min.
Press (bending)	60 times/min.

Materials stamped out with the blanking machine were placed on palettes and transported to one corner of the factory. Then, they were moved again for punching and the bending process as necessary. Furthermore, the blanking machine's capacity was excessive and was not in operation for one third of the month. Based on this information, I made the following suggestions:

- Stop the blanking machine after operating it for 40 seconds and stamping out 60 sheets of material
- Send the stamped–out sheets to the following punching process using a conveyor where they can then be stacked inside a chute
- Insert the sheets one by one in the chute for processing with the punch
- Install a limit switch that will activate once the remaining sheets are down to ten, and turn on the blanking machine for another 40 seconds
- Connect the drilling and bending process with a conveyor and send work pieces one by one to the next processed immediately

The company decided to follow my advice. In this case,

one–piece flow production was realized by stopping the blanking machine for one third of a minute, instead of one third of a month at a time, and connecting each process with conveyors. As a result, transportation worker hours and work–in–process inventory became zero and the production cycle shortened greatly without changing the downtime of the blanking machine at all. This shows that even if machine capacities are not level, flow production can not only still work but also be the preferred choice. In this case, however, cushion inventory was often required to absorb the deviation in machine capacities. In other words, the so called "full work control system" needed to be employed.

B. Assembly Process and Line Balance

So far, the issue of low operation rate has been discussed assuming that it applies to machines. However, operation rate needs to be considered differently when it is applied to human workers. As mentioned before, when machine operation rates are lowered, it just takes longer to pay back the initial cost. When human operation rates are lowered, however, the loss is incurred daily and continuously. Therefore, when workers take on a main role in production, such as in assembly processes, operation rates have to be examined very carefully. "Balance–Loss" is commonly used as a way to measures operation rates.

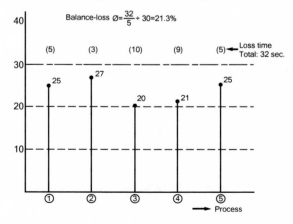

Figure 3.89 Calculation of Balance Loss

Take the case shown in Figure 3.89 as an example.

- Takt time — 30 seconds
- Sum of the difference between takt time and actual time required: 32 seconds
- Average loss time per process — 32/5 = 6.4 seconds
- Balance–Loss $\emptyset$ = 6.4/30 x 100 = 21.3 percent

Unless this balance–loss is less than 10 percent, one–piece flow production cannot be considered successful. The following are ways to improve this index.

1. Redistribute process task.

   Redistribute tasks that cause processing bottlenecks to processes with surplus capacity. In order to redistribute effectively, the process sequence of the product needs to be studied and detailed analysis charts need to be created. It is also good to do time analysis of each task unit and discern the benefit or redistribution quantitatively, as in "if task A is transferred to a different process, x seconds can be saved."

2. Alleviate bottlenecks through improvement.

   Reduce the cycle time of the bottleneck process by improving worker movement or through automation.

3. Improve non–bottleneck processes and redistribute tasks.

   Improve non–bottleneck processes by changing worker movement or through automation, and combine this with the redistribution of tasks.

In general, balancing assembly line process can easily be affected by factors such as changes in parts shape, tools, and workers. Therefore, supervisors at the shop floor always need to check the line balance and improve it. Paying attention to line balance is essential. By improving the productivity of one process by five percent, productivity as a whole can improve by five percent.

SUMMARY

Active improvement of delays means to eliminate lot delays by reducing the transportation lot to one, and eliminate process delays through synchronization. This greatly improves the relationship between delivery period (D) and production cycle (P). However, reducing the transportation lot to one means the amount of transportation increases, and this should be addressed through layout change. Finally, we need to understand that delays are what really decides the length of the production cycle.

CHAPTER THREE SUMMARY

Process is the flow in which materials transform into products. It is composed of processing, inspection, transportation, and delays. Of these four aspects, processing is the only activity that adds value, the other three only raise cost. Therefore, before anything else, reducing non–processing activities to zero should be considered. After that, active improvement of all four aspects followed by passive improvement, should be considered.

IV FUNDAMENTAL APPROACHES TO OPERATION IMPROVEMENT

When improving operation, each aspect of it—preparation and post-adjustment, principal operation, incidental operation, and allowance—needs to be improved. Improvement of preparation and post-adjustment (setup changeover) has often been neglected. A revolutionary improvement of setup time, namely the Single Minute Exchange of Die, SMED System, is going to be discussed in this chapter.

Principal operation often requires technical improvement. Incidental operations consumes the most worker hours, and machine use is often considered to be the improvement of these operations. However, many factories say that they could not reduce personnel even after doing so. This is a misunderstanding of the nature of automation.

True automation is not easy to achieve since it is technically and economically difficult. Instead, I suggest managers try to adopt "pre–automation."

Subject of operation / Content of operation	Operation — Active improvement	Operation — Passive improvement	Machine — Active improvement	Machine — Passive improvement	People — Active improvement	People — Passive improvement
① Preparation and post-adjustment	• Eliminate setup changeovers by standardizing products and operations • Adopt SMED	• Increase lot sizes to reduce the number of setup changeovers • Use economic lots • Conduct off-line setup of materials and tools • Make adjustment easier	Give SMED setup capability to machines	• Adopt pneumonic or hydraulic chucking method • Use electricity for adjustment	Use SMED method	• Organize materials, tools, and jigs • Improve clamping operation, etc.
② Main operations	• Value Engineering improvement • Improvement of processing • Combine processing	Improve cutting speed, etc.	Improve and combine processing (Process larger volume at once)	• Increase cutting speed • Adopt multiple-cutting method	Mechanization	• Improve movement
③ Incidental operations	Automation	Combine and speed-up chucking operation	Automation	Combine and speed-up chucking operation	Automation	• Mechanize chucking operation • Improve movement
④ Fatigue allowances	• Realize unattended operation • Introduce easier work method	Provide appropriate rest	—	—	• Periodical inspection • Realize unattended operation • Reduce work intensity by improving operations	• Provide appropriate rest • Improve workplace environment, provide rest area, etc.
⑤ Hygiene allowances	• Realize unattended operation • Improve work environment	Provide appropriate rest	—	—	• Realize unattended operation • Improve work environment	• Provide appropriate rest • Improve drinking fountains and restrooms
Operations allowances — ⑥ Lubricating	• Use oil retaining bearings • Conduct oilless cutting	• Automate lubricating • Adopt effective lubricating method	• Use oil retaining bearings • Conduct oilless cutting	• Automate lubricating • Adopt effective lubricating method	Automate lubricating (Lubricant and cutting oil)	Improve lubricating motion
Cutting scrap	• Use cutting methods that do not create cutting scraps	Eliminate cutting scrap automatically	• Use cutting methods that do not create cutting scraps	• Eliminate cutting scrap automatically • Create cutting scraps that are easier to remove	Eliminate cutting scrap automatically	Improve the motion of eliminating cutting scraps
Replacing blades	• Use durable blades • Use computerized machines that can change blades automatically	Use SMED method for blade replacement	• Use durable blades • Use computerized machines that can change blades automatically	Use SMED method for blade replacement	• Use computerized machines that can change blades automatically	• Use SMED for blade replacement • Improve the movement of blade replacement
Workplace allowances — ⑦ Material delay	• Eliminate delay through better process management	Increase inventory	—	—	—	—
Machine breakdown	• Check abnormalities continuously • Conduct preventive maintenance	• Periodical inspection • Prepare spare parts • Prepare for repair work	• Check abnormalities continually • Conduct preventive maintenance	• Periodical inspection	• Conduct preventive maintenance	• Prepare for repair work • Mechanize repair work

Table 4.1 Active & Passive Improvement of Operation

Active and Passive Improvement of Operations
Active and passive improvement of operations needs to be considered from three perspectives: operation itself, machines, and workers. Basic concepts are explained in Table 4.1.

Revolution in Setup Time
Development of Single Minute Exchange of Die (SMED) Method (Active improvement of preparation and post–adjustment operations).

In the past, preparation and post–adjustment (setup operations), were given only cursory attention in plant improvement. Conventional improvements were only passive ones, such as increasing lot size to decrease the number of setups, or calculating economic lot size which was supposed to balance out delays and setup time. Few if any efforts were made to improve setup operations themselves. In other words, no active improvements were done. As a solution to this situation, I would like to present Single Minute Exchange of Die (SMED).

4.1 Challenging SMED
A. Adversity of Low Volume–Mixed Model Production
When I visit companies, I often hear people say, "Production at our company includes many products produced at a low volume. It's such a pain." If I ask, "Why is low volume – mixed model production such a pain?" The answer would often be something like, "It just is ..." yet this response does not provide any real answer or solution to the problem.

There are two issues at hand that make low volume – mixed model production difficult. One, when products change, efficiency tends to go down and defects tend to go up. Two, frequent setup change leads to lower operation rates.

To address the first problem, operations need more standardization. As for the second problem, the common solution is to increase lot size in order to offset the percentage of time used for setup change. This approach actually lengthens production cycles and amasses excessive work–in–progress inventory. If setup time is taken into account, it is true that increasing the lot size decreases relative operation time per production item. As shown in Table 4.2, simply increasing the lot size from 100 to 1,000 reduces the relative operation time per production item by 64 percent. If setup time is longer (8 hours) as in Table 4.3, this ratio drops by an even greater 75 percent. This shows that increasing the lot size ten fold quadruples the operation efficiency. Thus, increasing the lot size seems to be an easy and effective way to raise efficiency, perhaps explaining why it is use is so prevalent.

	Setup Time	Principal operation time per item	Lot Size	Relative operation time	Ratio
Ⓐ	4 hours	1 min.	$l_1 = 100$	$1\text{ min.} + \dfrac{4 \times 60}{100} = 3.4\text{ min.}$	100
Ⓑ	4 hours	1 min.	$l_2 = 1{,}000$	$1\text{ min.} + \dfrac{4 \times 60}{1{,}000} = 1.2\text{ min.}$	36

Table 4.2 Effect to Setup Time 1

	Setup Time	Principal operation time per item	Lot Size	Relative operation time	Ratio
Ⓐ′	8 hours	1 min.	$l_1 = 100$	$1\text{ min.} + \dfrac{8 \times 60}{100} = 5.8\text{ min.}$	100
Ⓑ′	8 hours	1 min.	$l_2 = 1{,}000$	$1\text{ min.} + \dfrac{8 \times 60}{1{,}000} = 1.48\text{ min.}$	25

Table 4.3 Effect to Setup Time 2

However, this approach comes with a downside, as mentioned before. So, what is the best solution to low volume mixed model production? The best approach is to take an active improvement measure and decrease the setup time itself.

If we take a closer look at Tables 4.2 and 4.3, we can tell that the smaller the initial lot size, the greater the boost in efficiency when we increase lot size. If the initial lot size is 1000, reducing the setup time from eight hours to four hours increases efficiency by only 19.4 percent (*B'/B*). However, when the initial lot size is smaller (100), efficiency increases by 70.6 percent (*A'/A*). This means that the greater the diversity, the easier it is to reap the rewards of setup–time improvement.

Because of this, some companies tried to reduce setup times by standardizing dies or attachments. However, these efforts were often stymied by the staggering time and cost of improvements, sometimes tens of millions of yen.

If the concept of SMED is applied, setup time can be reduced dramatically with little time and cost. Reducing setup time by 95 percent, reducing one to two hour setup times to just three to six minutes, for example, is an attainable goal.

B. Considering Economic Lot
A section chief from N Die–casting Co., Mr. Y, attended a seminar where an extended lecture was given on the concept of the "economic lot" by university professor, Mr. E, using real shop floor examples.

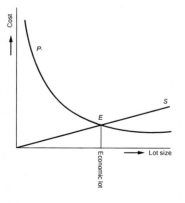

Figure 4.1 Economic Lot Calculation

An economic lot is determined as follows: if costs are plotted on y axis, and lot size on the x axis, labor costs gradually decrease as lot size rises (*P*). On the other hand, costs associated with inventory, storage, and the extended production cycle tend to go up (*S*). As Figure 4.1 illustrates, the intersection of these two lines is known as an economic lot (*E*).

During the lunch break, Mr. Y happened to sit across the table from the professor. The professor introduced himself and asked, "Are you one of the participants in today's seminar?"

Mr. Y said, "Yes, I am. Your lecture was very interesting."

"Thank you, that's good to hear."

As the conversation went on, Mr. Y told the truth, "At our company, we don't take the economic lot into consideration at all."

"That's not good," the professor replied. "If you don't think about economic lot, it will eventually lead to a large loss."

"In the past, it took us two hours to change casting dies. But we made a significant improvement to the process, and now it only takes five minutes. So there's no need to think about it."

"From two hours to five minutes? Really?"

Mr. Y proceeded to talk about the outline of the SMED method his company used. The economic lot is based on the premise that setups take a long time, and it is impossible to reduce it drastically. However, if a two hour setup can be reduced to just five minutes, the whole basis of the economic lot crumbles. The concept of the economic lot may be effective if long setup time cannot be changed. Nonetheless, it is a passive improvement, and dramatically reducing the setup time itself is an active and superior improvement.

C. Mind-set Reform for SMED

As mentioned before, frequent setup change is the biggest problem of low volume — mixed model production. Although switching to mass production may be the best solution, this is not possible at a majority of the small and medium–size businesses in Japan. Therefore, it is important to understand clearly that as long as low volume — mixed model production continues, frequency of setup changes cannot be changed. Yet, it is possible to reduce the time it takes for setup changes.

At the beginning of 1970, Y Auto Company succeeded in reducing their press setup time from four hours to an hour and a half. At that time the same operation took two hours at Volkswagen in Germany, so those involved in the improvements were delighted to know that they had beaten the German competition.

A few months later, however, an executive of the company gave the order to reduce the setup time to three minutes. The workers wondered how they could possibly reduce the setup time to just three minutes. At that point, I was asked to lend my expertise. I knew that conventional setup methods could not do the job; it had to be something entirely different. While I was thinking about how to solve this problem, it occurred to me that the press setup, which was done while halting the machine, should probably be done externally, without stopping the machine. The improvement team tried numerous setup methods based on this idea, and eventually succeeded in reducing the setup time to three minutes.

I presented this example to A Electronic Company, and suggested that the setup of the company's 300–ton press should also be done in less than 10 minutes. A month later I came back and asked how the improvement was going. "We're still discussing it," was the answer. Another month later, I visited the company and asked again if the goal of single–minute setup was getting any closer. The answer remained, "We are still discussing it." At this, I decided to press the matter further. "So, what did you really do?" I asked, and it turned out that nothing had been done. I was told that the press workers thought reducing the setup time from the current two hours to an hour and a half might be a possibility, but reducing it to less than 10 minutes would be impossible, and they would not consider trying it.

In order to change people's mind-set, I took the press section–chief and the setup operation leader to Y Auto Co. While there, they saw a die setup done in two minutes and fifty seconds. They were very impressed. Upon their return they told their subordinates, "Single–minute exchange is actually possible. Why don't we try it here?" However, the reaction was far from enthusiastic. "It might be possible with different products, but not with ours. Our situation is different," said one of the setup–operation members.

After I heard this conversation, I decided to take a tour of Y Auto Co. again, but this time with all the setup members. Again, the die setup at the auto maker was completed in less than three minutes. Everyone was so surprised and inspired after this visit, the setup crew completely changed their mind. A project team made up of six members from the design division, production technology division, and shop floor, was created. The team worked overtime, held discussions, and researched countless times on how to reach the goal of single–minute setup. As a result, the two–hour die setup time dwindled steadily as follows:

- 30 minutes after a month
- 17 minutes after two months
- 9 minutes after three months
- 7 minutes after four months

To their delight, what was first thought as impossible came true.

Another episode comes from K Metal Corporation. A senior staff member of the company, Mr. N, did not believe that the current 70–minute setup could possibly be done in less than ten minutes. However, after he attended a five–day industrial engineering seminar that explained the concept of SMED, he came back deeply impressed. Less than two weeks later, he succeeded in reducing the 70–minute setup time to only 4 minutes, 33 seconds. One day, he showed me the new setup method and said to me, "If I make a little more improvement, I think it can be less than four minutes." His mind–set had completely changed.

As these episodes show, having a positive attitude and believing what is attainable with SMED is the fundamental premise for successful implementation.

D. Past Achievements of SMED
(a) Examples of Presses, Plastic Molding Machines, and Die–Casting Machines
Table 4.4 (p. 246-47) shows actual achievements of SMED, related to presses, plastic molding machines, and die–casting machines, from 1971 to 1974. The biggest reduction in setup time was 98 percent, the smallest was 86 percent, with an average of

94 percent. One example is from Weidmann Plastics Technology in Switzerland. In 1951, the company succeeded in reducing the setup time of its plastic molding machines (50–ounce capacity) from 2 hours 30 minutes to just 6 minutes.

Setups in these examples were generally done with two people working in parallel. In about half of the cases, preparation took five to ten days, and in the remaining cases, preparation was less complete and took just 30 minutes to an hour. Setup times in the figure shows the time starting from the point a die was removed, to the point a new product was created with a new die.

Cost of installing a new setup system was 10,000 to 30,000 yen in cases of small dies, and 50,000 to 70,000 yen in cases of large dies. Even multiple dies or progressive dies could be installed for only 100,000 to 150,000 yen. As long as there is a will, SMED can be achieved with little time and cost.

A. Press Machine

No.	Company	Capacity	Old	New	1/*n*
Single-Die Press					
1	K Automobile	500 t x 3	1°~30'	4'~51"	1/19
2	S Automobile	300 t x 3	1°~40'	7'~36"	1/13
3	D Automobile	150 t	1°~30'	8'~24"	1/11
4	M Electronics	150 t	2°~10'	7'~25"	1/18
5	S Electronics	"	1°~20'	5'~45"	1/14
6	N Industry	"	1°~30'	6'~36"	1/14
7	A Auto Body	"	1°~40'	7'~46"	1/13
8	K Industry	100 t	1°~30'	3'~20"	1/27
9	S Metal	"	40'	2'~26"	1/16
10	A Iron Works	"	30'	2'~41"	1/11
11	K Press	"	40'	2'~48"	1/14
12	M Metal	"	1°~30'	5'~30"	1/16
13	K Metal	"	1°~10'	4'~33"	1/15
14	T Corporation (Press for springs)	80 t	4°~00'	4'~18"	1/56
15	M Iron	"	50'	3'~16"	1/15
16	H Corporation	50 t	40'	2'~40"	1/15
17	M Electronics	"	40'	1'~40"	1/27
18	M Electronics	"	50'	2'~4F"	1/18
19	H Press	30 t	50'	4'~51"	1/63
20	K Metal	"	40'	4'~51"	1/15
21	Y Industry	"	30'	4'~51"	1/12
22	I Metal	"	50'	4'~51"	1/18
Multiple-Die Press					
23	S Industry	150 t	1°~40	4'~36"	1/22
Successive-Die Press					
24	M Metal	100 t	1°~40	6'~36"	1/17
25	M Electronics	100 t	1°~30'	6'~28"	1/14
				Average	1/18

Table 4.4a Active & Passive Improvement of Operation

B. Plastic Molding Machine

26	M Corporation	140 oz.	6°~40'	7'~47"	1/53
27	TM Corporation	100	2°~30'	8'~14"	1/18
28	Y Corporation	"	1°~50'	4'~36"	1/24
29	N Rubber	"	2°~30'	6'~28"	1/23
30	N Rubber	50	2°~00'	4'~18"	1/28
31	T Industry	"	1°~20'	6'~46"	1/12
32	TT Industry	"	1°~10'	7'~36"	1/9
33	N Chemical	20	40'	3'~45"	1/11
34	D Plastic	10	50'	2'~36"	1/19
35	GA Electronic	"	50'	6'~45"	1/07
36	S Light	"	40'	3'~38"	1/11
37	Y Corporation	"	40'	2'~48"	1/14
38	W Plastics (Switzerland)	50	2°~30'	6'~00"	1/25
				Average	1/20

C. Die-Casting Machine

39	M Metal	250 t	50'	6'~24"	1/8
40	T Die-casting	"	1°~20'	7'~46"	1/10
41	S Corporation	"	1°~10'	5'~36"	1/13
				Average	1/10
				Overall average	1/18

Table 4.4b Active & Passive Improvement of Operation

4.1.1 Basic Concept and Techniques of SMED

The following section describes the basic concept and techniques of implementing SMED.

1. Separating Internal and External Setup

   Setup operations can be divided into two fundamentally different types:

   1. Internal setup (online setup), such as mounting or re-moving dies, that can be performed only when a machine is stopped.

   2. External setup (offline setup), such as preparing tools

and jigs, that can be performed while a machine is in operation.

The most basic step in implementing SMED is to distinguish whether your setup is internal or external. An external setup is the best option since it does not stop the machine. However, even setup operations that can be done externally are often done while stopping the machines. If we make an effort to conduct as much of the setup operation as possible externally, then the time needed for setup can usually be cut by 30 to 50 percent. To do this effectively, it is recommended to create a checklist of setup operations and determine what can be done externally.

2. Converting a Setup from Internal to External

Separating internal and external setup operations is the first step in achieving SMED. However, what is most effective is actually converting an internal setup to an external one. Many procedures that only seem internally possible can actually be done externally. For example, when die height varied, adjustment had been done while the machine was stopped. This can actually be done offline, simply by using an adjustment jig and making the die height uniform before mounting. This method reduces setup time drastically and required less technical skills.

In the case of plastic molding machines and die–casting machines, dies were conventionally preheated by conducting a trial shot. This preparation time can be reduced by preheating the dies with gas or hot water beforehand. In the case of die–casting machines, it is extremely effective to use the waste heat from the heating furnace for preheating. These measures save costs as much as time.

3. Implementing Functional Standardization

Many die designers say that standardizing setup operations would greatly reduce setup time. However, this often means standardizing the sizes and dimensions of all machine parts and tools. This method, called "shape standardization," requires too much cost and time.

In contrast, "functional standardization," used in SMED, is the standardization of only those parts whose functions are necessary for setup operations. For example, standardizing only the part the dies are clamped to, or using adjustment jigs to standardize the mounting position of the die. Functional standardization can reduce setup time without wasting time and money.

4. Using Functional Clamps (Figure 4.2)

To secure a die to a press, the "direct attachment method" is often used where bolts are passed through holes in the die and attached to the press bed. In this method, if a bolt has fifteen threads on it, it cannot be tightened or loosened unless the bolt is turned fifteen times.

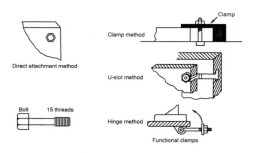

Figure 4.2 Setup Changeover Time

Functional clamps, on the other hand, are devices designed to attach and release the objects much faster with the same clamping functionality. For functional clamps, various methods can be used such as clamps, U–slots, and hinges.

5. Using Intermediary Jigs

The use of intermediary jigs is another useful method of achieving SMED. Instead of mounting dies and cutters directly to the machine, they are attached to a standardized intermediary jig that can then be mounted on the machine. As such, the attachment can be done offline. In addition, since intermediary jigs are standardized, there is minimal downtime for mounting. Intermediary jigs have already been successfully used for cutting machines and large–scale presses.

6. Using Parallel Operation

In the case of large dies, it is better for multiple workers to do the setup operation in parallel, instead of one. Two people can finish a setup operation in half the time as one person. Although the total worker hours are the same, the machine operation rate increases. In fact, if a setup operation is done by one worker, it often creates extra transportation or movement. Thus, procedures that take only five minutes with two workers often takes more than double. Parallel operation is recommended for this reason as well. When multiple workers collaborate, however, clear communication and attention to safety is a must.

7. Eliminating Adjustment

Adjustment operations during an internal setup are quite wasteful. They extend and cause variation to the setup time because much depends on the workers' skill level. Adjustments should be avoided by taking the following measures:

- Use functional standardization and intermediary jigs
- Use stoppers and gauges
- Learn about operational conditions such as air pressure, current value, place of limit switches, and predetermine the best place for a die

Cutting machines often allow the operators to move the machine parts freely and make adjustments within a certain range. In actual operation, however, the machine operators usually need only a couple of adjustment options.

Therefore, adjustments can be made easier by installing stoppers and gauges. To be functional, we generally do not need continuous adjustments.

Take a look at the example of adjusting the initial material feed volume for a press. In general, the appropriate degree of eccentricity of a feed cam, that determines the feed volume, is determined through a number of trials and adjustments (Figure 4.3). This time–consuming procedure can be eliminated, however, if appropriate eccentricity is predetermined for each product and a gauge is installed in the feed cam. By using this gauge, appropriate feed volume can be achieved with the first shot and save tremendous internal setup time.

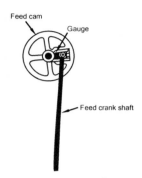

Figure 4.3 Setup Change-over Time 2

In the case of roll–feed style machines, using feed volume gauge plates (Figure 4.5) is also effective in achieving the appropriate feed volume from the first shot. Creating a function that keeps spooled material centered to the plates is also useful.

Figure 4.4 SMED Result Table

Figure 4.5 Feed Volume Gauge Plates

These examples show that eliminating the necessity of test runs and adjustments by using fixed settings is a very powerful tool in reducing internal setup time.

When measurements require fixed numerical values, gauges can be used for rapid settings for dimensioning and centering. However, as the types of measurements to be set increase, the number of gauges grows and the operation becomes cumbersome. In this situation it is possible to reduce the variety of gauges considerably by using combinations of a limited number of instruments. The proper combination can be determined by using numbers obtained as follows:

a

$a + 1 = b$

$a + b + 1 = c$

$a + b + c + 1 = d$

The numbers generated are 1, 2, 3, 8, 16 etc.

Any number up to 15 can be made using combinations of 1, 2, 4, and 8. Any number up to 30 can be made by combinations of 1, 2, 4, 8, and 16. Single digit numbers can be created by combinations of 1mm, 2mm, 4mm, and 8mm. However, if the increments get too small, 11mm, 12mm, 14mm, and 18mm can be used instead.

By just using two gauges, as shown in Table 4.5, numbers up to 35 can be created by combinations of 1, 2, 4, 6, 7, 8, 11, 12, 13, 16, 17, and 18.

Totals Numbers	1	2	3	4	5	6	7	8	9	10	11	12	13	14	15	16	17	18	19	20	21	22	23	24	25	26	27	28	29	30	31	32	33	34	35
1	◎		△		△																														
2		◎	△						△	△																									
4				◎	△																														
6						◎							△							△			△	△											
7							◎		△				△		△				△		△														
※8								◎		△					△							△													
11											◎														△		△	△	△						
12												◎							△							△				△					
14														◎						△	△	△			△	△					△	△			
※16																◎											△						△	△	
※17																	◎						△					△			△		△		△
18																		◎						△					△	△		△		△	△

Note: 1. ◎ – Only one gauge is necessary

2. △ – Combination of two gauges

3. Other combinations are also possible

4. ※ – May be omitted from the series if three-gauge combinations are permitted

Table 4.5 Reducing Gauges

8. Implementing Structural Improvement

Structural improvements like the following can also reduce setup time tremendously: using pneumatic or hydraulic pressure for transporting and mounting dies (instead of using bolts), and adjust ram stroke electrically, instead of manually.

The previous eight sections described the basic concepts and techniques of SMED. In the past, improvement was predominantly structural, as in section eight. Yet, this measure only saves about a minute of setup time. Measures one to seven, however, can reduce setup time from one hour to three minutes, thus making them far more crucial components of the SMED system.

9. Structure of SMED Concept

Figure 4.6 summarizes the measures used to achieve SMED.

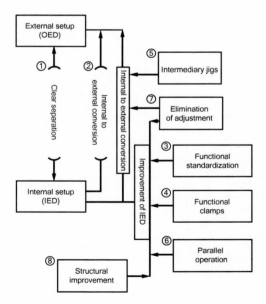

Figure 4.6 Structure of SMED

4.1.2 Conceptual Stages of SMED

The conceptual stages of SMED are shown in Figure 4.7.

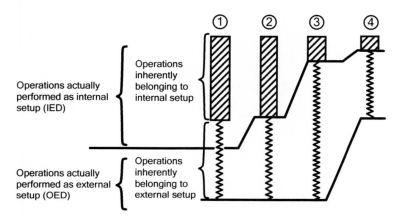

Figure 4.7 Mental Steps of SMED

First Stage

In this stage, internal and external setups are not clearly distinguished. After stopping a machine, unforeseen problems that could have been dealt with externally crop up due to insufficient preparation and checks. Such problems include: dies not being ready, bolts that do not fit, and not having blocks with appropriate thickness. This confounding of internal and external setup operations makes internal setup time and machine down time unnecessarily long.

Second Stage

In this stage, internal and external setup operations are clearly distinguished, and what can be done externally is properly done externally. To facilitate this success, a checklist of items required for internal setup, should be created so that everything necessary can be prepared as part of external setup. Moreover, the functions of the dies, jigs, tools, etc. should be checked.

Third Stage

In this stage, not only are internal and external setups separated, but people are actively trying to convert internal operations, previously thought impossible to be done otherwise, to external operations. Converting setup from internal to external is the most basic and important concept of SMED. Examples might include attaching adjustment jigs to press dies to create uniform height, thus eliminating the need for internal ram stroke adjustment.

Fourth Stage

In this stage, efforts are made to further improve both internal and external setup operations and reduce overall setup time. Examples include using hydraulics instead of bolts to mount dies, or standardizing the dimension of dies to facilitate or eliminate tightening and adjustment operations.

4.1.3 Technical Steps of SMED (Figure 4.8)

Figure 4.8 shows setup procedures (technical steps) which correspond with the conceptual stages of SMED.

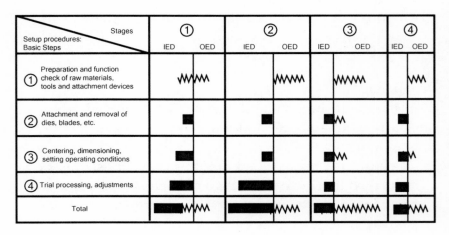

Figure 4.8 Technical Steps to SMED

Table 4.6 shows the distribution of time for these procedures in a traditional setup. Figures 4.9–4.12 are illustrative of concepts discussed through the stages. The following describes each SMED stage taking both conceptual and technical aspects into account.

Step	Operation	Proportion of Time
①	Preparation and function check of raw materials, tools and attachment devices	80%
②	Attachment and removal of dies, blades, etc.	5%
③	Centering, dimensioning, setting operating conditions	15%
④	Test runs, adjustments	30%

Table 4.6 Order of Setup Changeover

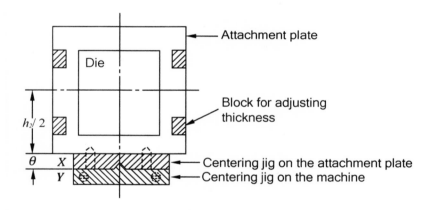

Figure 4.9 Centering Clamp Jig

Figure 4.10 Clamp Setting

257

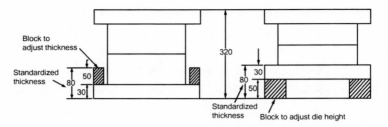

Figure 4.11 Standardizing Die & Clamp Height

Figure 4.12 Standardizing Die Height

First Stage

The preparation and function check of raw materials, tools, and attachment devices is not done properly. Therefore, issues regarding missing fastening bolts, improper block dimension, broken dies, etc., arise and are addressed after the machines are stopped. In other words, what could be done externally is done internally.

In order to transcend this stage, the following measures should be taken:

- Organize tools and attachment devices
- Make a checklist and complete all external setup procedures before stopping the machines
- Conduct a function check of equipment and make necessary adjustments before stopping the machines

By making these improvements, setup time can generally be reduced by 30 to 50 percent. Yet, steps two, three, and four are all still conducted internally, after stopping the machines.

Second Stage

In this stage, the preparation and function check of raw materials, tools, and attachment devices that were tackled in stage one, are now done externally before the machines are stopped. Setup steps two through four are still treated as internal setup.

Third Stage

The preparation of tools and raw materials, etc., is completely external. Attachment and removal is internal but the method is improved. Centering and dimensioning needs to be improved and converted to external setup as much as possible. By conducting centering and dimensioning accurately, test runs and adjustments should be eliminated as much as possible. If adjustments cannot be eliminated, follow the concept of "chose" rather than "adjust." If gauges are used, for example, the worker can chose a fixed numerical value, instead of relying on intuition, and achieve the optimal setting from the first shot.

Fourth Stage

In this stage, people are actively trying to convert internal operations (once previously thought impossible) to external operations. This is the most decisive stage of SMED.

The preparation of raw materials and tools is taken care of before stopping the machines. External setup time is further reduced by better tool management and transportation.

Attachment and removal procedures are also improved to save time. For example, adopting functional clamps or the so called "cassette–method," enables a one–touch attachment without bolts. Using oil pressure, air pressure, and electricity for attachment devices is also a good idea.

Centering and dimensioning procedures are eliminated by functionally standardizing dies.

Test runs and adjustment procedures are eliminated completely by accurate centering and dimensioning. For example, making die height uniform nullifies the need for shut height adjustments and test runs.

4.1.4 Practical Techniques of SMED
A. Metal Presses
As mentioned before, when implementing SMED it is important to separate internal and external setups clearly, and convert internal setup to external setup. Eliminating the need for test runs and adjustments through highly–accurate centering and dimensioning is an extremely effective way to achieve this. Using functional clamps is also effective in reducing internal setup time greatly.

(a) Single–Shot Presses
Improvement of Clamps
The thickness of attachment plates can be standardized by adding appropriate adjustment blocks. For example, if the thickest attachment plate is 40mm, a 30mm–plate would be matched with 10mm–block, 25mm–plate would be matched with 15mm block (30+10=40, 25+15=40). This way, the thickness of the attachment plates become uniform, and the same bolts and blocks (necessary for balance) can be used for any die, thus eliminating the trouble of searching for bolts and clamps.

In the case of metal presses, shims may be attached to both upper and lower dies to standardize die height. If this is the case, dimension of bolts and blocks need to be determined taking into account the thickness of both the shims and standardizing blocks.

Elimination of Shut Height Adjustment
When there is a wide variety of die height, adjustments can be

made by first attaching a thinner shim (4, 5, 6mm, etc.) followed by a thicker shim (20, 40, 60mm). This way, despite a wide variety of original die height, every die can be standardized before being attached to a machine. Moreover, if these dies are frequently used, adjustment shims could be welded or bolted to the die, making changeover even easier.

Table 4.7 shows how varying die heights can be adjusted to 320mm. Again, standardizing die height eliminates the need for the highly technical tasks of shut height and ram–stroke adjustment. This not only reduces time, but also allows workers of all skill levels to change dies.

Die thickness	Number of dies	Thickness of shims for 1st adjustment	Die thickness after 1st adjustment	Number of dies	Thickness of shims for 2nd adjustment
320	3	—			
315	1	+ 5 mm	320 mm	6	—
312	2	+ 8 mm			
295	1	+ 5 mm	300 mm	1	20 mm
280	4	—			
276	1	+ 4 mm	280 mm	8	40 mm
270	3	+ 10 mm			
260	3	—			
256	2	+ 4 mm	260 mm	6	60 mm
253	1	+ 7 mm			
(Based on the study of Machine # 1.)	Total 21			Total 21	

Table 4.7 Standardizing Die Thickness

Centering Improvement

Attaching a lower die to the middle of a bolster plate is yet another time consuming operation. Attaching centering jigs to the bolster plate makes this operation much faster.

Suppose that a centering jig is mounted on the far side of the machine (Figure 4.13), and the

Figure 4.13 Centering Jig (bottom)

261

distance from the center of the lower die to the centering jig is 200mm. If the distance from the center to the edge of the die is 160mm, then a 40mm centering jig is attached to the die (Figure 4.14). With the conventional method the operator needed to find the best position of the lower die by inching the upper die downward. However, if centering jigs are used this adjustment becomes unnecessary. As long as the two jigs fit snugly, the upper and lower dies align automatically.

Figure 4.14 Centering Jig (top)   Figure 4.15 Assembled Jig

Other Considerations

Treat die transportation as external setup. In other words, transport new dies to the side of the machine before it is stopped. Likewise, take old dies away after restarting the machine. If two cranes or forklifts can be used, transportation becomes more efficient.

- Electrical cables and air pipes can be pre–attached to a new die, thus necessitating only their attachment to the main, once the die is mounted on the machine.
- In the case of large dies, conduct parallel operation with two workers to eliminate wasteful transportation, minimize internal setup time, and machine downtime.
- In order to conduct parallel operations efficiently, procedural charts should be made (Table 4.8) to reduce mistakes and enhance safety.
- Using check lists and lights is also an effective way to insure worker and machine safety. If there is a procedural

check–list at hand, the workers can cross out the items as they finish them and make sure all the procedures are completed. If check lights are installed, the workers can press a switch after each setup procedure to turn on check lights. Unless all the lights are on the machine will not operate. This is called an interlock mechanism and it is a very effective safety measure.

(Information from Matsushita Electric, Laundry Machine Department.)

Task	Time (sec.)	Worker 1	Worker 2	Buzzer
1	15	Lower ram (to bottom dead point).	Prepare to remove rear bolts.	
2	20	Remove front mounting bolts securing upper die.	Remove rear mounting bolts securing upper die.	Yes
3	30	Raise ram (to top dead point).	Turn press switch off.	Yes
4	20	Remove bolster setting pons	Prepare to remove mounting bolts securing lower die.	
5	60	Move bolsters.	Remove mounting bolts securing lower die.	
6	20	Attach cable to transport metal die.	Attach cable to transport metal die.	
7	20	Hoist.	Move metal die for mounting.	
8	30	Position metal die.	Position metal die.	
9	20	Tighten front bolts securing lower die.	Tighten rear bolts securing lower die.	
10	50	Move bolster.		Yes
11	30	Set pins for bolsters.	Move crane.	
12	30	Set ram at bottom dead point.	Adjust ram stroke.	Yes
13	50	Tighten front mounting bolts securing upper die.	Prepare to tighten rear bolts securing upper die.	
14	20	Raise ram (to top dead point).	Tighten rear bolts securing upper die.	Yes
15	15	Test die action of empty press.	Check switches and meters. Set pressing lever.	Yes
16	40	Insert material and process.	Check for safety and quality, etc.	
	Total Time 470 sec. (7 min. 50 sec.)	Problems to watch for: (1) Twisted or severed cables or strands. (2) Vertical movement of dies while they are being exchanged. (3) Presence of any hazard on floor.	Actions to be confirmed: (1) Tightening of bolts. (2) Switch (on or off). (3) Bolster pin setting. (4) Meter. (5) Quality check.	OK On

Table 4.8 Order of Changeover

263

(b) Multiple–Die Presses

In the case of multiple–die presses in which two or three dies are used in a single machine, two intermediary jigs (30–50mm thick, about 80 percent of the bolster size) should be prepared. If the dies are placed on the jig as part of external setup, the prepared jig can be mounted on the bolster as it is (Figure 4.16). This meth-

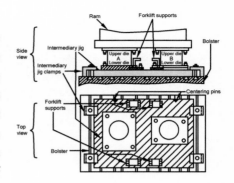

Figure 4.16 Multiple Assembly Jig

od can greatly reduce internal setup time. As for die centering, clamps, and standardization of die height, the same approaches used for single–shot presses, can be used.

(c) Progressive–Die Presses

In the case of progressive and transfer dies the pass line along which the material passes, must be constant. Thus, line and die height should be standardized by attaching adjustment jigs to upper and lower dies. Only after the pass line and die height are taken care of can die alignment and improvement of clamps be approached. Reversing this order may just lead to readjusting the pass line.

When new spooled material is used, its beginning has to be inserted between each set of dies manually. This is difficult and time consuming. However, this task can become much simpler if manual rollers are used in addition to a roller feeder. Manual feeders can adjust the feed volume more accurately, which makes this

Figure 4.17 Setting by Manual Roller

264

operation easier (Figure 4.17). Furthermore, it makes omission of new material easier if an operation is finished. If multiple spooled materials are used the beginning and the end of materials can be welded beforehand to reduce internal setup time.

Adjusting the feed volume of spooled materials with conventional methods takes a long time. If a crank–feed method is used, however, a feed cam gauge can eliminate the need for adjustments (as in Figure 4.3 p. 251). One company used a roll–feed method (as in Figures 4.4, 4.5, p. 251) to reduce setup time. In this method, plates were made corresponding to the material width and inserted to standardize stroke–adjustment.

(d) Cost and Time of SMED
The cost of implementing SMED is about 30,000 to 50,000 yen per die for single–shot presses. For multiple–die presses, cost is about 100,000 to 150,000 yen if large–scale intermediary jigs are created. The same goes for progressive–die presses. The time it takes to fabricate new equipment is generally three to five days. This, of course, varies depending on enthusiasm and ingenuity.

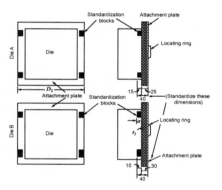

Figure 4.18a Standardizing Clamp Settings

B. Plastic Molding Machines
In Figure 4.18, the middle point of the dies, the height of attachment plates and middle point of the width are assumed identical for both dies A and B.

Figure 4.18b Standardizing Clamp Settings

(a) Fixed Dies (Figures 4.18)
Clamps

With plastic dies, direct attachment is generally used. However, mounting and dismounting dies is cumbersome due to the excessive turning of bolts, finding bolt holes, as well as the bolt position needs to be changed as the die width changes.

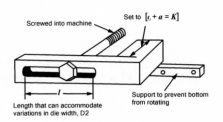

Figure 4.19a Mold Clamps

These two problems can be addressed by using a clamp with a long hole that can accommodate variations in die width (Figures 4.19). Furthermore, if clamping point thickness is functionally standardized via the welding of standardization blocks, the same clamps can be used for any die, greatly reducing internal setup time.

Figure 4.19b Mold Clamps

Centering, Dimensioning

With plastic molding the tip of the injection nozzle needs to be aligned with injection holes in the dies. There is usually a locating ring in the middle of the die as a guide. As with metal presses, using centering jigs (Figure 4.20 and 4.21) will solve this problem.

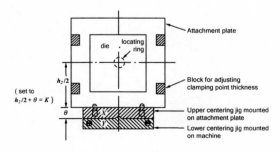

Figure 4.20 Centering Jig

In Figure 4.20, jig X is attached to the die, and Y is attached to the machine as part of external setup. The height of X is determined by die height, so that the middle point of

the dies are stan-
dardized ($h2'/2+\theta' = K$, $h2''/2+\theta'' = K$). By
simply fitting the jig
X with Y, the tip of
the injection nozzle
can be aligned with
injection holes on
the dies very easily.

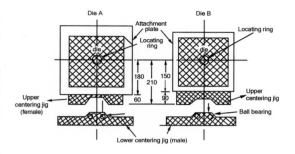

Figure 4.21 Centering Jig

Adjustment
Adjustment can usually be
eliminated if centering jigs
are properly used as above.

Figure 4.22 Centering Jig Example

(b) Movable Dies
Standardizing Die Thickness

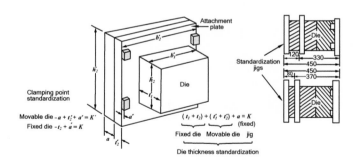

Figure 4.23 Standardizing Die Thickness

As with fixed dies, the improvement of movable dies can be approached by standardization clamping points. Centering, of course is inherently easier.
If die thickness varies, stroke adjustment becomes necessary. In
order to avoid this, the two–step standardization method, used

267

for metal presses, can also be used here. (Table 4.9) In this example, the goal is to standardized die thickness to 320mm.

Die thickness	Number of dies	Thickness of shims for 1st adjustment	Die thickness after 1st adjustment	Number of dies	Thickness of shims for 2nd adjustment
320 mm	3	—	320 mm	6	—
315	1	+ 5 mm			
312	2	+ 8 mm			
295	1	+ 5 mm	300 mm	1	20 mm
280	4	—	280 mm	8	40 mm
276	1	+ 4 mm			
270	3	+ 10 mm			
260	3	—	260 mm	6	60 mm
256	2	+ 4 mm			
253	1	+ 7 mm			
	Total 21			Total 21	

(Based on the study of Machine #1.)

Table 4.9 Mold Thickness & Standardization

Check the thickness of every die used for a certain machine.

By adding thin shims or scraping the back of the die, make initial adjustments, and make the dies either 260mm, 280mm, 300mm or 320mm.

Prepare two sets of thicker shims, 20mm, 40mm, and 60mm.

If the 300mm die needs to be used next, a 20mm–shim is attached as part of external setup. In this case, the dimension of push–out pins also need to be changed.

Shims can be welded to dies that are used frequently. Die thickness can be standardized using steps like these, thereby eliminating the need for stroke adjustment. After the die thickness is standardized, appropriate clamp dimensions (that

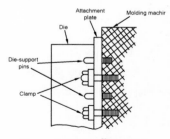

Figure 4.24 Installing Large Molds

268

match K or K' in Figure 4.23, p. 267) must be used. If a shim is inserted between an attachment plate and a die, clamp dimensions can be determined in the same manner as with fixed dies.

In the case of large–scale machines that use heavy dies, it is a good idea to use die–support pins in addition to clamps to distribute die weight (Figure 4.24).

(c) Die Transportation

When transporting dies with a crane, it is useful to mark the operating board so that the best die position can be determined easily without adjustment.

(d) Die Preheating

Depending on the type of resin, it is necessary to preheat the new die to about 70°C. Conventional preheating by injecting molten resin creates substandard items that cannot be used. Instead, if heated water is circulated through coolant pipes, not only is preheating much faster, but internal setup time is reduced by 30 to 60 minutes. Gas or electricity can also be used for this purpose as well.

Appropriate measures should be taken to prevent burning accidents. Even the simplest precautions such as wearing gloves are effective.

(e) Switching Resins

Cleaning the interiors of hoppers when changing resins is quite a chore. However, setting up the work to sequentially use materials from "weak to strong" in terms of quality and color, white to black, for example, greatly reduces the workload.

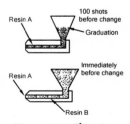

Figure 4.25 Changing Resin

Internal setup time can also be saved if hopper liners are used. When resins need to be changed, the liners are simply replaced instead of cleaning the hoppers.

100 shots before the time to change from resin A to B, the volume of resin should be adjusted to the line that shows the appropriate amount for 100 shots; any excess is removed. Then, resin B is introduced. This way the moment the resins need to be switched, resin B is right at the nozzle, while any remaining resin A is almost gone. This makes resin changeovers faster and minimizes loss.

When this method is used it may be necessary to use a purge agent between the two resins. Detergent, diluted to about 5 percent, can effectively remove the remaining color of resin A.

(f) Setting Air Pressure and Coolant Pipes
Depending on the quality of materials or the size of items, air pressure adjustment is often required. In this case, it is important to follow the basic concept of, "choose" rather than "adjust." Research the condition in which the work was done previously, record it, and create a chart. By doing this, adjustments become unnecessary and predetermined settings just need to be dialed in. It is also good to know that when laying coolant pipes, using one–touch connectors can save a significant amount of time.

C. Die–Cast Machines
To a great extent the setup of die casting machines may be approached in exactly the same way as the setup for plastic molding machines. One big difference is that the die pre-heating temperature is much higher than plastic molding machines — about 140 degrees Celsius. Therefore, gas or elec-

Figure 4.26 Pre-heating Die Cast Mold

tric heaters need to be used.

Furthermore, in the case of die–casting machines, exhaust heat from the heating furnace can be reused for preheating. At one company a metal plank was placed above the furnace and a die was set on top of the plank, then the die was covered to trap heat better. The company succeeded in heating the die in an hour and a half with just the exhaust this way. I strongly recommend this method since it saves energy, money, and time.

D. Machine Tools
(a) Machining Camera Bodies
A die–cast camera body is defective if there is even one hole in the film plate. In one factory, plates were cut on a milling machine and then inspected. This procedure required a high level of skill and was very time consuming.

The factory's parent company provided three types of jigs which corresponded with different types of cameras. The workers at the factory had to adjust the height of the cutting surface depending on the type of the jigs. Centering the camera body on the machine was not easy either. As a result, each cutting operation took about two and a half hours.

The factory workers attached a spacer and an intermediary jig to each provided jig so that height adjustment and centering would become unnecessary (Figure 4.27). After this improvement the setup operation was reduced to merely a minute and half. In addition, an operation that only skilled workers could do in the past became simple enough for any worker to do.

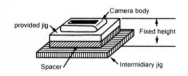

Figure 4.27 Camera & Body

(b) Profile Milling and Intermediary Jig
In one company, when a profile milling machine was used, the worker used to attach both a template and a work piece directly

to the machine. Work pieces also had to be centered while the machine was stopped. Since this setup operation was time consuming the company created two standard intermediary jigs. After this improvement, a template and a work piece were attached to each intermediary jig and centered as part of the external setup. When the processing of one work piece was done, all the worker needed to do was clamp the other standard intermediary jig to the machine. This successfully cut internal setup time from an hour and a half to merely 3 minutes, 30 seconds (Figure 4.28).

Figure 4.28 Milling & Jig

(c) Cut–off Operation with a Lathe

Figure 4.29 Lathe Blade Jig

When a cut–off operation is conducted with a lathe, its blade wears off and needs to be replaced frequently. At one company, the replacement took over 20 minutes since the blade had to be centered so accurately. However, this operation was reduced to merely 45 seconds after the company introduced standard-ized intermediary jigs (Figure 4.29). The worker could center the blade simply by attaching it to the jig, no adjustment was nec-essary. Since the blade setup could be done externally, internal setup time shortened dramatically.

(d) Milling Machine Blade Exchange
At one company, blades used to be attached directly to the tool posts of milling machines. Since this required precision, only veteran workers could do blade exchange, and even then it took 45 minutes.

This situation was improved by using a jagged intermediary jig, as shown in Figure 4.30. Any blade could be attached pre-cisely by simply fitting it to the jig. This reduced internal setup time to only 1 minute, 40 seconds.

Figure 4.30 Milling and Jig (a)(b)(c)

(e) Exchanging Bits for Bearing Processing
A lathe with four bits was used to process the end surface of

273

bearings. Every time a blade broke, it took about 40 minutes of internal setup time to align them accurately. This operation was reduced to only 1 minute, 40 seconds by using two intermediary jigs as shown in Figure 4.31. The bits could be aligned properly by simply inserting them into the jig during external setup. When the bits in one jig became dull, the whole jig was simply replaced by another jig.

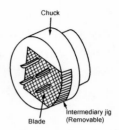

Figure 4.31 Blade Changeover

(f) Countersinking a Hole in Bearing Metal

At one company, there was an operation of countersinking the surface of an oil hole in bearing metal with a drill. Since the countersinking depth had to be precise, after the drill bit had started cutting into the metal, measurements were made and the degree of drill protrusion was often adjusted. As a result, changing drill bits used to take about 25 minutes.

The company improved this operation by making a dimensioning jig (Figure 4.32) and an additional socket for a drill. With this dimensioning jig, the precise drill protrusion could be achieved simply by inserting a drill into it. When the drill in the machine

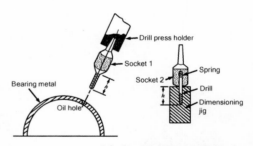

Jig for determining the precise drill protrusion

Figure 4.32 Drill Press Changeover

needed to be changed, the worker only needed to replace it with another drill and socket. As such, setup time drastically shrunk to 30 seconds after this improvement.

(g) Cutting Bearing Metal Ends

Company M had a machine that cut the ends of bearing metals (Figure 4.33). When the blades became dull the machine was

274

stopped and new blades were attached. After the new blades were in, however, their location and angle had to be adjusted through numerous test runs. As a result, each blade changeover took about 40 minutes.

This operation was improved simply by purchasing another arbor on which the blades are attached. During the external setup, the worker attached new blades to this additional arbor and adjusted their location and angle. Once the machine was stopped, the additional arbor simply replaced the existing arbor with the new blades already set precisely. In this case, the arbor worked as an intermediary jig and reduced internal setup time to just two minutes.

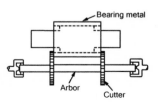

Figure 4.33 Changing Blades

(h) External Setup for Radial Drilling Machine (Figure 4.34)
In general, only one bed was used for radial drilling machines. Company G, however, added an extra bed within the radius of the machine arm's rotation. This way, while Bed A was being used for drilling, for example, Bed B could be prepared externally, thus reducing machine down time.

This method was also very convenient when expedited production sprang up. Before the improvement a work piece being processed had to be removed to accommodate the expedited production work piece. Once expedited work finished, the removed piece had to be mounted again. However, once the additional bed was installed these wasteful procedures, including unnecessary idle time, disappeared.

Figure 4.34 Drill Press Off–Line Setup

E. Wood Working Machines

(a) Gang Rip Saws

A gang rip saw is a machine fitted with several circular blades, used to make simultaneous parallel cuts. Out of a single plank, several planks with varying width can be made. When setting up this machine, positioning and mounting the blades takes quite a long time.

At one company this operation was improved using a metal bar which was the same length as the blade arbor of the machine. During the external setup new blades and distance–setting pieces were attached to this bar, then positioned and angled precisely as they would in the machine during external setup. When the blades on the machine needed to be replaced, the machine operator would bring the prepared bar to the machine and simply slide the blades into the machine arbor. This method led to tremendous savings in setup time.

(b) V–Cut Method

A v–cut method is sometimes used to make TV cabinets. In this method, three v–shaped cuts are made in a sheet of plywood.

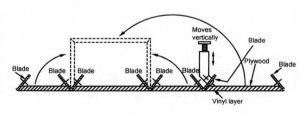

Figure 4.35 V–Cut Machine

The wood is then folded into a box (Figure 4.35).

These v–cuts have to be made accurately with two blades, while abstaining from cutting a vinyl layer on the outside of the plywood sheet. Setting the blades required skill and time.

At one company I worked with, the blade setup was taking about 40 minutes. I suggested that there might be a correlation between the blade dimension and the angle. A study found that there was indeed a perfect correlation. So the company made a chart showing blade dimension and appropriate angle. In addition, blade dimension was measured with slide calipers and the angle was set precisely based on the chart. After this improvement, blade setup time was reduced to merely three minutes. Since this eliminated the need for trial processing, it also saved on material. This improvement exemplifies the basic concept, "choose" rather than "adjust."

F. Assembly Operation and SMED

Assembly operation is comprised of a series of smaller operations. For each of these smaller operations the same SMED approaches that we have discussed so far—conversion of internal setup to external setup, elimination of adjustment, for example—can be used. How SMED is applied to assembly operation depends on whether this operation is viewed as either parts of the whole, or the whole itself.

(a) Products

Assume that the following two types of products are manufactured in assembly operation:

- A: Total assembly time = 800 seconds (13 min 20 sec)
- B: Total assembly time = 1,000 seconds (16 min 40 sec)

(b) Types of Setup Changes

1. Multiple–Line Change and Single–Line Change
(I) Multiple–Line Change Method

In this method an extra assembly line is prepared. While the main line is in operation, external setup is conducted at the extra line. In this way internal setup is eliminated, thus minimizing setup changeover time. However, machine operation rates go down and excessive floor space is required. Therefore, this method is suitable when the machines are inexpensive and the factory is spacious.

(II) Single–Line Change Method
In this method, a single assembly line is used to produce multiple products. Therefore, setup needs to be changed depending on the product type. The following explanation will focus on this more common changeover method.

2. Conclusive Change and Successive Change
Single–line change method can be divided into the following two types:

(I) Conclusive–Change Method
With this method of assembly, Product B does not start until Product A's last process is completed. This method is widely used because setup changes are easier. However, this method results in frequent processing down time.

(II) Successive–Change Method
With this method Product B follows Product A, while A is still on the assembly line. Although processing down time is minimized, many difficulties arise. The following discussion will focus on this method and provide solutions to its inherent difficulties.

3. Fixed Worker and Fixed Takt–Time
The following explains the single–line, successive change method.

(I) Fixed–Worker Method
When using this method, a fixed number of workers attend the assembly line even if there is a setup change. For example, if there are 20 workers, the takt time changes as follows:

Product A: Total assembly time = 800 seconds

Takt time = 800 / 20 = 40 seconds

Product B: Total assembly time = 1,000 seconds

Takt time = 1,000/20 = 50 seconds

Personnel management is very convenient when worker numbers are fixed. However, even though takt time varies depending on the product, the product with the longer assembly time is rate–limiting, and thus the assembly speed of all products must be slowed accordingly. If worker numbers remain as they are, an unnecessary waste of man–hours results. Moreover, although there are ways to match the speed to the faster takt time, they are too complicated and not practical.

(II) Fixed Takt–Time Method
Under this method, constant takt time is maintained by changing the number of workers. For example, if the takt time is set to 40 seconds, the number of workers changes as follows:

Product A: Total assembly time = 800 seconds

Worker = 800/40 = 20 people

Product B: Total assembly time = 1,000 seconds

Worker = 1,000/40 = 25 people

This method uses man hours more efficiently. However, personnel management is more difficult than the former method since workers have to move around every time a setup is changed.

4. Fixed–Worker, Fixed Takt–Time Method
With this method, problems with personnel management and inefficient use of man–hours disappear. However, the varying assembly time of different products still has to be offset somehow. The following are some of the ways to do just that.

(I) Cushion Method
The assembly time of Product B is longer than that of Product A by 200 seconds. Under this method, a "cushion work team" does 200–seconds worth of work on Product B outside the as-

sembly line beforehand (this is done in lot operation). Then, the partially–processed Product B can be brought to the assembly line where both A and B can be assembled with a fixed number of workers and fixed takt time—20 people and 40–second takt time, for this example.

Operations that are suitable for this cushion operation include initial and mid–process assembly that can be taken care of independently. Since cushion operation creates temporary delays, processes that either deal with small parts, or parts that do not change over time should be selected.

(II) Set Method
In this method one of Product A and one of Product B are sent to the assembly line together as a set. The takt time is 45 seconds ((40+50)/2=45). Naturally, each assembly process needs processing capability for both products. It is desirable if machines and tools can be shared. There are probably cases where two different machines must sit together in one process to handle the two products. Either way, setup change between Product A and B becomes unnecessary with this method. Desirable conditions for this method are as follows:

- Production volume of Product A and B are the same
- Machines and tools can be shared
- If they cannot be shared, they are inexpensive

When this method is used mistakes should be prevented by strategically using poka–yoke devices.

(III) Mix Method
This method is used when there are more than two types of products and their production volume varies—five A's, three B's, and two C's, for example. In this case, takt time is the average time of the three products. As with the last method, setup changes are unnecessary, and the use of inexpensive or sharable machines and tools, along with strategic used of poka–yoke, is desired.

Overview

The discussion on assembly production so far is based on the assumption that the assembly times of Product A and B are different. Of course, it is the most convenient if they are the same. Thus, efforts should always be made to standardize assembly time first. It should also be noted that each machine and tool is likely to require setup change, even when setup change between different types of products is not necessary. The concepts and techniques of SMED should, of course, be used in that case.

In general, setup change in assembly operation is done within a minute by applying methods such as ones discussed above. An appropriate method should be chosen based on the level and environment of production management, as well as the techniques used at your factory.

Summary

The idea of "pre-setting" has been talked about for a long time in the field of machining. With the SMED method, the same concept is described as "converting internal setup to external setup." There is no doubt that it is the most effective measure to achieve setup change in less than ten minutes. In order to realize this, it is also important to use effective intermediary jigs, functional clamps, and implement functional standardization. Above all, the most crucial element of success is the belief that SMED can and should be realized.

4.1.5 Cost of SMED

The cost of implementing SMED is about 30,000 to 50,000 yen per die for single-shot presses. For multiple-die presses it is around 100,000 to 150,000 yen if large-scale intermediary jigs are created. As for plastic molding machines, Figure 4.36 shows actual examples of cost at one company. This particular company fabricated items required for SMED in-house. In general, the cost is about 30,000 to 50,000 yen per die.

4.1.6 Effects of SMED

Effects of SMED were shown in Table 4.4 (p. 246–47), Time Reductions Achieved by Using SMED. If setup time is reduced like the examples in the table, the following effects can also be expected.

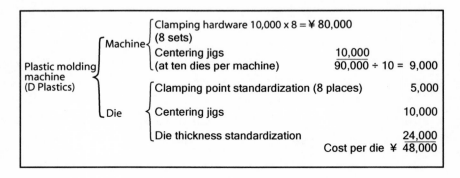

Figure 4.36 Cost of SMED

Increase in Machine Operation Rates

Company M's machine operation rate increased by 30 percent. Since the company had 18 machines, this increase was equivalent to having 5.4 additional machines. It was also equivalent to having five extra skilled workers. This was an enormously significant improvement for the company, especially since skilled workers were in short supply.

Small Lot Production

In the past, large–lot production was often used because of long setup times. However, if a two–hour setup can be reduced to six minutes, for example, changing from a monthly lot to weekly lot becomes a reasonable choice. As a result, companies that accomplish single–minute setups can switch to small–lot production and enjoy its benefits: decrease of work–in–progresses, storage space, pallets and production cycle, as well as better fund turnover.

Increased Production Flexibility

Increased production flexibility is especially beneficial when expedited production springs up. If a two–hour setup time can be reduced to six minutes, responding to such unexpected situations becomes much easier.

Having production flexibility is also advantageous when a new model is introduced. In the past, conducting trial shots of the new model between castings of the old model posed incredible difficulty. However, using SMED substantially eases this.

Lower Skill Level Requirement

Previously, the job of setup change was limited to skilled workers. However, SMED makes it possible for anyone to conduct setup changes, thus eliminating problems associated with the unavailability of skilled workers. Naturally, this reduces worker and machine wait time. In addition, a feeling of responsibility is fostered when workers are able to perform setup changes by themselves.

Elimination of Setup Mistakes

Since SMED eliminates internal adjustments, common mistakes such as breaking the molds or machine parts, also disappear. In addition, simpler setups lead to safer operation.

Positive Change in Worker Attitude

If setups take as long as two hours, workers tend to dislike and avoid setup operations as much as possible. This attitude changes completely if setups can be done in less than ten minutes.

Material Yield Improvement

If the die height of metal presses is standardized, shut–height adjustment, as well as trial shots become unnecessary, thereby raising material yield. As for plastic molding machines and die-casting machines, pre–heating eliminates the need for trial shots, thus reducing production cycles and minimizing material waste.

Better Organization of Tools

In the past, many attachment tools (bolts, blocks, and clamps) needed to be used for each die. However, once SMED is implemented attachment tools are specialized so that each machine requires just one type of tool.

When height and thickness of dies need to be standardized in stages, appropriate shims are used. In this case the shims need to be organized. However, since the number is limited, organization is not difficult. In the case of small dies, shims can be welded or bolted to the dies instead of using shared shims. This also leads to better tool organization.

Reduction in Internal and External Setup Time

Although SMED is meant to reduce internal setup time, it also reduces external setup time as well. Figure 4.37 shows Company M's example of time reduction in both types of setups through SMED.

			Before	After	Ratio
Die exchange 120 min (27 min) 5:1	External setup 60 min (19 min) 3:1	Transporting die to press	5 min	(10 min)	1 : 1
		Transporting die to maintenance area	5 min		
		Organizing maintanenance area	15 min	(10 min)	4 : 1
		Exchanging die block	35 min	(5 min)	7 : 1
	Internal setup 60 min (8 min) 7:1	Removing die	10 min	(5 min)	6 : 1
		Disposing scrap material in machine	5 min		
		Attaching die	15 min		
		Positioning die	15 min	(3 min)	10 : 1
		Various adjustments	15 min		

Setup time after improvement is shown inside ().
(Matsushita Electric Industrial Co., Ltd., Washing Machine Division)

Figure 4.37 Reduction of Overall Setup Time

So long as there is a will to do so, SMED can be achieved with little cost and time. You may wonder why such easy improvements were not made earlier. One reason might be the ease and availability of passive solutions like increasing the lot size if setup time is long. Another reason might be a lack of willpower and thorough study — despite the desire to reduce setup time.

In my case SMED began as an inspiration. When the company I worked with asked me to reduce their setup time to single-minutes, it occurred to me that internal setup could be converted to external setup. After that, like a knotted string untangling, other ideas followed suit, and single-minute setup was achieved relatively easily.

As long as one believes SMED is possible, and the difference between internal and external setup is clear, all you need is decision and action.

In 1956, at M Heavy Industry's Hiroshima shipyard, an open-sided planer created a bottleneck in production. Although the shop floor requested the company to purchase one more machine, it was too expensive. Extending work hours was not an option either, since the plant was already operating around the clock with three shifts a day. The plant manager, Mr. Okazaki, and I had a discussion on this issue and we started to wonder if the setup time could be shortened somehow.

In those days, a whole day was needed to change the setup of the planer which was used to cut ship engine parts. Based on my suggestion, the shipyard created an extra bed for the machine, so that the next engine part could be mounted on it externally. Once the processing of one engine part was done, the prepared bed was lifted with a crane and replaced the existing bed. To our delight, this method worked brilliantly and the company succeeded in doubling its production volume as a result.

I recognized this as an improvement at the time, however, it did not occur to me that what I actually did was "convert internal setup to external setup." If I had clearly recognized this as the key formula for single-minute setup, SMED might have been realized in Japan 15 years earlier. I still regret my slow awareness to this day.

SUMMARY
SMED can be achieved quite easily as long as the difference between internal and external setup is clearly understood and there is a will to convert internal setup to external setup.

Elimination of adjustment is also important in reducing setup time. Many people believe that adjustment, along with highly-skilled workers, are an indispensable part of setup operations.

Yet with SMED there is no need for highly–skilled workers. Indeed, it can be achieved easily without them as long as its key concept — conversion of internal to external setup — is understood.

4.1.7 SMED Case Studies
Single–Minute Exchange of Dies in Press Operation
(Matsushita Electric Industrial Co., Ltd., Washing Machine Division, 1973, January, Fukuda Masakatsu)

(a) Factory Profile
At the press factory of our Washing Machine Division, various types of washing–machine bodies were manufactured. All the mass–produced models had the same body size, so a fast die–exchange method, which replaced only a part of the die, was being used. For small–volume models, however, the whole die had to be changed since each model had a different body dimension. The following discussion focuses on how we reduced the die setup time for a 150–ton press, as shown in Figure 4.38.

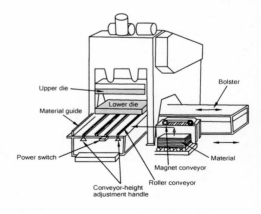

Figure 4.38 150–Ton Blake Press

(b) Background of Improvement

As the competition in the laundry machine industry grew fierce, we made efforts to expand our customer base by providing a wide variety of products. As a result, long setup times began to be problematic and needed to be addressed. Before our improvement, setup time was long, as shown in Figure 4.39. We kicked off our improvement project with the help of Mr. Shigeo Shingo, from the Japan Management Association.

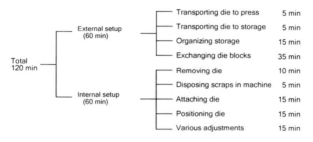

Figure 4.39 Current Setup Procedure

(c) Formation of Project Team

First, we set a goal of reducing 60–minute internal setup time to less than 10 minutes. Then, a project team was formed with the following members: press operator, die designer, die producer, management engineer, and foreman. Each aspect of improvement was assigned accordingly. Some key deliberation points are shown below.

Die improvement: Die designer, die producer

Die–height standardization

Appropriate handling of scrap material

Equipment and machine improvement: Press operator

Elimination of adjustment

Improvement of product–removal device

Setup–operation improvement: Foreman

Improvement of die transportation and other preparations

Management improvement: Management engineer

Standardization of setup operation

Minimizing wait time

(d) Points of Improvement
The team members deliberated their aspect of improvement and decided to move forward focusing on the following five points.

- In order to minimize machine down time, convert internal setup to external setup
- Standardize die height in order to eliminate stroke adjustment and conveyor height adjustment
- Setup operation is done with two workers, make changes so that they can work in parallel, rather than in series
- Make improvements so that scraps would not be left on the bolster
- Make an improvement so that different shapes of dies can be mounted to the machine and centered easily

(e) Improvement Examples
If there were many ways to achieve similar effect, the team chose the most cost–effective one. Following are some of the improvements the team implemented (Figures 4.43-4.46):

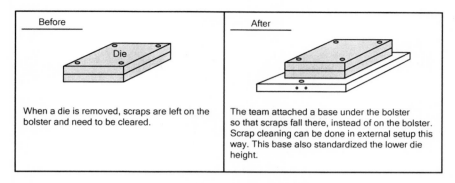

Before	After
When a die is removed, scraps are left on the bolster and need to be cleared.	The team attached a base under the bolster so that scraps fall there, instead of on the bolster. Scrap cleaning can be done in external setup this way. This base also standardized the lower die height.

Figure 4.40 Elimination of Scrap Removal

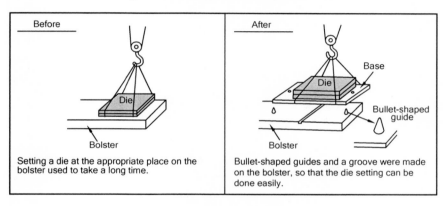

Before	After
Setting a die at the appropriate place on the bolster used to take a long time.	Bullet-shaped guides and a groove were made on the bolster, so that the die setting can be done easily.

Figure 4.41 Simplified Mold Setting

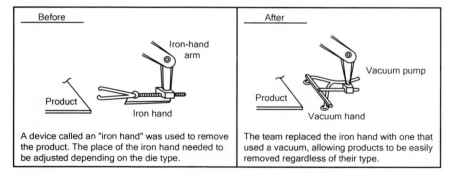

Before	After
A device called an "iron hand" was used to remove the product. The place of the iron hand needed to be adjusted depending on the die type.	The team replaced the iron hand with one that used a vacuum, allowing products to be easily removed regardless of their type.

Figure 4.42 Material Feeding Equipment

289

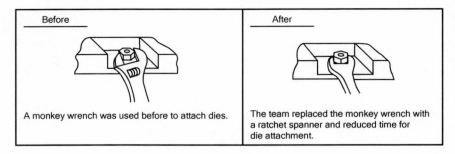

Before	After
A monkey wrench was used before to attach dies.	The team replaced the monkey wrench with a ratchet spanner and reduced time for die attachment.

Figure 4.43 Improved Clamp

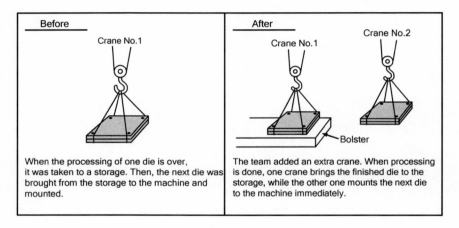

Before	After
When the processing of one die is over, it was taken to a storage. Then, the next die was brought from the storage to the machine and mounted.	The team added an extra crane. When processing is done, one crane brings the finished die to the storage, while the other one mounts the next die to the machine immediately.

Figure 4.44 Improvement in Mold Installation

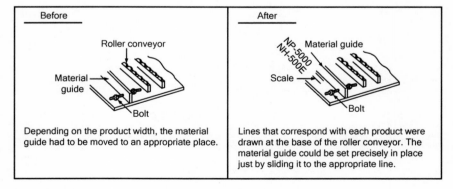

Before	After
Depending on the product width, the material guide had to be moved to an appropriate place.	Lines that correspond with each product were drawn at the base of the roller conveyor. The material guide could be set precisely in place just by sliding it to the appropriate line.

Figure 4.45 Improved Guide

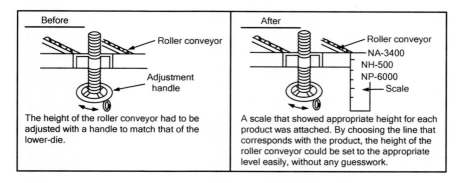

Figure 4.46 Method of Changing Chute Height

In addition to improvements shown in Figures 4.40 to 4.46, the project team made the following improvements.

- Crane positioning

The crane girder was painted to denote the place the crane became centered with the bolster.

- Bolt receptacle

A receptacle for bolts, used to attach dies, was placed on the bolster.

- Bolster cover

The machine operator had to attach and detach a bolster cover regularly. A new type of cover which did not require this tedious operation was installed (Figure 4.47).

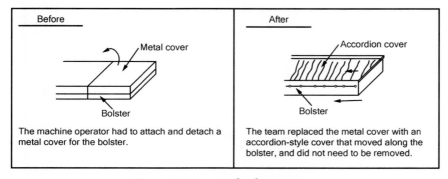

Figure 4.47 Improved Bolster Cover

• Safety Measures

Two people worked to-
gether to change the dies.
Safety measures such as confirmation lights as shown in
Figure 4.48 were installed.
After each setup procedure
was finished, corresponding
confirmation lights came on
to notify the other worker. In
addition to these lights the
workers started to communicate with each other after each
procedure using a whistle or gesture.

Figure 4.48 Check Lamps

• Work sequence

Sequence and method of setup operation were spelled out on
paper, so that the workers all had the same understanding.

(f) Effects of the Project

The project team's effort brought forth the following results.
First, machine down time for setup operation dropped from 60
minutes to 8 minutes (Figure 4.49).

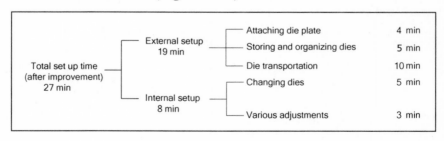

Figure 4.49 Reduction in Setup Time

The reduction in setup time brought about other benefits:

• Production volume increase

The production volume increased by 15 percent. This was

equivalent to a 300,000–yen cost reduction per month.

15,000 products (after improvement)/ 13,000 products (before improvement) x 100 = 115 percent

- Boosted morale

Workers' attitude toward die changes and press operations changed for the better.

- Quality improvement

Defects after setup changes decreased because of pre–setup inspections, maintenance of dies, and better mid–setup communications. Although we succeeded in bringing the setup time below ten minutes, we were determined to reduce it even further by improving the bolster speed and die attachment method. In all, we hoped the knowledge gained through this project could be used for other machines as well.

It should also be noted here that the project would not have succeeded without the hard work of these people: the project leader, Teruhisa Itonaga from Production Technologies Department, Shuji Takagi, Koujiro Yamatani, Kazuo Tsuji, and Minoru Fukuda from the press shop.

Single–Minute Exchange of Dies in Press Operation
(Toyoda Gosei Co., Ltd., Inasawa factory, January, 1973, Nori-hiro Hayakawa)

Since its founding in 1949, Toyoda Gosei contributed to the development of the Japanese automobile industry by supplying rubber and plastic auto parts. Our steering wheels and brake fluid hoses occupy the largest share in the industry. In total, about 5,000 types of products, ranging in size from clips to radiator grills, are produced by our factories. The following example is from our Inasawa factory, which succeeded in reducing its die setup time, which ranged from 60 to 160 minutes, to less than 10 minutes. Guidance from Mr. Shigeo Shingo, of the Institute of Management Improvement, and the efforts of related departments brought about this improvement.

(a) Background and Goal of Improvement

In the 1970's, the Japanese auto industry was pressured to raise its safety standards and take measures against automobile pollution amidst a labor shortage, reduction of work hours, wage increases and price escalation. Naturally, parts manufacturers were pressed to fulfill demands for quality and performance, and to supply items at low prices.

In order to meet these challenges, our company began a movement to eliminate waste under the guidance of T Motor Corporation, with the motto "streamlining without cost." As part of this movement, Toyoda Gosei's Inasawa factory was chosen as a model plant to implement what was called the Kanban system.

Under the Kanban system, the worker in one process obtains only "necessary amount of parts from the previous process, whenever they are needed." The previous process replenishes what is lost. This system has various merits: it synchronizes processes, simplifies production, eliminates work–in–process, and has positive effects on overall quality and costs.

In order for this system to run smoothly, the following twelve conditions need to be met through various improvements:

1. Continuous production
2. Stable production volume
3. Streamlined and stable production processes
4. Invariable quality
5. Thorough operational understanding
6. Defects or mistakes are addressed immediately
7. Establishment of clear defect criteria
8. 5S — Seiri (organization), Seiton (orderliness), Souji (cleanliness), Seiketsu (standardized cleanup), Shitsuke (discipline), is observed
9. Schedule is managed by the Kanban system
10. Swift and thorough execution of all decisions
11. Short setup time
12. Preventive maintenance (PM) and timely machine repair

Although Toyoda Gosei worked hard to make these improvements, condition number eleven was not satisfied; setup times remained long and problematic. Since we pursued the production system which would "make only what is necessary when it was necessary," the number of setup changes inevitably increased when machine capacities stayed the same. If setup operations stayed long, keeping the necessary production volume was impossible.

In the case of large–scale injection molding machines, large–lot production was preferred in the past. As production lots became smaller, although work–in–process decreased, the number of setup changes inevitably increased.

If the number of setup changes tripled, the setup time needed to be one third to compensate for the increase. Likewise, if the number of setup changes became fivefold, the setup time needed to be reduced fivefold. Otherwise, the loss would outweigh the benefit of small production.

It was the contention of most that long setup times were un-avoidable. Workers on the shop floor often showed resistance to the Kanban system, assuming that drastically reducing setup times was impossible.

In 1972, Toyoda Gosei started a company–wide campaign to promote preventive maintenance (PM). During this campaign, it became clear that setup time was the most influential factor in lower-ing machine operation rates (Figure 4.50). This finding drove home the necessity to reduce setup times. When our company was seeking a completely different way to cut back setup times, Mr. Shigeo Shingo, director of the Institute of Management Improvement, intro-duced the concept of SMED. We

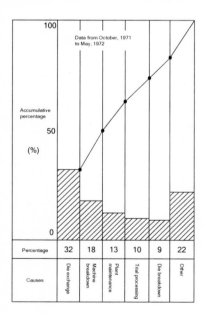

Figure 4.50 Factors for Machine Shutdown

decided to adopt this method and formed a workers group in order to heighten creativity and motivate others to make SMED a reality.

(b) Concept and Outline of Setup Improvement

The most important concept of SMED is to clearly separate internal setup from external setup. External setup is any setup operation that can be done without stopping the machines. This includes preparing materials, tools, dies and transportation equipment. Conversely, internal setup is any setup operation done while the machines are stopped. This includes putting new material in, attaching and removing dies, and centering and adjustment. Internal setup operations are not fixed, however. They can be converted to external operations. Indeed, that is the essence of SMED. Increased external operations are not a problem as long as the machine down time is low. Figure 4.51 shows the stages of setup improvement.

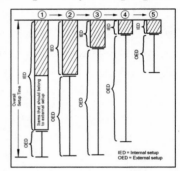

Figure 4.51 Stages of Setup Improvement

In stage one, external and internal setups are not separated clearly. Operations that can be done externally are done internally. In stage two, external and internal setups are distinguished and what can be done externally is done externally. In stage three, internal setups are converted to external setups through improvements. In stage four, internal setup time is reduced. In stage five, external setup time is also reduced. These stages can and should be repeated.

(c) Planning and Implementation

Our company succeeded in bringing the setup times of different types of machines to less than ten minutes: a middle–scale injection molding machine (500–ton level clamp capacity), a large–scale injection molding machine (1,250–ton level clamp capacity) and a protrusion molding machine. However, the following discussion will focus on the middle–scale injection molding machines.

1. Setup Time Study

Figure 4.52 shows the shift in setup times of all the middle–scale injection molding machines in the six months leading up to July, 1972, when the SMED improvement started. Line A shows the overall setup time (including die and material change, preparation for molding, internal and external setup combined) and its average is 160 minutes. This was equal to machine downtime because even external setups were done internally back then. Line B shows the duration of die change itself and its average is 60 minutes.

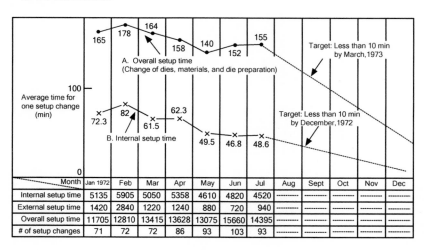

Month	Jan 1972	Feb	Mar	Apr	May	Jun	Jul	Aug	Sept	Oct	Nov	Dec
Internal setup time	5135	5905	5050	5358	4610	4820	4520	-------	--------	--------	--------	--------
External setup time	1420	2840	1220	1240	880	720	940	-------	--------	--------	--------
Overall setup time	11705	12810	13415	13628	13075	15660	14395	-------	--------	--------	--------
# of setup changes	71	72	72	86	93	103	93	-------	--------	--------	--------

Figure 4.52 Shift in Setup Time

2. Improvement Plans and Goals

The duration of each setup procedure was studied; improvement started from the most time–consuming procedure.

a. Improvement Steps (Figure 4.53)

No	Setup Procedure	1st	2nd	3rd	4th	Point of Improvement
1	Wait for a crane			O		Shorten through better planning
2	Get tools	O				Use a designated cart
3	Get a crane	O			O	
4	Apply anti-corrosion treatment	O				
5	Set wires	O			O	
6	Remove bolts			O		Use an electric wrench slide device
7	Remove pipes		O			Replace the pipes with special quick joints
8	Look for a die	O				Print die type on each die
9	Make sure right side is up	O				Print direction on dies
10	Attach hook bolts	O				Attach the bolts in advance
11	Move a die to the machine			O		Print the center of the die on the crane
12	Locating ring					
13	Look for clamps and blocks					
22	Adjust ejector knock pins			O		Standardize the ejection volume
23	Attach a hydraulic knock-style pipe		O			
24	Remove rear safety door	O				Switch to a rail type

Figure 4.53 Difficulty & Improvement of Changeover

Steps of improvement were planned as follows:

- First step: Separate internal and external setups (August, 1972)
- Second step: Convert internal setups to external setups (October, 1972)
- Third step: Shorten internal setup times (November, 1972)
- Fourth step: Shorten external setup times (March, 1973)

The goal was to make the total setup time equivalent to the die–exchange time after the first and second steps. From there, we wanted to reduce the die–exchange time to less than ten minutes with the second and third steps. Finally, by repeating steps one through four, we planned to reduce the overall setup time to less than ten minutes.

b. ABC Analysis of Setup Procedure Time

Our company studied the duration of each setup procedure of all the machines and dies and conducted an ABC analysis. Figure 4.54 shows one of the analysis charts created as a result. In this case, regular machine operators — not setup specialists, changed the setup. Items are listed in order of duration, not in actual operation sequence.

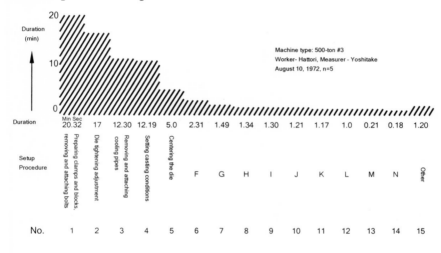

Figure 4.54 Mold Changeover Time Chart

c. Improvement Plan for Each Setup Procedure

We divided setup operations into four areas: die attachment, material, worker, and system–related. Then, we listed all the operations related to each area (Figure 4.55 on the next page) and decided in which improvement step each operation should be addressed. All improvement ideas were written down, even if they were not immediately applicable.

3. Implementation

We implemented as many as fifty different kinds of improvements based on our detailed plans. The following examples were very effective.

Example 1: Elimination of Die Thickness Adjustment

Die thickness ("a" in Figure 4.55) varied from die to die and adjustment was necessary every time a new die was mounted. Moreover, adjustments were made through trial and error, often taking 15 to 40 minutes depending on the clamping mechanism. This

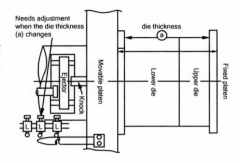

Figure 4.55 Mold Setup Adjustment

was improved by narrowing down the die thickness to just two types by scraping or adding spacers. Molding machines were also divided into two accordingly. This improvement eliminated the need for adjustments.

Example 2: Improvement of Die Removal Method

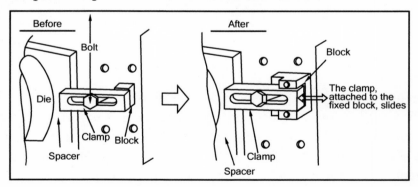

Figure 4.56 Changeover Method

In the past, dies were secured with removable bolt–operated blocks and clamps. Preparing and assembling the necessary parts was time consuming. Because there were multiple bolts, it took 20 minutes to change a die. Our company invented a sliding jig in which a bolt, clamp, and block became one set (Figure 4.56). With these jigs, a die could be secured or released by sliding the clamps on or off. This invention reduced the time for removing and attaching bolts from 20 minutes to merely one minute.

Example 3: Improvement of Die Positioning

Before improvement, dies were centered using a locating ring. However, this five–minute operation was reduced to 30 seconds simply by using a guide block as shown in Figure 4.57. With this guide block a die, lifted with a crane, could be centered simply by fitting its edge to the block. Implementing this improvement was made easier by the standardization of die thickness using a spacer (Example 1).

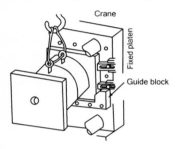

Figure 4.57 Improved Guide Block

Example 4: Heating Resin Externally

Heating resins initially took two hours and was done internally. Since this was time consuming, our company invented a special device to connect a hot air dryer to a molding machine and enable the heating process to be done externally. This improvement drastically reduced the machine downtime from two hours to two minutes.

(d) Results

Figure 4.58 shows the shift in setup operation times for one machine that we created about a month after Mr. Shingo taught us the methods of SMED in July, 1972. White bars and shaded bars show the setup times before and after improvement respectively. Lack of a shaded bar indicates that operation was eliminated or externalized. The 80–minute machine down time shrank to merely 4 minutes 45 seconds in this machine.

No	Setup Operation	Time Before (Min Sec)	Time After (Min Sec)	Time (min)
1	Prepare, remove and attach clamps, blocks and bolts	20.32	1.10	Switched to sliding clamps
2	Adjust die clamps	17.00	0.00	Standardized die thickness
3	Attach cooling pipes	12.30	0.00	Improved the pipes
4	Set casting conditions	12.19	0.45	Standardized the conditions
5	Center the die	5.00	0.00	Used a guide block
6	F	2.31	0.00	Converted to external setup
7	G	1.48	1.00	Improved clamps
8	H	1.34	0.00	Converted to external setup
9	I	1.30	0.00	Converted to external setup
10	J	1.21	0.00	Converted to external setup
11	K	1.17	0.34	Partly converted to external setup
12	L	1.00	0.00	Standardized the knock dimension
13	M	0.21	0.00	
14	N	0.18	0.10	Standardized the application method
15	O	0.15	0.00	Attached the piece in advance
16	P	0.12	0.15	
17	Q	0.06	0.06	
18	R	0.06	0.00	Improved the pipes
19	S	0.00	0.15	Added the final confirmation
	Total	1 hr 19min 40 sec	4 min 45 sec	Before improvement / After improvement

Figure 4.58 Comparison of Changeover Time

On September 16th, 1972, Mr. Shingo and our company executives received a demonstration of the new method for the first time. After the setup, which was completed in less than five minutes, the first product came out of the machine. Everyone was looking at it with the same question in mind: *does this product meet quality standards?* When the setup worker checked the product and declared, "It's good," and passed it around, we were extremely proud. This success was extremely motivating and dissipated any doubts regarding the new setup method. The same method was then implemented on other machines, such as large–scale injection machines.

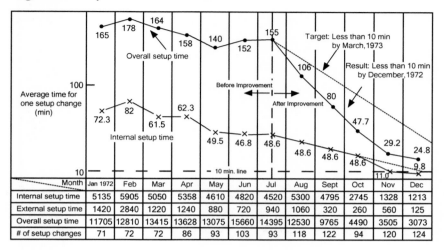

Figure 4.59 Shift in Setup Changeover Time

Mr. Shingo gave us some advice as well as his own "IE Award" to us. The company president emphasized the importance of heeding attention to operation safety, as well as pursuing speed. This comment led us to install a safety interlock system. The machines with this system do not operate unless all the setup procedures are properly taken care of. This improvement was also made in other machines and we eventually succeeded in bringing the average internal setup time of all the middle–scale injection machines to less than ten minutes (Figure 4.59). After January, 1973, we worked on the fourth step, reducing external setup time, and bringing the overall setup time (external and internal) to less than 10 minutes.

Cost and Benefits

The cost of the improvement was 200,000 yen per machine. Since the expected boost in profits was 600,000 yen per machine, the investment paid for itself in just three months. The expected profit was calculated taking into account two factors: a decrease in machine down time and a decrease in man–hours.

In addition there were other improvement benefits as follows:

- Increased material yield due to decreased trial shots
- Decreased initial defects
- Increased production capacity
- Increased morale
- Drastic decreases in work–in–process

Standardization
The improvement resulted in modifications and standardization in various areas such as the setup–procedure instructions, molding conditions, die design, and machine purchasing guidelines.

(e) Summary
Our company had tried to decrease setup times before. However, these efforts paled in comparison to the ease of implementation and dramatic results achieved with the SMED system. After realizing setup times under ten minutes, worker confidence skyrocketed and our notion of what was possible or not changed forever.

The SMED system can be applied to any machine that requires setup. Therefore, now that we have established SMED with molding machines, we would like to expand its use to other areas of the company to bring overall machine setup time to less than five minutes.

Finally, we would like to express our deepest appreciation to Mr. Shingo from the Institute of Management Improvement, our management team (which swiftly decided to introduce the SMED method), and the workers whose exceptional efforts made this improvement possible.

4.1.8 Shift From SMED to OTED

The goal of the One Touch Exchange of Die (OTED) method, on the other hand, is to lower setup to under a minute. In addition to the basic SMED concept, the following ideas need to be considered to achieve OTED.

(a) Elimination of Adjustment

As in the case of SMED, adjustment needs to be eliminated entirely. In order to eliminate adjustment, easy setting methods such as one that uses precise intermediary jigs, need to be conceived.

(b) Liberation from Bolts

When it comes to attaching dies or blades, many engineers think of using bolts. However, using bolts is not the only way to go. There are other ways, such as the dovetail–groove or wedge methods, that can attach things as easily as inserting a CD into a stereo. Fast setups are possible even without using expensive hydraulic, pneumatic, magnetic, or electric clamping methods. Using functional clamps such as U–slot or hinge methods, are also effective. If a U–slot method cannot be used, pear–shaped slots (Figure 4.60) may also be effective.

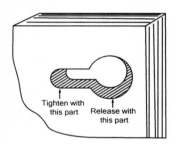

Figure 4.60 Liberation from Bolts

(c) Magnitude and Direction of Force

When bolt operated clamps are used to secure dies, people generally only consider the forces necessary to tighten the bolt. However, if we shift our focus more specifically to the magnitude and direction of forces necessary to secure the die, better and simpler fastening methods might emerge.

(d) Precision and Adhesive Joints

When centering a die, tapered joints fit together better and more precisely than cylindrical joints. Some think about using bolt holes for centering, but this is a mistake. Doing so results in time consuming adjustments. Bolt holes may be effective for fastening but are not helpful for centering. If bolt holes are used for centering, they should be used in conjunction with knock–pins and tapered joints to make precise centering easier.

(e) Separation of Machine and Die Function
When press machines are used, it is common to attach the upper die to the ram and the lower die to the machine bed. However, if the machine's movement is not precise, centering the dies can take a long time. The two dies need to fit together in relation to one another, not in relation to the machine. The machine's function is just to apply load. Therefore, if we omit consideration of machine position and focus only on the dies themselves, centering them becomes much easier. Such a method can be achieved using a mechanism that positions only the dies within a machine called a "die–set mechanism." This mechanism should be designed so that different types of dies can be inserted, making it more cost–effective. In addition, dies should have guide sticks, holes, or grooves in order to facilitate centering.

(f) Separation of Metal and Mold
Metal molds are usually used for press machines and plastic molding machines. Interestingly, separating the functionality of "metal" and "mold" can actually lead to setup improvement. Metal has a function of adding weight, whereas a mold has a function of molding material. In rugby, dies are like the scrum center that controls the ball, whereas metal is like the back rows that add force.

If the outer surface of small molds is standardized to fit into one large metal mold, benefits such as easier and faster mold exchange are realized, resulting in a 30–percent drop in production cost. Furthermore, if a die–set mechanism is installed in a "metal" part, centering molds becomes easier. Again, using the concept of separating functionality — machine and die and that of metal and mold — is one of the fundamental methods of implementing OTED.

(g) Insert Method

When I went to a die–casting factory in Germany, I saw the workers change dies extremely fast using plates that dies could simply be inserted within (Figure 4.61). In Japan, standard dies that could be exchanged relatively swiftly are often used. However, the methods that demand the outer surface of dies to be finished with high precision still drive up the die production cost unnecessar-

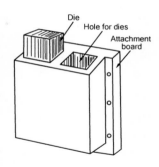

Figure 4.61 Insert Method

ily. We need to understand that while increasing the accuracy of dies themselves adds value, increasing the accuracy of the outer dimension of dies only increases cost. Again, thinking beyond precision to matters like direction and magnitude of force will lead us to better setting methods, such as the insertion method.

(h) Sharing and Minimizing Approach

The fastest way to change setup is not to change. Therefore, using an approach that shares what can be shared and minimizes setup changes is very convenient.

- Share and use a minimum number of stoppers.
- When placement of limit switches differs from product to product, use detection bars so that the same switches can be shared.
- When the width of a material feed conveyor needs to be changed depending on the product, install a mechanism, such as spring loaded spacers, so that one conveyor can accommodate multiple products.

B. Examples of OTED

(a) Steering–Wheel Inspection Jig (Figure 4.62)

At one company, there was an inspection tool used to check steering wheels. Since there were four different types of steering wheels with different shaft diameters, adjustments had to be made every time a different type of product was mounted. This tedious operation was improved by introducing a box–shaped inspection tool that had an appropriate adjustment jig on each side. Therefore, when a product type needed to be changed, all the inspection worker needed to do was to turn the box to bring the appropriate side of the box to the top.

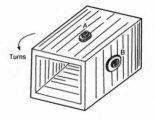

Figure 4.62 Rotary Inspection Jig

This improvement reduced the setup time from 30 minutes to 15 seconds. It also made the complicated setup operation, which could only be done by the foreman, simple enough for part–time workers.

(b) OTED for a Molding Machine (Figure 4.63)

At one company, two types of handles made of different materials were manufactured for electronic appliances. Since the materials were different the dies had to be changed between each product. However, this setup operation was greatly improved by using a new die with a simple flow–control mechanism. The die was partitioned into die A and die B with a channel that could be rotated to allow resin to

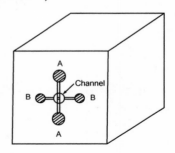

Figure 4.63 One–Touch Switchover Die

flow into either, depending on what handles were being produced. In this way two different handles with different resins could be created in one die. Setup change took only 10 seconds with this method.

(c) Cassette–Style Mold for a Molding Machine (Figure 4.64)

At one company, bolts were previously used to hold down dies of a 250–ton molding machine. However, an improvement was made and the bolts were replaced by standardized die attachment boards that would fit into board–holders installed on the machine. Therefore, the dies could be inserted and removed just like cassette tapes. High pressure is applied when the dies are closed; however, little force is applied when they are open. As long as the holders could center and hold the dies firm enough so that they would stay in place when the molded materials

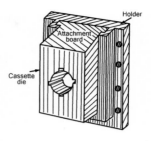

Figure 4.64 Cassette Die

were removed, the dies did not need to be bolted at all. The new method required only 28 seconds for setup changeover.

(d) Bending Die for Front Forks (Figure 4.65)

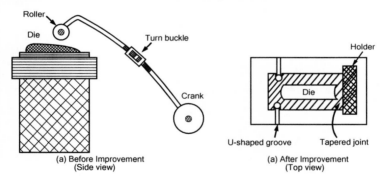

(a) Before Improvement
(Side view)

(a) After Improvement
(Top view)

Figure 4.65 Front Fork Bending Operation

There was a machine used to bend front forks at one company. Since the setup operation of this machine was time consuming, the company made some improvements. First, an intermediary jig was installed at the bottom of each die so that the surface level of the dies would stay the same even if product types were different. Before this improvement, the turn buckle on a roller had to be adjusted depending on the die surface level. Second, a U–shaped groove and tapered joints were used to attach the dies to the machine, instead of bolts. This vastly reduced mounting

309

and dismounting time from an hour to 25 seconds as a result.

(e) Cutting Median Planes (Figure 4.66)

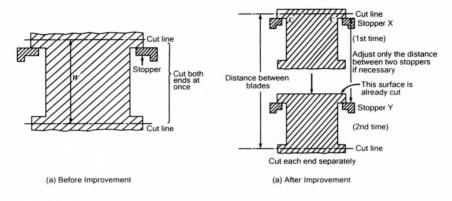

Figure 4.66 Cutting Median Planes

There was an operation of cutting median planes into 18 different widths. In the past, the upper and lower end of each plane was cut at once using two blades. This method took about an hour since the blades' positions had to be adjusted precisely. This operation was improved as follows:

- Make the distance between the two blades wider than the width (w) of the largest plate
- Place a median plane so that its edge (c) touches stopper X—then cut just the upper end with Blade A
- Slide the median plane downward until the edge (c) hits stopper Y, and cut the lower end

With this method, when the product type was changed, the worker just needed to move the stoppers to the appropriate positions. This new method required only 20 seconds for a setup change.

(f) Press Machine for Washing Machine Bodies
At one washing machine factory, various models of machine

bodies were manufactured. For example, machines with left sided or right sided pipe fittings, or standard and deluxe models. Deluxe models had holes on four corners for decoration. In total, eight different molds were used and a setup change took an hour and a half each time.

The company developed a standard mold by taking advantage of the fact that the exterior design of all the models was exactly the same — except for the position of holes. The standard mold could accommodate all the models and change the hole positions. In order to make holes at desired places, metal blocks were inserted between the press machine's ram and the die as necessary. Attachment and removal of the metal blocks was done electronically through a switch. As a result, the hour and a half setup change was drastically reduced to only eight seconds.

There was another advantage. Products were previously manufactured in lots causing much floor space to be used as storage. The new mold was able to create different models one after another, which eliminated work–in–process.

4.1.9 Assembly Line and SMED

As discussed earlier, the basic concepts of SMED can be applied for an assembly line with multiple machines in much the same way as it is for a single–machine. However, there are some issues associated with assembly line production that should be discussed here. In order to reduce setup times of assembly line production, it is important to look at it at from two different levels: each specific process of an assembly line, and the assembly line as a whole.

A. Setup Changes of Each Process

For each process of an assembly line, the concept of SMED can be applied in the same way.

(a) External Preparation of Parts

When changing setups in an assembly line, it is absolutely essential that necessary parts never go out of stock. Inventory of parts needs to be managed well so that the parts are properly replenished. In addition, necessary parts need to be brought to the assembly line before the machines are stopped.

(b) Setup Change of Machines, Tools and Jigs

Company H manufactured single and twin calibrators using two corresponding assembly lines. While one line was in operation, the other line's setups were changed. Once the production in one line finished the workers all moved to the other line. Although this method worked it was far from desirable since the machine operation rates were so low and the two lines occupied excessive floor space.

An improvement plan was made to allow extras of only those machines that have long setup times. This seemed effective, but it still made the operation rates low. Plus, buying extra machines was only possible when machine prices were reasonable.

The company reached a conclusion that reducing setup times would be the best measure, not increasing the number of machines. The company eventually succeeding in cutting back setup times by using SMED concepts such as using intermediary jigs, functional standardization, functional clamps, and adjustment elimination.

B. Setup Changes of Entire Assembly Lines

When changing setups of an entire assembly line, the following needs to be considered.

(a) Effects of total assembly hours

Assume that three types of products, A, B, and C are going to be manufactured in a single line. Two cases can be considered: total assembly times are the same or different.

1. When total assembly times are the same.

When total assembly times are the same, the same number

of workers can manufacture all the products at the same takt time.

Takt time is the time it takes for a product to go through each process, and can be calculated as follows:

Takt time (t) = daily operation time/daily production volume

The number of workers necessary can be calculated as follows. A is Product A's total assembly time.

Number of workers (n) = A /t

Even if the monthly production volume of Product A, B and C varies, it can be handled simply by adding extra production days for products with larger production volume. Therefore, problems associated with setup changes are not likely to occur.

Even so, in order to make production work, proper groundwork needs to be laid. Assembly workers need to be trained so that they can handle different types of work, and SMED should be introduced in each process.

2. When total assembly times are different.

Difficulty arises when total assembly times are different. Assume that the assembly time of each product is as follows:

Product A: 8 minutes

Product B: 6 minutes

Product C: 5 minutes

If the assembly times of Product A and B could be reduced to match that of C, that would be ideal. But oftentimes, this is not possible and setup change becomes necessary.

(b) Conclusive Change and Successive Change

Depending on the timing of setup change, conclusive and successive–change methods are possible.

Setup change methods / Line method		Application of SMED method	
		Conclusive change method	Successive change method
Fixed-worker method		O	
Fixed-takt-time method			O
Fixed-worker, Fixed-takt-time method	Cushion method		O
	Mix method		O

(i) Conclusive–Change Method

With this method, assembly of Product B does not start until Product A's last process is completed. This method results in longer assembly–line down time and setup time.

(ii) Successive–Change Method

With this method, Product B follows Product A, while A is still on the assembly line. Assembly line down time, as well as setup time can be minimized.

(c) Fixed Worker and Fixed Takt Time

As setup methods change, the following methods can be considered.

Fixed Worker Method

When using this method, a fixed number of workers attend the assembly line, even if there is a setup change. Naturally, takt time changes when products are switched. For example, when switching from Product A to B, the takt time becomes shorter. When switching from Product B to C, the takt time becomes longer. In other words, takt time imbalance occurs.

This issue can be addressed if a conclusive–change method is used. However, operation rates will decrease. If a successive–

change method is used, the following adjustments need to be made when the products are being switched:

- Match the shorter takt time to longer takt time — loss from the difference in takt–time results, although it is not as bad as that of conclusive–change method
- Match the longer takt time to shorter takt time, give assistance to slower operations and match the speed of faster ones — this sounds possible in theory, but not practical

Overall, this method has one benefit: personnel management is very convenient when worker numbers are fixed.

Fixed Takt–Time Method

Under this method, constant takt time is maintained by changing the number of workers. Although this is suitable for the successive–change method, personnel management is more difficult than the former method since workers have to move around every time a setup is changed. Workers tend to dislike this method as well.

Fixed Worker, Fixed Takt–Time Method

Under this method, fixed takt–time and fixed number of workers are maintained even if total assembly times differ from product to product. If possible, this is the best method, since it minimizes the loss from setup changes and makes personnel management easier. However, the varying assembly time of different products still has to be offset somehow. The following are ways to do just that.

Cushion Method

The assembly times of Products A and B are longer than that of Product C by three minutes and a minute, respectively. Under this method, a "cushion work team" does three-minutes of work on Product A and a minutes worth of work on Product B outside the assembly line beforehand. Then, the partially processed products are brought to the assembly line where A, B, and C can be assembled with fixed number of workers and fixed takt time.

The cushion work team literally works as a cushion to absorb the difference in assembly times between products. As the team is often responsible for difficult and fast–changing operations, skilled workers are essential.

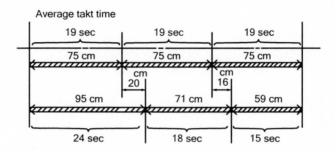

Figure 4.67 Takt Time & Work Area

Mix Method
With this method, one of Product A, B, and C are sent as a group. If there are 20 workers, the takt time of each product will be as follows:

Product A: 24 seconds

Product B: 18 seconds

Product C: 15 seconds

As a group, the takt time will be 57 seconds. A fixed number of workers and takt time will be maintained this way. However, the following needs to be taken into account.

First, different products come one after another. Therefore, setup changes need to be either eliminated or simplified so that they can be done quickly.

Second, appropriate poka–yoke devices need to be installed

so that mistakes will be prevented even if different products come at once.

Third, average takt time for each product is 19 seconds (57/3 = 19). In general, it is said that appropriate length of work area per person is 75cm in an assembly line. This means that in this example, appropriate length of work area for 19–seconds worth of work is 75cm (29 and a half inches). Although the workers use the same length of space, each product actually requires different length.

Required length	Difference from the given length
Product A: 95cm	+ 20cm
Product B: 71cm	–4cm
Product C: 59cm	–16cm

Therefore, the workers have 20cm less, 4cm more, and 16cm more length when handling Product A, B, and C correspondingly. Although deviation from the required length is not desirable, up to 20cm is considered to be permissible. If greater deviation is likely to occur, it should be addressed by changing the product combination.

The above mix method example using Product A, B, and C was actually taken from a factory which succeeded in establishing very efficient assembly lines via effective one–touch setups and poka–yoke devices.

At O Electronics, parts such as transistors were mounted to printed circuit boards. There were two different sizes of products, A and B, and their assembly times differed significantly. Therefore, Product A was manufactured for half a month in the assembly line, then Product B was manufactured for the rest of the month. Although this production system worked, it created excessive work–in–process, and made meeting delivery deadlines quite a challenge. After much deliberation the company took up the mix method. Product A and B were set in one attachment jig and sent to the assembly line as a set. This method turned out to be a success. The large volume of work–in–process disappeared and delivery deadlines were never missed again.

C. Summary
In summary, the following are the keys to improving setup changes of assembly lines.

1. Apply the concept of SMED and OTED for each process.

2. For an entire assembly line, implement the fixed–worker, fixed–takt time method if possible. In order to realize this either a cushion method or a mix method needs to be used.

The mix production method can be used even if total product assembly times vary. However, it is important to take appropriate measures beforehand, such as implementing one–touch setups or poka–yoke devices. Many companies realized improvement using the above methods and succeeded in reducing assembly–line setup times greatly, from 40 minutes to 30 seconds, for example.

SUMMARY
Whether SMED can be realized or not is often more a matter of mind-set, rather than technical ability.

Every operation requires setup changes. If the concepts of SMED are applied, a dramatic reduction in setup times can be realized in any type of work.

4.2 Development of Pre–Automation
(Improvement of Principal Operations and Allowances)
Many managers I meet tell me, "We can't reduce the number of workers even after automation." This kind of comment stems from the misunderstanding of what automation really is. Automation is different from simply mechanizing human movements. A machine is truly "automated" when it has the functionality to detect and fix abnormalities. As a way to implement automation more reasonably, I would like to explain "pre–automation."

4.2.1 What is Pre–Automation?

Scholars explain that there are 23 stages separating manual labor from complete automation. The first through the 20th of these stages are called "mechanization." Sometimes, "automation" is often used prematurely to describe what, really, is still mechanization. A machine is truly "automated" when it has the functionality to detect and fix abnormalities. In many cases, so called "automated" machines do not have this functionality.

I would like to propose what is called "pre–automation" here. If a machine is pre–automated it stops and alerts workers when abnormalities occur so they can come and fix the problems. It is a stage between mechanization and automation, hence the term "pre–automation."

Pre–automation and automation both encompass an element of human intelligence. However, it is only "automated" machines that have the ability to actively respond.

4.2.2 Contents of Operations

Operations can be classified as in Figure 4.68.

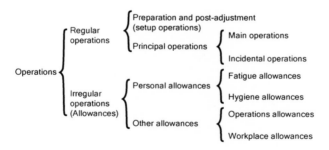

Figure 4.68 Classification of Operations

A. Regular Operations

Regular operations are made up of setup operations and principal operations.

(a) Preparation, Post–adjustment Operations (Setup Operations)

This refers to the operations which occur only once before and after processing of each lot. These operations can be reduced up to 95 percent if the concepts of SMED are applied.

(b) Principal operations

Principal operations are repetitious and are comprised of two operational subtypes:

- Main operations

These are literally the main operations such as cutting, molding, forging, and assembling in which products are worked upon.

- Incidental operations

These are the operations that support principal operations, such as attaching and removing items, and operating switches.

B. Allowances

Irregular occurrences are called allowances and can be divided as follows:

(a) Personal allowances

These allowances are for human physiological and psychological needs.

- Fatigue allowances

These allowances are designed to accommodate recovery from physical or mental fatigue.

- Personal hygiene allowances

These allowances are used mainly to satisfy the physiological needs of thirst, lavatory needs, wiping off sweat, and so on.

(b) Other allowances

These are the allowances given to operations themselves,

irrespective of human physiology or psychology.

- Operational allowances

These allowances are for operations that are usually unique to a specific operation and occur irregularly, such as fixing machine breakdowns, lubricating, removing cutting scraps, etc.

- Workplace allowances

These allowances are for things that happen irregularly, yet are common for any work place, such as power outages, waiting for cranes, material delays, and meetings.

4.2.3 Conditions of Pre–Automation

There are five conditions necessary for pre–automation: the automation of main operations, incidental operations and allowances, the capability to detect abnormalities, and large–scale machine feeding and product storage.

1. Automation of Main Operations

Automation of main operations using various machines: lathes, milling machines, machine tools, metal presses, and die–casting machines has long since been accomplished and therefore, does not require further discussion here.

2. Automation of Incidental Operations

(a) Mounting materials

When attaching a type of material to a machine, the following three functions are required: one piece is fed at a time, it must be properly aligned, and attached.

The two ways that materials are sent to machines include the single–piece method in which materials are separated into pieces, and the continuous method in which they come in such shapes as bars, rolls, and resin. In the case of the continuous method, feeding is relatively easy. However, in case of the single–piece method, an appropriate feeding device such as a parts feeder (Figure 4.69), rotary feeder, (Figure 4.70) and magazine feeder that can correct material direction, need to be installed. When implementing pre–automation, mounting materials smoothly is a very important issue to think about.

Figure 4.69 Parts Feeder   Figure 4.70 Rotary Feeder

(b) Detaching products

There are various ways to detach products such as dropping them naturally or by force (pushing or using air), or grabbing them. When dropping products, it is necessary to think about ways to prevent scratches and how to separate products from cutting scraps. If products are fitted tightly to the machines, alternative ways to separate them need to be considered.

(c) Switch operations

There are two ways to automate switch operations.

• Continual running—Keep the machines running even when materials are being attached or detached
• Intermittent running—Machines run only after sensing that new material has been attached; once processing stops, the machine stops so that the product can be taken out—all these operations are automated.

(d) Cutting

After processing, products that need be cut should be

done so by an automated cutting process.

(e) Others

Other incidental operations that occur repeatedly, such as applying cutting oil or mold lubricant, also need to be automated.

3. Detecting Abnormalities

The main distinction between pre–automation and mechanization is that pre–automated machines have the functionality to detect abnormalities.

A. Detection methods

Table 4.10 shows the commonly–used detection methods.

Detection method	Category	Passing	Turning	Position	Low accuracy	High accuracy	Flaw	Color difference
Limit switch	Contact type	●	●	●		▲		
Micro switch	Contact type	●	●	●		▲		
Touch switch	Contact type	●	●	●		●		
Differential transformer	Contact type	●	●	●		●		
Trimetron	Contact type			●		●		
Proximity switch	Non-Contact type	●	●	●		●		
Optoelectronic switch	Non-Contact type	●	●	●	▲			
Reflective optoelectronic switch	Non-Contact type	●	●	●	▲		▲	●
Fluid element	Non-Contact type	●	●	●				

Detection method	Pressure	Temperature	Electrical current	Quantity	Time	Timing
Barometer	●					
Pressure-sensitive switch	●					
Meter relay			●			
Nugget tester			●			
Thermostat (Thermometer)		●				
Thermistor (Thermometer)		●				
Thermo coupler (Thermometer)		●				
Counter				●		
Programmable counter				●		
Timer					●	
Delayed relay						●

Table 4.10 Classification of Detection Methods

Detection Based on Product Movement, Position, & Dimension
• Contact type

This is a method that detects abnormalities based on whether or not contact was made, or on the amount of contact.

- Limit switch, Micro switch (Figure 4.71(a))

These are the most commonly–used contact–type detection devices.

- Touch switch

Touch switches are highly sensitive devices that can detect abnormalities based on whether or not their antennas are touched. They are not suitable for places that vibrate, because of their high sensitivity and can detect 1/100mm movement with their antennas.

Figure 4.71 Limit, Micro, & Touch Switches

- Differential Transformer (Figure 4.72)

Differential transformers are placed so that when products come into contact with them, abnormalities can be detected via changes in magnetic lines, which are displayed as changes in current value. Highly accurate detection is possible with this method.

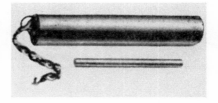

Figure 4.72 Differential Transformer

- Trimetron (Figure 4.73)

324

Trimetrons have dial indicators that can be set to the upper and lower limits of a normal range. There are three lights that signify whether the contact force is below, above or within the normal range (measurement accuracy of 1/100mm can be attained). By linking trimetrons with devices like air cylinders, defects can be separated easily and accurately.

Figure 4.73 Trimetron

• Non–contact type

Non–contact type devices can be placed outside the processing range of product movements.

Figure 4.74 Proximity Switches

• Proximity switch

Proximity switches sense the difference in the distance between products; they are highly accurately and can thus detect abnormalities.

• Optoelectronic switch

Since proximity switches are magnetic, they can only be used for metal products. However, optoelectronic switches can be used for non–metals as well. Each device has a part that emits light and a part that receives it, and products pass between these parts. The devices can detect abnormalities in products by the way lights are blocked.

• Reflective optoelectronic switch (Figure 4.75)

Reflective optoelectronic switches have light emitters and receivers on the same side. The devices can detect abnormalities in product position and color by the changes in reflected light. At one factory, a reflective optoelectronic switch was connected to two chutes—A and B—that separated spooled spring material. When springs were made, ten spools were welded into one and the joints marked with black tape. Unwelded material lacked tape and thus passed through the light and entered Chute A. When products with welded joints passed through the light however, the tape activated the switch, allowing them to fall in Chute B instead. In this way, products with welds could be separated automatically. When using such a switch, distance and angle of reflection need to be determined carefully, as they can greatly affect precision.

Figure 4.75 Optoelectronic Switch

- Fluid element (Figure 4.76)

By placing products in a flow of air, the flow changes. Abnormalities can be detected by the changes in flow.

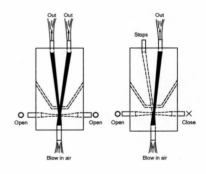

Figure 4.76 Fluid Device

Detection Based on Product Damages or Color Variation

- Magnetic flaw detector

This is a device that detects flaws by changes in the magnetic field. These detectors are highly expensive and take up space.

- Reflective optoelectronic switch

As mentioned above, reflective optoelectronic switches can be used to detect flaws, although tiny flaws may be missed. The devices are also effective in detecting color differences between two sides of a board, or welded sections in boards or pipes. These functions help lead to the realization of pre–automation.

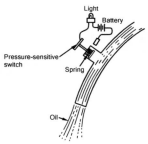

Detection Based on Pressure Change

Barometers and pressure–sensitive switches can be used to detect abnormalities. For example, one company used a pressure–sensitive switch to successfully alert workers to lowering oil level in an oil tube (flow switches can also be used to alert workers to lowering oil level).

Figure 4.77 Pressure Sensitive Switch

Detection Based on Temperature Change

Thermostats, thermistors, and thermocouples are used to detect temperature changes.

Detection of electrical current change (Figure 4.78)

Figure 4.78 Meter Relays

- Meter relay

There are many ways to detect changes in electrical current, using meter relays is one of them. Upper and lower limits for normal electrical current are set before hand, such as 25 amps to 35 amps. If the current goes outside of this normal range, the machine stops. However, to prevent shutdown during normal operations, a delayed relay mechanism needs to be installed.

When using meter relays, condition changes that affect current also needs to be taken into consideration. S Ironworks started pre-automation one spring, but by winter the meter relays stopped working properly. After some research, the workers found that change in lubricant viscosity was causing the problem. In the winter time stagnant lubricant became very viscous, but became smoother after the machines ran for about an hour. So, they addressed the problem by warming the lubricant before starting the machines. This example highlights the importance of considering environmental conditions when using meter relays.

- Nugget Tester (Figure 4.79)

This device detects fluctuations in electrical current during welding. If electrical current goes beyond pre-set limits, the device alerts the operators and shuts off the machine. With this device defective welding can be found without destruction tests.

Figure 4.79 Welding
Inspection Device

Inspection of Numbers

Counters — especially programmable counters, are quite useful in production. For example, assume that 8,000 products need to be processed with a machine after regular work hours while no one is attending it. If a programmable counter is set to 8,000 products it shuts down when the machine reaches 8,000. Programmable counters are used widely in pre-automation.

Inspecting time

- Timers (Figure 4.80)

Timers can be used to effectively stop or resume machine functions at predetermined times.

- Delayed relay system

328

Delayed relays can also be used to stop or resume machine functions at determinable time intervals.

Figure 4.80 Preset Counter & Timers

As mentioned before, machines capable of detecting abnormalities is an absolute pre–requisite for realizing pre–automation. Moreover, these capabilities must take into account abnormalities in both the machines and the products. Although machine troubles and product defects are related, the two are discussed separately below.

B. Machine Abnormality (Table 4.11)
Nature of Abnormalities

Consequence	Nature of abnormalities	Detection Timing	Source (S) Before trouble	Source (S) After trouble Immediately after	Source (S) After trouble Sometime after	Result (S) Before trouble	Result (S) After trouble Immediately after	Result (S) After trouble Sometime after
A Discard	a. Unexpected		◎	○		◎	○	
A Discard	b. Machine wear		◎	○		◎	○	
B Repair	a. Unexpected			◎	○		◎	○
B Repair	b. Machine wear			◎	○		◎	○
C Continue using	a. Unexpected				◎			◎
C Continue using	b. Machine wear				◎			◎

Table 4.11 Detection of Machine Abnormality

329

There are two types of machine troubles: unexpected breakdown and regular machine wear.

Unexpected breakdowns are the most troublesome. However, there are ways to deal with them. First, find and address signs of machine troubles through regular inspections. Second, take preemptive measures using machine breakdown statistics as a guide.

Although the term "unexpected troubles" is used here, their causes are usually cumulative and detectable. The results only appear unexpectedly because checkups were not done. Therefore, it is wise to check for signs of trouble beforehand so as to prevent them from happening in the first place. Truly "unexpected troubles" are very rare. And because they usually occur for reasons that are unknown, they can be difficult to address technically or financially.

Machine wear on parts such as blades and bits, happens gradually over time. When the speed of wear differs from part to part, the duration that parts can be used safely should be determined statistically. To make accurate statistics, timers and pre–set counters come in handy. Making a cumulative time record for each tool, is very useful in determining the tool's lifespan.

Consequences of Machine Trouble
Several consequences resulting from machine trouble are possible:

- Machines or machine parts such as molds and blades have to be thrown away
- Troubled parts can be repaired and continue to be used
- Machines can continue to be used as they are

Responding to Trouble
How workers respond to trouble can have varying conse-

quences on production and the use of the machine.

- Early detection and treatment

The best way to respond to breakdowns is to address them before they actually happen. However, this can be difficult since machines often break down soon after abnormalities are detected. If the cause of trouble is unknown, intervention is especially challenging. Nevertheless, prior detection is very important, especially in cases where troublesome machines are discarded rather than repaired.

Characterizing possible sources of trouble is essential for quick detection of abnormalities. It is also necessary to think about quick response methods, such as a break that can immediately halt the machine.

- Late detection and treatment

Detection is considered late when it occurs after the dies or machines have incurred damage. Treatment can be done immediately or sometime later, depending on the impact of damage.

Means of Detecting Abnormalities

Abnormalities can be detected either by the physical alteration of the product, or at their source.

1. Type S—Source Detection

With die-casting machines and plastic molding machines, make sure that the previous product was taken out before tightening the die.

Install a mechanism in plastic molding machines that replenishes main resin hoppers when they become low, and stops replenishing when they are filled.

With a progressive die press use limit switches, proximity switches, or optoelectronic switches in order to make sure that spooled material is moving accurately one pitch at a time. If feeding is not done accurately, the machines should stop.

Install a device that detects the end of spooled materials and stops the machines before the end comes into the dies.

Figure 4.81 Detection of Material Feed Error

When manufacturing screws, use a programmable counter so that the machines will stop when a set number of screws are made.

In order to prevent bearing metals from burning, install a mechanism that checks the surface level of lubricant and alerts the workers if the level gets low.

In order to detect when lubricant pipes clog, install a pressure sensitive switch that signals an alarm when oil pressure drops.

Attach a thermistor to a bearing, and then connect it to a meter relay. When the bearing temperature gets more than 15 degrees above normal operating temperature, the thermistor activates the meter relay and stops the machine. One company took up this system and completely prevented bearings from overheating during unattended operations after regular work hours (Figure 4.82).

Figure 4.82 Detecting Overheat Conditions

Although it is effective to implement devices that detect abnormalities, it is far better to prevent them from happening in the first place. The following is an example of how one company did just that by eliminating a problem at its source.

At this company, a press machine was used to punch out small holes, but the machine punch often broke unexpectedly. Rubber rings were placed around the punches to help secure them to the work pieces. However, while these rings improved punching, they did not prevent breakage. The

Figure 4.83 Prevention of Punch Machine Breakdown

workers wondered why punches broke so often and realized that they broke when bent. The workers used metal covers around the punches and succeeded in preventing them from bending and breaking altogether.

2. Type R — Result Detection

The following are examples of Type R detection — detecting abnormalities after they develop into problems.

After screw heads are made with a header machine, the products are expelled by push-out pins. However, the push-out pins often broke and created resistance when new material was inserted. The factory experiencing this problem connected a meter relay to the machine so that it would detect current increases caused by such resistance and shut down the machine.

Within a header machine, there was a device that carried cut rods to a position where they would be punched. But this device sometimes malfunctioned and dropped the rod, causing the machine to punch air. Since the current dropped when the machine punched air, as in the previous case, a meter relay was attached in order to stop the machine when the problem occurred. A delayed relay was also installed in order to prevent the machine from shutting down at current drops during the normal operation.

Meter relays were also used to detect material shortage

or abnormal material feeding in cutting machines.

Spring–loaded bars were sometimes installed next to punches in press machines, or taps in cutting machines. When these parts broke, the bars moved and activated limit switches.

In a machine that produced leaf springs, a panel with lights that corresponded with each operational step was installed. When machine trouble occurred, the operators could pinpoint which step caused it, making it easy for them to take appropriate and immediate action (Figure 4.84).

Figure 4.84 Abnormality Signal

C. Product Abnormalities (Table 4.12)
Nature of abnormalities

There are two types of product abnormalities: isolated defects and continuous defects.

Consequence	Nature / Timing	Source (S) Sensory Before defects	Source (S) Sensory After defects Immediately after	Source (S) Sensory After defects Soon after	Source (S) Physical Before defects	Source (S) Physical After defects Immediately after	Source (S) Physical After defects Soon after	Result (S) Sensory Before defects	Result (S) Sensory After defects Immediately after	Result (S) Sensory After defects Soon after	Result (S) Physical Before defects	Result (S) Physical After defects Immediately after	Result (S) Physical After defects Soon after
A. Discard	Single defect					◎	○					◎	○
A. Discard	Continuous defects					◎	○					◎	○
B. Fix	Single defect				◎	◎	○				◎	◎	○
B. Fix	Continuous defects				◎	◎	○				◎	◎	○

Table 4.12 Detection of Defects

Isolated defects are the kind of defects that appear abruptly for a couple of products then stop. In general, these defects are caused by partial defects in material, or irregular material feeding. If the rate of occurrence is low, it is often better to keep the machines running and either take out the defective products on the spot, or remove them upon final inspection. However, if the rate of occurrence is high, problems should be detected and dealt with as soon as possible.

Continuous defects are the kind of defects that continue once they happen. These defects should also be detected and dealt with as soon as possible.

Consequences of Product Abnormalities
Several consequences resulting from product abnormalities are possible:

- Defective products must be discarded
- Defective products can be repaired and used

Responding to Defects
When it comes to product abnormalities, timing of detection and reaction tend to be after—not before—defective products are created. However, if poka–yoke devices are installed, it is still possible to detect abnormalities prior to product finalization. In cases where resulting defects need to be discarded, poka–yoke should to be implemented as much as possible. However, if poka–yoke are not possible and detection comes after defects are created, immediate reaction is required if the defects are continuous. Reactions can be slower if the resulting products are repairable.

Means of Detecting Abnormalities
Abnormalities can be detected via the defects themselves, or at their source. Detecting at the source is called a Type S detection whereas detecting the resulting defect is called a Type R detection. In either case, there are also two ways of inspecting for abnormalities:

- Visual inspection: Inspections of color, tone, etc., that rely on human senses
- Physical inspection: Inspections conducted using gauges and other measuring devices

Pre–automation is impossible as long as visual inspections are used. However, if abnormalities are isolated and rare it is permissible to set aside products for later visual inspections. But if the abnormalities are continuous, or happen at a high rate, it is best to detect them at their source using methods like those below.

- Check the temperature of molten–metal in die–casting machines
- Check die temperature and the spray volume of mold lubricant
- Check the nozzle pressure and temperature in plastic molding machines
- Check the material feeding volume
- Use nugget testers when spot welding to monitor abnormal current fluctuations

Physical inspections are used to check dimension, shape, strength, hardness and roughness, etc., using gauges and other measuring devices. Devices such as micrometers, proximity switches, optoelectronic switches, and trimetrons are usually used. Measuring tools that combine micrometers with electronic displays, are especially useful. Physical inspections can be used both for type S and R detections. Here are some examples.

> In a drilling operation, parts advanced without being drilled when the drill broke. However, a sensor to inspect the existence of drill holes was installed and connected to a limit switch. When holes were missing, a buzzer alerted the workers and shut down the machine (Type R detection, Figure 4.85).

> A trimetron was installed in a chute which fed cut metal parts from a machine, to check the exterior dimension of products as they slid down. When defective products were detected, the device alerted the workers and shut down the machine (Type R detection).

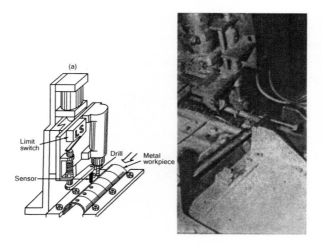

Figure 4.85 Hole Detection Device

Inappropriate feeding can occur when feeding spooled material between dies of press machines. This can be prevented by installing proximity switches, or limit switches on feeding devices. If feeding is incomplete, the switches stop the machines (Type S detection).

Bolts were sometimes double threaded at a bolt factory. However, the company astutely noticed that the heads of double–thread bolts rose higher than normal bolts when they are being threaded. Therefore, an electronic micro sensor that could detect height differences was installed. When abnormalities were detected, the sensor alerted the workers and the machine was shut down (Type R detection, example from S Iron Works).

D. Additional Notes on Abnormality Detection
Type S Detection and Type R Detection
As mentioned earlier, there are two types of abnormality detections:

Type S detection: Detecting abnormalities at the source and preventing them from developing into actual machine breakdowns or defective products.

Type R detection: Detecting abnormalities via machine

breakdown or product traits.

An R type detection is permissible in cases where the resulting products or affected machines can still be used as they are; the rate of occurrence is low and the defects are not continuous. However, a type S detection is always preferable. In other words, a few abnormalities are permissible, but they should not be allowed to develop into machine troubles or defective products. Using a S type detection can accomplish this very effectively.

In many cases people are content as long as problems are detected at some point, and thus do not distinguish between type R and S detections. Yet, this differentiation can lead to major improvements.

Detection and Poka–Yoke
As discussed before, poka–yoke is an excellent way to detect abnormalities. Therefore, it is going to be explained again.

The following examples highlight the three different poka–yoke detection types: contact type, fixed–value type, and motion-step type.

1. Contact type

As in Figure 4.86, hole location differed in left and right sided parts. When the wrong part was attached, a limit switch installed in the hole position, was activated and shut down the press machine.

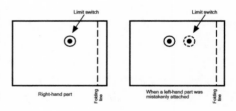

Figure 4.86 Preventing Reverse Installation

2. Fixed–value type

At Q Company, there was an operation in which workers inserted two leaf springs inside each push button. However, springs were sometimes forgotten. Discussions about ways to prevent this mistake settled on the simple idea of isolating the necessary number of springs needed for installation so that the worker could visibly see whether or not all were installed. After this poka–yoke was in place, the same mistake never happened again.

3. Motion–step type

There was an operation to inject grease inside axles, but the workers sometimes forgot it. The factory installed the following poka–yoke device to prevent this. When an axel was brought to a certain position, a bar was raised to block the axel. The bar did not move until the grease gun was used against a grease hole. This system made it impossible to forget injecting the grease.

There are also two different types of poka–yoke feedback.

Control type: If abnormalities are detected, the work is obstructed and cannot be continued.

Warning type: If abnormalities are detected, the workers are alerted with a buzzer or a light.

Poka–yoke should be used broadly in pre–automation since it can prevent machine breakdowns and defective products.

100% Inspection and Sampling Inspection

Many people still believe that since sampling inspections are backed by statistics, they are better than 100 percent inspections. But sampling inspections are only a method for improving inspection operations, not a method for guaranteeing quality. Although sampling inspections tend to take less time, it is still possible for defective products to slip through inspections. The chance may be one in a million, but defects should never leave factory doors. Therefore, 100 percent inspections are preferable, especially if worker hours can be reduced to match that of sampling inspections. Efforts should be made to conduct 100 percent inspections without spending much time or money.

E. Preventive Maintenance and Periodic Inspections
To control abnormalities at the source it is effective to conduct pe-

riodic inspections and preventive maintenance. However, many times people misuse the term "preventive" in cases where maintenance is actually done after abnormalities are detected. This is not preventative, but rather sampling–type maintenance.

Because type S detection and 100 percent inspection are conducted in pre–automation, moving to pre–automation can drastically reduce or prevent machine breakdowns. At S Iron Works for example, motor burnout accidents disappeared completely after installing a voltage meter relay.

Preventive maintenance and periodic inspections are effective as long as they are conducted properly. We should also know that successful pre–automation can prevent problems just as well as, or even better than, preventive maintenance.

Automation of Allowances
A. Automating the Feeding of Cutting Oil, Lubricant, and Mold Release Agent
In order to implement pre–automation cutting oil, lubricant, and mold release agent, should be provided automatically. If mold release agent is applied manually, for example, workers tend to generously apply it initially and then reapply it only when it becomes noticeably ineffective. This application imbalance is not ideal. However, this can be amended by mechanizing this process so that the appropriate amount of release agent is applied every time.

B. Blade Exchange and Machining Center
There is much room for improvement when it comes to blade exchange due to wear–out, especially for tools that wear out fast, such as parting tools.

A few years ago, I had a chance to tour plants in Europe and the United States, as part of a delegation to study automation and labor saving methods for machine tools. I was told at that time that the most innovative advancement was "machining centers" which could replace blades automatically. In fact, at **Cincinnati Milacron Inc.**, in the United States, I saw a machine that had 36 blades of a single type. When one wore out, the following blade took over and continued processing. I was very impressed. However, I soon realized that I had already seen some machining–center type tools in Japan. They were turret lathes that held multiple bits. Although those in Japan held different types of blades, it occurred to me if they could hold multiple bits, they could just as well all be the same type.

Figure 4.87 Machine with Multiple Cutoff Tools

This realization led to improvements at several factories. At the first factory there was a machine that used a parting tool. I made a circular tool holder that could hold four parting tools at once and installed it in the machine. It successfully quadrupled the machine's pre–automated running time without blade change. At another factory, I made multiple cuts into a circular blade and changed it into a machining–center type fluting blade. This made it possible for the machine which

Figure 4.88 Machine Fluted Blade

used this blade to run for a month without a blade change. Lastly, the idea of machining centers was taken further at T factory. At this factory, a limit switch used to control a machine's tool movement sometimes malfunctioned. Therefore, an additional limit switch was installed. This improvement extended the machine's pre–automated running time significantly.

In any case, these machine–center improvements can be used very effectively for blades and other tools that wear out after a certain amount of use.

C. Clearing Cutting Scraps and Cleaning

When implementing pre–automation, clearing and cleaning cutting scraps and other deposits often pose a major challenge. In order to remove cutting scraps mechanically, the following strategies may come in handy:

Use covers for bit holders to prevent cutting scraps from accumulating.

In addition to cutting oil, shoot pressurized oil to remove or control the direction of cutting scraps.

Use sheathes to remove cutting scraps that cling to drill bits.

Figure 4.89 Pressurized Scrap Removal

Use pressurized oil to remove cutting scraps as they fall (Figure 4.89).

In case of rotor cutting, place a vacuum pipe right underneath the cutting surface to immediately remove cutting scraps from the machine (Figure 4.90).

Figure 4.90 Vacuum Scrap Removal

At one factory, cutting scraps from a press machine were blown away by air. However, with this method, scraps spread everywhere. They sometimes landed on top of dies and caused problems. The factory placed a powerful magnet at the tip of an oscillating bar inside the machine so that scraps would adhere to it. When the bar moved to a certain position, scraps were scraped off into a chute and collected in a box. This improvement completely prevented the scraps from spreading.

Figure 4.91 Magnetic Scrap Removal

Large–Scale Machine Feeding and Product Holding
Since pre–automated machines run without operators, large–scale machine feeding and product holding become important issues.

A. Large–Scale Machine Feeding Hopper Method
In case of plastic molding machines, install a large–scale material storage tank by a machine, and place a limit switch within a hopper that is part of the machine. When the amount of material within the hopper hits the lower limit, the limit switch is activated and triggers the material to flow in from the tank. Likewise, when the material within the hopper hits the higher limit, the limit switch stops the flow in from the tank.

Welding and Rewinding Method
At one factory, workers welded 10 spools of material for a press machine into one spool, annealed the joints, smoothed them with a grinder, and rewound the material into a large–scale spool. Due to this modification, the machine's pre–automated run time was extended from two hours to 24 hours.

When welding the ends of spooled material together this way, there is one problem that needs to be addressed — as the material unreels, the joints need to be separated somehow from the other parts. At this particular company, workers marked the joints with permanent markers and detected them using a built–in reflective optoelectronic sensor. Upon detection, jointed parts were shunted into an alternate collection location for defects. This method worked remarkably well and led to a 24–hour unattended operation.

Welding Method (Without Rewinding)
When welding the ends of spooled material, it is also possible to use the material without unwinding and rewinding it into a bigger spool. For example, if the end of material A1 and the

beginning of A2 are welded and then rotated in the same axis, when A1 ends, A2 starts automatically.

Initial Setting Method

Welding spooled material is useful when the material width is narrow, but not when it is wide. If it is wide, devices for initial material setting need to be developed. The following are the basic steps of the initial setting:

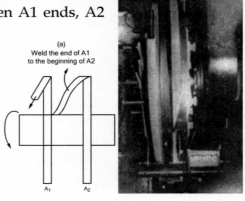

(a)
Weld the end of A1
to the beginning of A2

A₁   A₂

Figure 4.92 Connecting Spooled Materials

- As a part of external setup, cut the beginning of one material properly and deburr it
- A holder grabs this material and positions it close to the machine
- Once the end of the previous material goes into the die, a limit switch detects it and brings the following material to the feeding position
- The holder moves one pitch at a time and sends the material into the die
- The dies should have a guide inside so that the beginning of incoming material does not get stuck
- Once the material is set to the proper position inside the die, the holder is released and goes back to its original position
- Mechanically insert consecutive material into holder

Many factories have already developed initial setting devices like these and are now making efforts to improve them. As for materials that are separated beforehand, each material can be stored in a turn–table style holder, and fed into the same type of initial setting device one at a time. Although it is best to realize automated large–scale machine feeding, if it is not possible,

344

workers can still manually feed the materials.

B. Large Scale Product Holding

When holding finished products, there are cases where the products can be randomized and cases where they have to be lined up appropriately. The former is relatively easy, but the later usually requires a complicated placing mechanism. "Stepping relays" are one of the most effective devices to place each product while changing the position one pitch at a time. Even in case of random holding, improvement can always be made.

Large Box Method

Use a conveyor and move finished products from the machine into a large box.

Roller Conveyor Method

Place multiple empty boxes on a roller conveyor next to a machine. When one box is filled a timer or counter releases it and another empty box comes in. When only box is left, a limit switch activates a buzzer and notifies the workers. If all the empty boxes are used, the limit switch shuts down the machine.

Figure 4.93 Conveyor Style Storage

Merry Go–Round Method

Use a device that can hold and rotate empty boxes like a merry go–round and fill the boxes one by one.

Figure 4.94 Merry Go–Round Style Storage

Parking Tower Method

Make two towers where boxes are held. Finished products are put into the lowest box on the left tower. When filled, it moves to the lowest position of the right tower. On the left tower, the following box comes down. On the right box, the boxes rise by one level, making space for the next.

Figure 4.95 Parking Tower Style Storage

V Shaped Flow Rack Method

Prepare a flow rack that has a sideways V shape (Figure 4.96). Empty boxes slide down to the tip of the V, products are put in, and the filled box is sent to the lower rack.

Figure 4.96 V Shaped Flow Rack

Guide Pole Method

This is an example of one factory which used this guide pole method. At the factory, 15 guide poles were installed at the last process of a transfer press. Car headlight components, which were made with the press, were loaded onto the poles. When one pole was filled to the top, the next pole came to receive the products. When all 15 became full, the next set of 15 poles took their place. This method enabled the machine to run continuously.

Figure 4.97 Guide Pole Type

Pallet Exchange Method

At a factory that made auto parts, the following pallet exchange method was implemented for a press machine. When a pallet placed by a machine was filled with products, a counter detected it, and a light notified the worker. The pallet was then pushed to the side mechanically and an empty one took its place. The filled box was taken

Figure 4.98 Pallet Changeover Type

away to a storage area by a forklift. In the past, when there was no counter or notification light, the forklift operator had to constantly check the amount of products on the pallets. Different methods of large–scale holding have been discussed so far, and there are still many other ways. Appropriate methods should be decided based on the style of production.

4.2.4 Individual Production and Pre–Automation

Pre–automation is usually used for mass production. However, the basic ideas of pre–automation can also be applied for individual production.

A. Shaper Pre–Automation

Figure 4.99 Pre–Automated Shaper

Figure 4.100 Limit Switch Material Feeder

An electronics company used a shaper to make press dies and jigs. The company pre–automated this operation successfully by creating a device that allowed workers to program up to five cuts of varying sizes (2.0mm, 1.5mm, 1.0mm, 0.5mm). For example, the device could be programmed as follows: two 2.0mm cuts, one 1.5mm cut, one 0.5mm cut. A built–in limit switch detected the

movement of work pieces and the machine performed the programmed operations, including cutting and moving work pieces all by itself. When the programmed operations finished, the machine alerted the worker. After this pre–automation was introduced, all the worker needed to do was to program the device.

Figure 4.101 Feed Direction Switch

Figure 4.102 Automatic Feeder

B. Face Lathe Pre–Automation (Figure 4.103)

At Factory G, there was an operation of cutting the surface of a large material type using a face lathe. Each cutting took about 40 minutes, and once it started it needed to be finished since stopping would make the surface rougher. Therefore, if the workers had 30 minutes before lunch, for example, they could

not start the operation, so the remaining time ended up being wasted. The factory installed a limit switch in the lathe so that it would come to a stop when it should by itself. After the switch was installed the workers could start the machine even when they had less than 40 minutes.

Figure 4.103 Pre–Automation Face Lather

This improved the machine operation rate by nearly 10 percent.

C. Rolling Machine Pre-Automation

At one factory, there was an operation for grinding material before it was put in a rolling machine. Because grinding took two to four hours, the factory installed limit switches so that feeding and grinding would be done mechanically. After this improvement the operation could be done during lunch time or after regular work hours, resulting in a 50 percent rise in machine operation rate.

D. Pre-Automation of Planers and Other Machines

Planers and milling machines have also been successfully pre-automated at multiple factories. The challenge of pre-automating machine tools is that multiple aspects need to be done mechanically — the moving of work pieces, and the moving blades. Using air rotors is a great way to realize this with little cost.

Figure 4.104 Pre-Automated Planer

E. Variables and Invariables

Contrary to the widespread belief that pre-automation is a concept limited to mass production, many factories actually use it for individual production. They do it by differentiating variables between invariables.

Even if a machine is used for individual production, there are always variable and invariable aspects of operation. For example, cutting, moving, changing orientation, and stopping work pieces are all things that are invariable. On the other hand, cutting dimensions and cycle count can vary from product to product. By pre-automating invariables and simplifying the steps required to accommodate variables, pre–automation can be applied to individual production as well.

4.2.5 Obstacles for Pre–Automation

There are many issues that arise when implementing pre–automation.

A. Machine Lunch Break

When I visited Company F, a production chief who showed me around told me a number of times that many of their machines are pre–automated. Toward the end of the factory tour, I asked him, "Do these machines work during the lunch break?"

He said, "Ah… no, they don't," as if he was wondering why I asked such a question.

I continued, "If these machines are really pre–automated, they can keep working even if the operators are away. "

"Hmm, you have a point there," he agreed. Like many other companies, this company stopped the machines while the worker was away, and did not even question it. When I talk with people who have this type of mind-set, I sometimes tease them by asking, "Do your machines go to lunch along with your workers?"

When I visited F. M. Company in the United States, I had a chance to discuss pre–automation with some people. I asked a production chief, "Are there pre–automated machines here?"

He said, "Of course, many of these machines are pre–automated."

I asked, "Do they work during the lunch break?"

"What do you mean?"

"At companies I consult for in Japan, machines keep working as long as they are oiled, even when the workers are off to lunch."

"I see. Well, it seems like all the machines at our factory go out to eat hamburgers then, " he said, triggering laughter from everyone. It turned out the phenomena of machines going out to lunch was not unique to Japan. At factories that have truly translated pre–automation into reality, machines keep working even when people are away at lunch. I believe it is not against labor laws to do so.

B. Monitoring is Nonsense

I often hear managers say, "We still need the same number of workers even though we have 'automated' machines." At K factory, its department chief told me that one worker is in charge of five "automated" machines. So I asked, "Why do you need people attending 'automated' machines?"

He said, "Well, we need people just in case."

"What kind of case to be exact?"

"In case the machines breakdown or defective products are created," he answered.

I said, "If that's the case, it's nonsense to make people attend the machines. Since each person has five machines to look after, only sample–type monitoring is possible. And the chance of machine breakdowns and defective products starting the moment the workers happen to come by is very slim.

If a touch switch is installed to detect feeding problems, for example, 100 percent monitoring can be done fairly easily. Indeed, using people for monitoring often makes little sense."

C. "Since It's an Expensive Machine…"

At one factory I visited there was a high–speed press used to punch out motor cores. When I suggested to the managers to keep running the machine during lunch break, they all showed reservations.

A group leader said, "It's an expensive high–speed machine and we can't afford to let it break down. Someone has to be there all the time." A section chief said, "I agree, I don't think we should run it unattended."

I asked, "I understand that the machine is expensive and it seems better to have someone attending it. But the machine is running so fast, is it even possible for a person to stop it the moment a feeding mistake happens, so the die won't break?"

The section chief said, "When you put it that way, I doubt if it's possible."

So I told them that it is more logical to use a touch switch, for example, so that the machine can be stopped immediately after abnormalities are detected. They were quickly convinced.

While the idea of having a person attending machines is re-assuring, we need to realize that there are other, more reliable options available.

D. Gate Problem on a Plastic Molding Machine

At D Plastic Company, the workers were tending a plastic mold-ing machine during the lunch break. I told a section chief that the machine did not need to be attended at all. The section chief was not sold on this idea and decided to monitor the machine himself during one lunch break.

The machine was designed so that it would not mold a product unless the previous product went down the chute, pushed a gate, and left the machine. When the previous product was stuck somewhere, the machine shut down.

Soon after the section chief came to the machine, it stopped. When he checked the die, the product was not there. Then he noticed that the product was simply unable to open the gate with its force and was stuck there. He opened the gate and

Figure 4.105 Plastic Molding Machine Gate

the machine resumed running normally. After a while, however, the machine stopped again for the same reason. It turned out that by the end of the lunch break, this abnormality happened ten times.

He later asked the operators about this problem. One worker shrugged and said, "It's normal. I just open the gate every time it happens."

After some research the cause became clear: the gate was too heavy and its hinges too stiff. As it turned out other machines were having the same issue and operators were dealing with it the same way. After these issues were solved, this problem never happened again.

When small problems occur that can be easily remedied by worker intervention, they can sometimes linger indefinitely while the manager remains unaware. Removing workers from the equation not only helps elucidate these issues, but brings production closer to realizing pre–automation.

E. Unspoken Problems

Here is another example of a small problem being brushed under the rug on the shop floor. At one factory, there was a machine that inserted parts such as resisters, onto printed circuit boards. I suggested to the managers to run the machine unattended and they decided to give it a try.

When unattended operation started, however, it only lasted for 15 minutes. It turned out that there were some resisters whose legs were longer than usual, causing them to stick in the machine.

I talked with the machine's operator and asked if it was a recurring problem.

Figure 4.106 Printed Circuit Board

He said, "Yes, it happens all the time."

"How do you deal with it?"

"If you tap the machine guide with a hammer, things start flowing again."

I wondered why the resister leg length varied in the first place and looked into it. The problem lay in a blade that cut the legs; it was attached loosely. After fixing this, the same problem never occurred again. The company also carried out more than 20 little improvements such as enhancing the shape of the cutter and the guide pin, and succeeded in running the machine unattended throughout the lunch break.

As in the previous example, when machine operators can circumvent problems relatively easily, the problems tend to remain on the shop floor and not reach managers. If those in management pay closer attention to the shop floor and implement necessary improvements, these hidden problems will disappear much faster.

F. Rotor Short Circuit

There was an operation of heating up rotors with gas, inserting a shaft inside, and submerging them under water to anneal. Rotors are made up of layers of thin silicon–steel sheets, and the water between the layers was supposed to evaporate. However, it sometimes remained and caused short circuits during later product testing. This phenomenon did not happen if the cooling water temperature was high. But if it was too high, annealing ended up being insufficient. The water temperature demanded precision and the worker in charge was required to check it every 30 minutes.

The company decided to pre–automate this annealing process. And along with its decision came a device that could check and control the water temperature at all times. After this device was installed, the short–circuit problem never happened again.

This problem was a direct result of using a sampling–style inspection to control the water temperature. When pre–automation was implemented with the new device, and a 100 percent inspection evolved, water temperature variation was finally controlled successfully.

G. Distrusting Stage

At Company M, I suggested that management should try out pre–automation and the company agreed. Soon after pre–automation started, however, its labor union expressed its opposition to the new system, "Even if the machines do not need to be attended, workers still worry about them and end up going to the shop floor repeatedly during their lunch breaks to check the machines. They cannot rest properly as long as pre–automation is in place."

The company decided to place section managers on the floor during the lunch break for one week, so that workers could relax without worrying.

A month later, I visited the company and happened to see the workers taking a lunch break. I asked one of them, "What are the machines doing now?" He replied, "The machine should be running by itself."

The initial distrust felt by the workers toward unattended machine operations is one of the issues managers should expect to face when implementing pre–automation. Although workers might not trust pre–automation at first and worry about their machines, they will eventually be won over.

H. Perfection is Not Required

A stereo factory decided to try unattended operation of a machine called an inserter, which inserted parts such as resisters onto printed circuit boards. Through various improvements, the factory succeeded in extending the unattended operation time from 15 minutes to 50 minutes. However, the factory manager told me that it could never go beyond that point.

I went to the shop floor and learned that the most frequent

cause of machine stoppage was resister insertion failure. When the machine inserted resisters onto the circuit boards, they sometimes did not fit properly due to imprecise machine movement or defective resister legs. It seemed these two problems were causing the machine to stop.

I said to the manager, "The insertion mistakes are isolated defects, not continuous defects, and the machine's imprecise movement does not cause breakage. Therefore, even if insertion mistake happens, it's best to just let the machine remember it electronically and continue operation. When the board with the problem is finished, it can be set aside separately. Once this system is in place, the machine can continue running even if the insertion mistakes happen—defective products can be fixed later."

The manager said, "We can do that with a simple change on the electronic circuit."

The difference between true and pre–automation is that in automation, machines detect abnormalities and fix them; in pre–automation, machines detect abnormalities, but people fix them. Yet, both are similar in that in both cases, abnormalities are accepted.

People sometimes think that they can start pre–automation only if the machines can keep running indefinitely without producing any abnormalities. This is a bit unrealistic. The truth is, continuing to run machines despite small amounts of abnormalities is acceptable. Pre–automation does not require perfection.

I. "Since Someone is There…"
A spring factory implemented pre–automation upon my advice. About three months after the implementation, Mr. H who was in charge of die maintenance said to me, "Mr. Shingo, in the past I used to hand over dies even if I thought their maintenance was imperfect, because I was too busy. However, those dies often caused problems which I had to fix, which left me even less time to maintain other dies, which in turn, caused even more prob-

lems. It was a vicious circle.

"However, after pre–automation started and the machines started running around the clock unattended, I felt like mistakes could no longer be tolerated and started making sure the all the dies were maintained perfectly. As a result, the number of die problems dropped, which correspondingly gave me more time to maintain other dies. It was a virtuous circle.

"Before starting pre–automation, devices to detect abnormalities were installed. Of course, these devices helped prevent major breakage, but the most beneficial thing of all was the change in my attitude. Prior to pre–automation I was less thorough with the dies because of my over dependence on workers being there to field a problem if and when it occurred. Now that's all changed.

"My wife is happier now, too. There aren't any more phone calls waking us up in the middle of the night because of a die breakdown."

People are often hesitant about switching to pre–automation due to over dependence on people taking care of the machines if problems occur. Yet, by adjusting their mind–set, many times these problems can be prevented from happening in the first place.

4.2.6 Steps of Pre–Automation Implementation

Pre–automation can be initiated beginning with the following three time periods:

1. Lunch break.

2. A few hours after the regular work hours.

3. From the end of regular work hours until the following morning.

1. Implementing Pre–Automation During Lunch Break

When pre–automating for the first time, it is usually best, for a number of reasons, to start during lunch break.

- Workers can take immediate action against the occurrence of abnormalities
- Workers can confirm the proper working order of abnormality detection devices and make necessary improvements
- The added functionality of turning on and off the main power switch, air compressor, and lubrication system is not required
- In general, special equipment to feed machines and hold products on a large scale is not required

Although initiating pre–automation during the lunch break is relatively easy for these reasons, its benefit is not small. In general, lunch breaks are an hour long. Assuming that there are eight working hours in a regular day, running machines just during lunch break can lead to 12.5 percent increase in production volume (1 hour/eight hours=12.5 percent). In a year, this is equivalent to a production increase of one and a half months.

2. Implementing Pre–Automation for a Few Hours after Regular Work Hours

If pre–automation during lunch break is successful, the next step should be to try it for a few hours after regular work hours. Feeding machines and holding a few extra hours of finished products is not much of a challenge. However, ways to automatically turn off the main power switch, air compressor, and lubrication system need to be developed.

Using pre–automation during lunch and two hours after work will lead to 37.5 percent increase in production. In a year, this is equivalent to a production increase of five months.

3. Implementing Pre–Automation from the End of Regular Work Hours till the Following Morning

After pre–automation is used successfully during lunch break and a few hours after the end of regular work hours, the next step is to try it from the end of regular work hours until the following morning. However, before advancing to this stage the following conditions need to be satisfied:

- Occurrence of abnormalities is reduced to minimum
- Devices to detect abnormalities reliably have been developed
- Ways to automatically turn off the main power switch, air compressor, and lubrication system have been developed
- Devices to conduct large–scale machine feeding and product holding have been installed

If a complete transition to this stage poses a challenge, it can be buffered by placing a small number of people on the shop floor outside of regular work hours in order to help handle material and finished products.

If pre–automation is conducted during lunch break and outside of regular work hours, production volume can be tripled. This will shorten machine depreciation periods and eliminate unpopular night shifts.

Pre–automation can be initiated gradually via these steps. When doing so, in addition to relevant technical issues, special attention should be paid to worker psychology. As mentioned before, workers often have a sense of distrust for pre–automation. Worker complaints regarding an inability to relax during lunch break is not uncommon. To dispel this uneasiness, managers need to make one thing very clear — even if troubles happen during pre–automation, workers are never to be blamed.

On the first week, managers may need to place someone from management on the shop floor during the lunch break to ease worker concern and to prove that defect detecting devices are working properly to prevent trouble. Usually, workers can be won over after running pre–automation smoothly for a month.

Another common complaint involves noise from machines during lunch time. If the lunch room is in close proximity to the shop floor and the noise interferes with their activities or relaxation, a different area may need to be provided.

Worker psychology and comfort is sometimes overlooked when implementing pre–automation. However, it is a very serious factor that needs to be taken into account.

4.2.7 Effects of Pre–Automation

Successful implementation of pre–automation has the following effects:

> Worker hours and defect rates can be reduced by more than 90 percent (pre–automation can also reduce work-hours during attended operation).
>
> Workers tend to carry out maintenance of machines and dies more thoroughly.
>
> Due to abnormality detection devices, the number of machine breakdowns — especially serious ones, drop, thus raising machine operation rates and productivity significantly.
>
> Internal costs decrease significantly.

At one iron works factory, the percentage of internal costs out of total costs dropped from 70 percent to 40 percent. This was possible because during pre–automation, labor costs and management–related costs were reduced to almost nothing. In other words, products can be manufactured for just the cost of material and power required to make them. In times when cost reduction is essential, the benefits of pre–automation do not require much explanation.

SUMMARY

Some people mix up pre–automation with multiple–machine operation. It is important to understand these concepts are different. In multiple machine operation, machines stop mechanically when they finish the main operation, such as cutting. While machines are cutting work pieces by themselves, the workers mount and dismount work pieces to and from the stopped machine. In pre–automation, however, workers do not attend the machines at all. When the machines are operating normally, they only come when there is a problem. The number of workers necessary for pre–automation is therefore dependant on the frequency of troubles and the time it takes to fix them.

The term "mechanization" is used when machines are doing what people did in the past. The difference between "pre–automation" and "mechanization" is that in pre–automation, machines also have the capacity to intervene when problems occur.

Pre–automation can produce extraordinary returns from a relatively small investment. For example, at S Iron Works, it cost 300,000 yen to pre–automate five machines; at an iron factory, 160,000 yen for a 60–ton press; and at a laundry machine factory, 140,000 yen for a shaper. These are not large investment numbers. At N chemical company, it cost only a few hundred thousand yen to pre–automate eight molding machines. The return was phenomenal; during the first month of pre–automation, stoppage occurred only one time (on one machine out of eight), due to an abnormality.

True automation means that machines need not only find abnormalities, but also to fix them. However, this is often technically difficult and financially prohibitive. For many companies, pre–automation is the most realistic and effective method of improvement.

When it comes to pre–automation, although every company will need to adapt it to their style of production, it is less a matter of finances and more a matter of will that opens the door to make improvements that reap enormous benefits.

4.2.8 Pre–Automation Examples
The following are various examples of pre–automation from three different companies.

A Electronic Company, Laundry Machine Department

1. Pre–Automation Line of Shafts

Figure 4.107 shows the pre–automated production line for shafts. All processes, including cutting and grinding, are completed unattended. The line runs by itself during lunch time and a few hours after regular work hours as well.

Figure 4.107 Pre–Automated D–Shaft Production Line

2. 100 Percent Inspection of Knurled Shafts

Figure 4.108 shows a device with a built–in electronic micrometer that inspects all the shafts following a knurling process. The external diameter of the shaft is checked by the micrometer and defective products are separated from normal products and sent down a chute.

Figure 4.108 100% Inspection of D-Shaft

3. Shaft Holding Device

Figure 4.109 shows a device that holds finished shafts, according to their diameter. It can hold a half–days worth of product, and the production line can run unattended until this device fills up.

Figure 4.109 D–Shaft Storage System

4. Spin Dryer Production Line

Figure 4.110 shows a pre–

automated production line of spin dryer bodies. Sheet metal is rolled and the seams welded to make a cylinder. Then it is fitted with a bottom, which comes from a different line, and the joint is seam welded to make a spin dryer.

Figure 4.110 Dryer Production Line

5. Spin–Dryer Bottom Production Line

Figure 4.111 shows a pre-automated production line to make the bottoms of spin dryers. Two press machines make the bottoms and the finished parts go on the conveyor that goes up on the right side of the picture. The conveyor goes on a path that connects to the line producing spin–dryer bodies.

Figure 4.111 Dryer Bottom Production Line

6. Spin–Dryer Bottom Holder

A portion of spin–dryer bottoms are held as shown in Figure 4.112. The holding device turns in synchronization with the press machines, so that the parts are stacked in consecutive piles.

Figure 4.112 Dryer Bottom Storage

7. Constant Grinding of Seam–Welding Electrodes

In Figure 4.113, a spin–dryer body and bottom are being seam welded. When the company was trying to introduce pre–automation, this seam–welding process posed a great challenge. During welding, sparks sometimes burned holes in the electrodes which then led to defective welding. Therefore, a worker needed to check the electrodes and grind them about twice a day using a hand grinder. This was a problematic hurdle for pre–automation.

Figure 4.113 Continuous Grinding

The company solved this issue by changing their approach completely. In the past, the electrodes were ground only after holes were burned on them. The new approach, however, prevented holes from developing in the first place. A small–scale grinder with a built–in air cylinder and timer ground them mechanically every 15 minutes. Workers expected this extra grinding to wear out the electrodes faster. On the contrary, the opposite became true. As it turned out burned electrodes only exacerbated the sparking that was causing the burning to occur in the first place — thus accelerating wear. Therefore, grinding immediately not only controlled defective welding, but it also greatly increased the lifespan of the electrodes. Constant grinding also proved effective for seam welding kerosene stove tanks whose zinc based material tended to stick to electrodes and cause defective welding. Constant grinding can be used for blades as well as for electrodes. By preventing blades or electrodes from becoming problematic in the first place, their performance and lifespan will improve significantly.

8. Pre–Automated Feeding

Figure 4.114 shows a pre–automated feeding mechanism for a press machine. When a photo tube senses that work pieces reach a certain height, a device pushes one piece to a roller that sends it into the machine.

Figure 4.114 Press Pre–Automation Line

9. Laudry Machine Spot Weld

In order to inspect spot welding of laundry machine bodies, welded products were randomly chosen and destructed in the past. Although this served as an inspection to a certain degree, it could never guarantee zero defects as a 100 percent inspection could. Therefore, the company decided to inspect the

Figure 4.115 Laundry Machine Spot–Weld

welding, instead of welded products, and introduced a nugget tester. The tester monitored the electrical current value during spot welding. If the value was below a predetermined level, the product was not released from the machine until additional welding happened. This prevented defective welding altogether and made destruction inspections unnecessary. This is a good example of type–s detection.

10. Machining–Center Type Blade

When trying to implement pre–automation, blade changing procedures often pose a challenge. Many insist that it must be done by workers. Company A developed a special blade holder that could change blades by itself, like a ma-

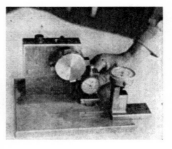

Figure 4.116 Multiple Cutter Machine

chining center. Four blades were centered and attached to the holder beforehand. When one blade wore off, the next blade took its place and continued cutting. Figure 4.116 shows a worker setting blades as part of external setup.

Electronic Company, Iron Department

1. Pre–Automated Product Holding

In order to hold finished products on a large scale, boxes were placed on a roller conveyor in front of a 60–ton press machine. Products were placed inside each box and once the number reached 5,000, the filled box was released from a stopper, sent down a roller conveyor, and the next box took

Figure 4.117 Pre–Automated Press

its place. In this way, finished products could be boxed unattended for a half a day. When boxes ran out, a limit switch detected it and alerted a worker. The worker then moved the filled boxes and placed empty boxes on the roller conveyor. The company installed other devices in addition to this product–holding mechanism, and succeeded in implementing pre–automation for just 160,000 yen.

2. Control Box

Figure 4.118 shows a control box for a 60–ton press machine. When abnormalities happened, such as missed strokes — or shortages of boxes, lubricant, or spooled material happened, a signal alerted the workers.

Figure 4.118 Control Box

3. Oil Shortage Alert Device

A box-shaped tank in Figure 4.119 holds oil which is

applied to the surface of spooled material. Since it needed to be replenished about once a day, a worker would periodically come and check the oil level. After the company installed a float inside the tank that alerted the worker when the oil level became low, the worker could then concentrate on other work.

Figure 4.119 Oil
Shortage Alert Device

4. Spooled Material Shortage Prediction Device

There was a device to alert workers when spooled material ran out. However, alerting them before it ran out was actually more desirable rather than after the fact. Therefore, the company installed a lever mechanism onto which the spooled material was attached. As the spooled material decreased, the decrease in mass cause the lever to shift, triggering an alarm and alerting the work-

Figure 4.120 Material
Prediction Device

ers. The lever was designed so that the mass required to activate it would occur five minutes before the material ran out completely. This mechanism successfully prevented the machine from stopping every time material ran out.

5. Bimetal Line Control Box

Figure 4.121 shows the control box for three machines used to process bimetal. The box could display information such as which machine had a breakdown, and in which cycle it happened. When abnormalities happened this device made it easy to address them faster and more effectively.

Figure 4.121 Bi–Metal
Production Line Controller

367

6. Bimetal Line

Figure 4.122 shows the bimetal production line composed of three machines. The line runs unattended even during lunch time and about three hours after regular work hours.

Figure 4.122 Bi–Metal Production Line

7. Welding of Spooled Material

At the bimetal production line, when one spool of material ran out, a worker used to come and initialize new material in the machines. This procedure took about 30 minutes every time. The company purchased a small welding machine that could weld, anneal, and grind the beginning and end of two spools. This made it possible to feed spools continuously and eliminated the time consuming set–up procedure. Welded joints were detected in the final process and separated mechanically to a different box.

Figure 4.123 Welding Spooled Material

Figure 4.124 Steam Iron

8. Steam Holes for Steam Irons

Each steam iron had 37 holes for steam to escape (Figure 4.124). These holes were drilled in a few different processes. However, since drill bits were small, they sometimes broke, creating products with fewer holes (Figure 4.125). Finding these defective

Figure 4.125 Broken Drills

products was a time–consuming process. In order to find abnormalities much
faster and easier, the production chief,
Mr. Ibata, came up with an innovative
device, called a "buckling system."

Within the device there was a board with
37 holes, about one centimeter in diameter. In each hole, there was a cylinder
with a length of piano wire in it. When a
drilling process finished, the piano wires
in the cylinders were pressed against
each product to check the existence of
holes. If there was a missing hole, one

Figure 4.126 Defect Detection

of the wires buckled. The buckled wire contacted the
edge of the cylinder, created an electric current, and shut
down the drilling machine. The worker was also alerted
at the same time. This system made it possible to detect
broken drill bits immediately and accurately. In addition,
installation was quite easy and reasonable. The company
applied for a utility model patent for this system.

9. Maintenance Counter (Figure 4.127)

Machine troubles often stem from
physical wear incurred by long–time
use. At the iron department, a "maintenance counter" was developed. If a
press machine had eight dies, for example, the device counted the total
number of times the press machine
itself and each die was used, and displayed the numbers on a screen. (On
the right side of Figure 4.127, there is
one display screen on top for the press
and eight screens for each die.)

Figure 4.127
Maintenance Counter

Due to this device, workers could accurately learn the lifespan of each die,

and each part of the die. This enabled workers to make necessary changes before troubles materialized. Workers also became more proactive about maintenance work after this device was installed.

Figure 4.128 Pre-Automation Line

Since the prototype proved quite effective, the department installed the device for every press machine. The counters were fabricated in-house for just 70,000 yen each.

S Iron Works

S Iron Works is a bolt manufacturer. The company succeeded in pre-automating its five machine production line. The production line ran unattended during and after regular work hours. The total cost of pre-automation was about 300,000 yen.

1. Control Box

Figure 4.129 shows a "control box" for the pre-automated production line. There is a programmable counter on the lower right of the box. If a worker set this counter to 8,000 when he left work, for example, the line shut down when it produced exactly 8,000 products. There was also a meter relay in this box. If electric current went outside of the normal range, the machine shut down.

Figure 4.129 Control Box

For example, if a push-out pin broke and a piece got struck twice in a header machine, excessive current activated the meter relay and shut down the machine. If there was a problem with a feeding mechanism, and the machine struck air continuously, the meter relay detected inefficient current and shut down the machine. On a return stroke during normal operation, the current went down, but in this case, a delay relay prevented the machine from stopping.

2. Defective Rod Cutting (Figure 4.130)

There was an operation in which rod material for bolts were cut. Before a rod was cut, it was supposed to hit a stopper within the cutter so that the length would be uniform. However, when a rod was slightly bent, or the feeding device malfunctioned, the rod was cut without hitting the stopper, resulting in short pieces, which then became defective bolts.

Figure 4.130 Defective Cutting

The company realized the lack of contact with the stopper was the origin of defects and installed a device with a limit switch at the stopper. If a rod was cut without making contact with the stopper, the device successfully separated the defective piece from other normal pieces.

3. Double Threaded Bolts (Figure 4.131,132)

The last bolt manufacturing process was thread rolling. At this company, about one in 100,000 bolts were double threaded. Double–threaded bolts do not match their counterparts and can cause breakage, making it imperative that they be found at the factory. In the past, only visual inspections were used; after bolts were threaded, workers used a visual inspection and tried to spot defective products. However, it was extremely hard to see them and, moreover, they were very rare.

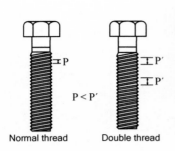

Figure 4.131 Double Thread

Figure 4.132 Thread Inspection

The company learned that the double–thread bolts had a wider pitch. Therefore, when they are being rolled, their head raised slightly higher than normal bolts. The company installed a mechanism to detect this height difference electronically. When a taller bolt was detected, the gate to a regular chute was shut, and the defective product was sent down a different chute. This mechanism worked very effectively, and made the in-efficient and unreliable visual inspection unnecessary.

4. Pre–Automated Box Change

Finished products were put into boxes as shown in Figure 4.133. In the past, when one box filled up, it needed to be replaced with an empty box immediately. Therefore, a worker used to come and check the box and the amount of bolts inside repeatedly.

Figure 4.133 Automatic Box Change

The company pre–automat-ed this procedure as follows.

First, several boxes were linked together. Second, a chain conveyor to move the boxes was installed underneath.

372

Then, a limit switch was placed at the position where bolts were filled.

When a box filled up, the limit switch sensed it and the conveyor moved the boxes so that the next box would come to take its place. When the last box moved into position, the worker was alerted. After this system was implemented, incessant checking was unnecessary. Moreover, new boxes could be set without needing to hurry. This also made it possible for the machine to run unattended after regular work hours.

SUMMARY

Do we understand the difference between mechanization and automation? If machines are truly automated, they can not only detect abnormalities, but fix them as well. However, true automation is often technically and financially unrealistic. With pre-automation, however, we get many of the extraordinary benefits associated with automation at only a fraction of the cost. Therefore, once operations are mechanized, the next step should be pre-automation.

CHAPTER FOUR SUMMARY

Operation improvements can be divided into active and passive improvements. More often than not, we are satisfied only pursuing passive improvement. For example, companies that take the idea of "economic lot" seriously, but never consider how to reduce setup time itself. The same can be said about pre-automation. We should always think about what would really lead to more fundamental forms of improvement.

V NON-STOCK PRODUCTION SYSTEM

5.1 What is Non-Stock?

The term "stock" refers to raw materials, in-process products, and finished products.

5.1.1 Is Stock a Necessary Evil?

In production management, stock has been considered a necessary evil, but perhaps with a bit too much emphasis placed on "necessary." For example, it is commonly believed that increasing the lot size, although it results in increased stock, is preferable because of the associated reduction in setup time per product, which therefore drives down production cost.

The validity of this thinking is negated, however, if setup times are reduced dramatically with SMED. With setup time no longer a factor, there is nothing "necessary" about stock at all, thus transforming it from a "necessary" evil to nothing but evil. It is this premise that the basic idea of non-stock production is based upon.

5.1.2 Numerical Stock and Schedule Stock

There are two types of stock as below:

Numerical Stock

The word "numerical stock" is used to describe the situation where more products than necessary are manufactured. For example making 1,200 products when only 1,000 are necessary. This is usually done in order to compensate for instability in production, such as those caused by defects. However, if predictions are inaccurate, excess stock becomes a problem.

Scheduling Stock

The term "scheduling stock" is used to describe the situation when the necessary number of products are created, but done so ahead of time; completing them on August 20th when the deadline is actually August 30th, for example. Even among those people who conceive numerical stock as bad, there is little acknowledgement that this scheduling stock is also bad. In fact, some believe that it is actually preferable. This misconception comes from the fact that the contrary phenomenon of schedule delays lead to missed delivery deadlines. Ideally, however, production should be done when products are needed. Therefore, products produced too early should be considered stock, and thus evil.

Of these two types of stock, scheduling stock remains the most misunderstood. It is no surprise that overcoming this challenge remains one of the biggest obstacles in achieving non-stock production.

5.2 Basic Methods to Achieve Non-Stock Production

As mentioned before, production is a network of processes (processing, inspection, transportation, delay) and operations (setup operations, principal operations, allowances). Non-stock production aims to eliminate delays and the stock that results. However, delays are merely unfortunate side effects created by an uncertainty in other aspects of production: processing, inspections, transportation, setup operations, main operations, and allowances. Therefore, delays can be successfully eliminated only by thoroughly improving all other production factors.

5.2.1 Introducing Flow Production

By synchronizing production processes and realizing one–piece flow production, stock between processes, namely process delays, can be eliminated. By implementing one-piece flow, lot delays also disappear. Furthermore, flow production can shorten the production cycle greatly, therefore making it possible to reduce the stock of materials and finished products. (See 3.4, Delay Improvement for details.)

5.2.2 Introducing SMED

With press machines and plastic molding machines, large-lot production is often chosen in order to reduce the setup time per product, thereby cutting costs. However, if setup time is reduced to less than ten minutes with SMED, or even to less than a minute with OTED, large-lot production no longer has any benefits.

5.2.3 Introducing Pre-Automation

Stock produced to compensate for unexpected machine breakdowns and product defects becomes unnecessary if abnormalities of machines and products can be detected with total inspection of pre-automation. Moreover, pre-automated factories can handle demand fluctuations much better.

5.3 The Path to Non-Stock Production
5.3.1 Speculative and Build-to-Order Production

Many companies forecast demand and conduct speculative production. However, predictions should never be mistaken for actual production needs. Indeed, forecasts of any kind are notorious for being off target, and relying on them for production can potentially result in dead stock.

Instead of trying to predict the future, production should adhere to this policy: make only what you can sell. For example, T Motor Company never holds stock. It assembles cars in two days, transports them in six days, and delivers within ten days of receiving orders. Furthermore, its factories receive dealer inventories everyday and change production plans as necessary.

Many companies do not have such close communication between factories and dealers. They assume that the cars are sold simply by handing them to dealers, only to find out at the time of settlement that there is large-scale bad stock.

It is essential to produce based on actual demand. Only if doing so is absolutely impossible, should production based on forecasts—and then only highly accurate ones— should be used.

5.3.2 Handling External Factors for Non-Stock Production
A. Seasonal Demand Fluctuation

The demand for certain products can fluctuate greatly depending on the season, such as heaters and air conditioners. To prepare for seasonal demand, companies often implement off-peak production. However, is this kind of production and the large-scale bad stock that results really necessary? The answer is no.

We should always make an effort to make our production more flexible to demand fluctuations, and thus manufacture based on existing demand, not on predictions. The following are some methods to help achieve this:

- Increasing the number of people and machines

T Industries has a two-shift system with four hours of gap between each shift. The company can handle up to 50 percent increase in demand by extending the work hours of both shifts.

- Increasing the number of people

At Y Industries, lines are run at 50 percent capacity during normal operation. If demand increases, the company can double production by adding additional temporary workers on the line.

- Increasing machine capacity

It is possible to increase just the capacity of machines by implementing pre-automation and running the machines unattended during lunch break and after regular work hours. Incidentally, this is the best method and it has proven effective at many factories.

Although producing after receiving orders is always best, in cases where products have extraordinary sales fluctuations it is acceptable to make a certain number of products beforehand, but only for the proportion of demand that is absolutely certain.

B. Short Delivery Period and Speculative Production

When making production plans, it is necessary to do so in a way that delivery deadlines can be met. However, making plans later is better because the demand forecast will be more accurate. Nevertheless, despite its negative drawbacks, when the delivery period is shorter than a factory's production cycle, speculative production is often believed to be the only useful compensatory method. Yet, irrespective of whether the delivery period can be changed or not, the production cycle can—and doing so eliminates the need for speculative production in the first place.

K Auto Body, which makes refrigerated delivery trucks, used

to consistently carry about 20 finished trucks in stock, due to a managerial problem. In the past, the production cycle was 20 days, yet orders were confirmed only a week before the delivery deadline. Hence, finished trucks were always in stock. However, the company succeeded in reducing its production cycle to five days by introducing small-lot production with flow production and SMED. Therefore, the company was able to eliminate its stock and restore profitability.

C. Two-Step Planning

Many companies make a month's worth of production planning by the 20th of the previous month. However, with this method planning towards the end of the month relies more and more on prediction. Consequently, when situations change with time, production changes have to happen frequently as a result.

Changes in production plans often create bad stock of finished products or works-in-progress. Sometimes, work pieces may even go missing. These are all side effects of premature production planning. Yet, if no future plans are drawn at all, the proper preparation of materials and allowances cannot be made. To address this issue, the following method can be used.

1. On the 20th of the month, predict as accurately as possible what and how much is going to be manufactured in the following month. However, as for "when," provide only approximate time lines. Procure materials and plan allowances based on this.

2. Divide the month into three periods (or weeks). Prior to the start of each period, determine "what," and "how much" is going to be produced "when" during that period.

How many days in advance these decisions are made (five days in this case) depends on how long the longest production cycle at the factory is. Therefore, minimizing the production cycle is highly advantageous.

Using the method above makes it possible to minimize prediction errors and corresponding changes in plans amidst production, thus stabilizing production and reducing stock.

5.3.3 Handling Internal Factors for Non-Stock Production
A. Stock between Processes
The best way to reduce stock or delays between processes is to realize one-piece flow production. This can reduce both process delays and lot delays. When implementing flow production, synchronization is essential.

The application of flow production is effective even if it is limited to one shop floor within a company. However, it becomes even more powerful if it is extended to different shop floors and work places of the company.

Flow production is effective not only in reducing stocks between processes, but also in shortening production cycles.

B. Stock for Setup Operations
If small-lot production is realized along with SMED, stock for setup operations will naturally decrease. This will also make it possible to reduce stock of materials and finished products.

C. Stock Due to Load Concentration
When load or demand concentrates and surpasses a factory's production capacity, companies usually deal with it by producing early and leveling the load. However, this will naturally drive up the amount of stock. In order to avoid this problem, the following methods are taken.

- Increasing production capacity flexibility

By increasing the flexibility of production capacity, it is possible to handle fluctuations in demand without making stock. Pre-automation is the best way to do just that.

- Divided Small-Lot Production Method

Even if there is a large-scale order once a month, it is often permissible to divide the load into three, for example, and manufacture the ordered products in three cycles. This will make it possible to level the load, thus it is called the divided small-lot production method. In order to implement this, it is better to realize SMED first.

At one washing machine factory, two models of washing machines were produced in the first and the second half of each month, respectively. However, the company made improvements and started producing each model every other day. As a result, its stock of materials and finished products diminished significantly.

- Using set production method

With this method, a set of different products are sent to the same assembly line. For example, a sink, a kitchen counter, and a cooking stove are assembled at once. Compared to the conventional method — making sinks in the first week, kitchen counters in the second week, and cooking stoves in the third week — stock of materials and finished products can be much smaller. However, when this set production method is used, in addition to OTED, poka-yoke needs to be used in order to prevent assembly mistakes.

- Using mix production method

With this method a set of different products are sent to the same assembly line as in the previous method. However, the number of products in a set varies depending on production volume, such as four of model A, two of model B, and one of model C. This can standardize load in addition to reducing stock of materials and finished products. As in the last case, OTED and poka-yoke are prerequisites of this method.

D. Compensate for Machine Breakdowns & Defective Products

If unexpected machine breakdowns or defective products arise production will stop and delivery deadlines may be missed. In order to compensate for these problems, stock between processes and stock of finished products are often made.

If pre-automation is adopted, abnormalities can be prevented from ever developing into actual breakdowns. Defective products are also minimized since they can be spotted and addressed immediately. Therefore stock created for these occasions become unnecessary.

E. Stock Due to Different Operation Hours

There are cases where different operations have different operational hours. For example, machining is done for eight hours during the day, whereas heat treatment and plating are done for 24 hours using three shifts. Another example might be, machining is done five days a week, whereas heat treatment and plating are done seven days a week. In situations like these, stock becomes unavoidable. However, if machining is synchronized with heat treatment and plating as much as possible through sophisticated pre-automation, stock will decrease significantly. As a rule, stock needs to be zero at the beginning of each day, when the latest shift ends, and at the start of all operations.

F. Meaningless Stock

When trying to introduce non-stock production systems, the first stock that needs to be expelled is "meaningless stock." Stock is often considered to function like a safety valve that compensates for production instability. However, this often leads to the misconception that more stock is better, which then leads to the creation of unnecessary stock, which ultimately leads to excess stock eventually becoming the norm.

Take a look at Figure 5.1. The top line shows cumulative incoming material weight. Running almost parallel to it is another line showing outgoing product weight. The distance between these two lines is equivalent to the daily work-in-progress stock. The daily stock weight is also shown along with the overall average stock weight, plus or minus 3σ.

Average =6,000 kg

3σ=2,500 kg

6,000 kg-2,500 kg=3,500 kg

According to statistics, stock weight equivalent to 3σ (2,500 kg, in this case), can compensate for 99.73 percent of production instability. In this case, 3,500 kg is therefore meaningless stock.

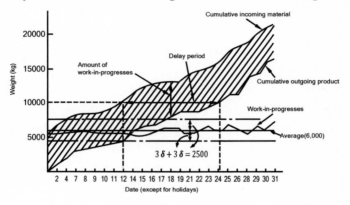

Figure 5.1 Flow Curve & 3 Sigma

Meaningless stock needs to be eliminated and can be done using measures as follows:

Minimize allowances in production time lines.

Ensure there are no products lining up on conveyors that are not being worked on. Some factories consider these products as "being assembled," when really they should be considered as stock.

Parts manufacturing should make what the assembly lines need, when it is needed, and in the amount needed. Therefore, monthly production schedules should only be given to assembly lines and they should make production orders to parts manufacturing as necessary.

Minimize transportation lot.

In addition to these measures we should know that planning and arranging things too early is always something to be cautious about.

5.4 Shift to Non-Stock Production

Using the following methods will assist in shifting to a non-stock production system.

5.4.1 Stock Compression Method

If no measures are taken stock will remain as is. When shifting to non-stock production, it is necessary to compress existing stock, which can be done using the following methods:

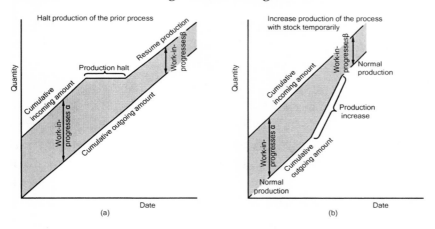

Figure 5.2 Stock Compression

Temporarily halt production of the process immediately prior to the one with excess stock. While production is halted, workers can do machine maintenance, fix products if necessary, or help the subsequent process.

Temporarily increase production of the process with stock. Regardless of the demand, increase production in order to consume the existing stock. It is possible to outsource this process while stock is being reduced in-house. It is necessary to have ways to handle this temporary increase in production.

It should be noted that reducing stock does not mean reducing sales. It is more akin to trimming off excess fat.

5.4.2 Cushion Stock Method

Stock is often created in order to compensate for production instability. It is similar to money in a savings account in that it should be withdrawn only when it is necessary. However, this is what happens at many factories: deposit all the income into a savings account and withdraw living expense every day from it. This makes it hard to know how much is in the account and how much really needs to be withdrawn. In cases like this, the "cushion stock method," explained below, should be used:

- Disconnect existing stock from the flow of production
- Conduct normal production without using the stock
- Only in case of problems, use the stock

This method has three advantages. First, this makes it possible to clarify how much stock is really necessary, thereby eliminating excess stock. Second, it clarifies why the stock is used, which expedites necessary improvements. Thirdly, these improvements ease delivery deadline concerns caused by the shift to non-stock production. Because of these advantages, the cushion stock method is the safest way to shift to non-stock production.

When this method is used the upper and lower limits of cushion stock need to be established. When stock reaches the lower limit it should be replenished. Also, in order to prevent the stock from being too old or obsolete, it needs to be replaced if necessary.

5.4.3 Stock Control and Order Point System

An Order Point System is one way to control stock. Using this system helps determine when orders should be placed to replenish stock. Calculations are done as follows:

Daily consumption amount: @

Delivery period: D (Period between order and delivery)

Minimum stock: a (the minimum amount of stock to compensate for daily consumption and delivery period instability)

Order Point = @ x D + a

Orders are made when stock drops down to the order point. Minimum stock, which is an important factor in determining the order point, can be reduced by addressing instability of production.

The amount of order (Q) is determined by each assembly line. If it is large, inventory will grow; if it is small, orders need to be made more frequently. Q is also affected by setup times and delivery periods. If they are short, Q can be smaller.

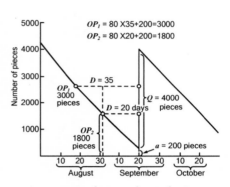

Figure 5.3 Stock Control & Order Point System

Lastly, it should be noted that this Order Point System is used for repeated production, and is not suitable for individual production.

5.4.4 Relation to the Kanban System

Kanban means "tag" or "ticket." The Kanban system, T Motor Co.'s unique production control method, plays an important role in the company's production system, and works as follows:

- Carry out "Just-In-Time" production which means only make what is needed, when it is needed, and only in the amount needed
- When a process uses parts retrieved from a preceding process, it uses a Kanban to communicate what parts have been used
- Based on the Kanban, the preceding process makes just what is needed, when it is needed, and in the amount needed

The Kanban system is well known and has many advantages.

However, simply introducing the Kanban system will not decrease stock. Indeed, having too many Kanban could actually increase stock. Regardless, meaningless stock should decrease by introducing the system, if only because workers become more conscious about stock in general.

In order to decrease inventory more thoroughly, a non-stock production system, which runs on minimum stock, has to be established first. Only after that should an appropriate Kanban system come into play to maintain it.

The number of Kanban necessary can be determined using the concept of the Order Point System as follows:

(Amount of order + Minimum inventory)/Number of items in each pallet

In this sense, the Kanban can be considered as a type of Order Point System.

Although the Kanban system is sometimes over emphasized, it does have the following important advantages:

- It allows visualized control of production
- Changes in assembly processes can be communicated to prior processes easier, faster, and more accurately
- It simplifies clerical work
- Finding bottle-neck processes and making appropriate improvements are simplified

It should be noted that the explanation of the Kanban system here is only superficial, and that a complete application of this system can be quite broad. At T Motor Co., the Kanban system is used ubiquitously in order to control and improve all aspects of its production.

5.5 Benefits of Non-Stock Production

The following are benefits of non-stock production systems:

Stock will decrease significantly. This in turn leads to other benefits: elimination of bad stock, decrease in regular stock, reduction in interest payments, better funding turnover, reduction of inventory space, reduction of processing time, and efficient inventory control.

Significant reduction in production cycles can be realized. This makes handling orders with short delivery periods easier. SMED will contribute largely toward this end.

Bottle-neck processes will be clarified, making it easier to improve these processes and, ultimately, overall production efficiency.

CHAPTER FIVE SUMMARY

Non-stock production's foundational principal is that stock is evil. However, superficial reductions will not be successful. Stock reduction has to come from solving the fundamental issues causing stock to exist in the first place.

A non-stock production system can only be established by thoroughly improving all aspects of processes and operations, and is realized as the culmination of these fundamental improvements.

Final Notes

Sometimes we view things as conclusive when, in actuality, we have only scratched the surface. In order to successfully solve problems, we must explore every layer of a problem, continually seeking out answers in quantitative detail.

Although all phenomena in the world are governed by causal relationships, the phenomena we actually perceive are only the effects of these relationships and not necessarily definitive of the relationship itself. In other words, causality is often not apparent, excepting the coherency forged through intellectual scrutiny. Therefore, in order to grasp a problem's true nature, we must be relentlessly inquisitive, a mental state that can be easily sustained simply by asking the question, "Why?"

Things that we know happened or will happen based on our experience, are called facts. Systemized facts are called science. While knowing individual facts may not be very effective, a systematic knowledge of these facts can be a very effective means of elucidating the true nature of problems.

Production improvements should be fundamental and ubiquitous. Doing so requires not only choosing active over passive improvement, but also a lucid understanding of the structure of production. Indeed, improving only fragments of production could be harmful rather than beneficial in the long run.

When making technical improvements, it is extremely important to be revolutionary in our thinking.

In plastic molding, burrs on molded products often pose problems. In many cases, people might start by thinking about better ways of removing burrs. Some may go one step further and consider why burrs are created, perhaps reaching the conclusion that they are caused by air in the molds and that this air should somehow be reduced. The best option is actually to create a vacuum in the molds. Yet, to ever reach such a conclusion requires a willingness to not just remove burrs, but completely deviate from the current production method, a truly revolutionary leap indeed.

Even though mechanization has made inspections seemingly more efficient, as long as they are segregation inspections — which simply separates defective products from others — defect rates will not decrease. However, the purpose of inspections should be to eliminate defects, not just decrease them, let alone just to separate them. The best inspection style should always be chosen with this in mind.

In order to completely eliminate defects, inspections must be 100 percent. Those who believe in sampling inspections may find it difficult to even consider adopting total inspections. However, if they can break out of their thinking and realize that sampling inspections can never assure quality, even the most blindly adherent people can think of many ideas for creating efficient total inspections.

Transportation is a crime—those who lack this conviction tend to be satisfied by reducing transportation through passive measures such as forklifts. However, the best option is to improve production layout to eliminate transportation altogether.

Mastering the relationship between D (delivery period) and P (production cycle) is the biggest challenge in daily production management. Maintaining the misconception that the production cycle is equivalent to processing time stymies efforts to reduce the production cycle, often leading to the implementation of less than ideal means to meet deadlines, like using speculative production and creating work-in-process.

In truth, it is delays that make up the majority of production. As such, the production cycle can be reduced by 90 percent through reductions in process and lot delays. Realizing this important aspect helps focus improvement efforts in a way that effectively eliminates issues between D and P.

99 percent of people are incredulous when they are first told that setup times can be reduced by 95 percent. However, drastic reduction is not difficult as long as the difference between internal and external setup is understood and that all aspects of adjustment are eliminated from internal setup.

When I visited Ford Company in the United States, I told the company executives about SMED.

"Toyota Motors in Japan, which originally introduced technologies from your company, now performs setup procedures in less than nine minutes. The same setup procedures take seven hours here."

"That's impossible. You have to do a trial shot. After that, there's a tremendous amount of fine tuning necessary," said one of the executives.

"If you conduct highly precise setups externally using jigs, adjustments are not necessary," I said. However, the executives were not convinced. I left the company saying that they should come see it with their own eyes. Later in the year, the executives from Ford Company came to Japan and saw Toyota's SMED system firsthand. They were finally convinced that it was real and something they should consider seriously. This experience really punctuated that changing one's mind-set is indeed the most important prerequisite of any improvements.

I often meet company executives who tell me, "We still have the same number of workers after introducing automation." After asking them why they need workers on the shop floor, they often say that the machines still need workers to function properly. Furthermore, it is assuring to have workers present in case of machine breakdowns. Experiences like these are a poignant reminder that improvement efforts can easily be undermined by failing to maintain an active focus on underlying sources of problems.

One of the most overlooked issues in factory improvement, including setup operations, is stock. Though considered as a "necessary evil" for a long time, the idea that stock should be eliminated completely has been gaining momentum on factory floors in recent years.

When eliminating stock, it is wrong to simply try to remove visible stock superficially. Doing so may cause problems such as missed delivery deadlines and lower operation rates. Stock will only disappear by addressing the fundamental issues creating it in the first place. This is the basic concept non-stock production is built on. Non-stock production can only be realized after fundamental improvements are made in all aspects of processes and operations.

Successful improvement is always edifying, yet it needs to be continuous. Therefore, it is important to not become overly satisfied with what we have achieved. Tomorrow the bar will be raised again, and lest we want our gains forfeited, we can not afford to become complacent. Instead we must use the momentum from our improvement successes to continue to propel the advancement of our production. Only through relentless, fundamental and inquisitive thinking will we ensure this comes to pass.

In 1937, I took a two-month-long training course in industrial engineering, sponsored by the Japan Industrial Association. It marked the beginning of my life-time pursuit of factory improvement. Incidentally, that year also marked the beginning of my marriage.

I would like to dedicate this book, a culmination of my 40 years of firsthand factory-improvement experience and ideas, to my wife, for all her support over the years.

LIST OF FIGURES

List of Tables

Index

E

F

G

H

M

Machine Tools 271, 321, 349

Machine Troubles 330

Marker Check 51

Matching Wood Grain 3

Material Yield 283, 304

Matsushita Electric 263

Mechanization 319, 323, 361

Mix Production Method 318, 382

Multiple–Line–Changeover Method 277

N

N–Line 218

Non–Stock Production 96, 375–381, 383–389, 392

Benefits of 388

Numerical stock 376

O

One–Piece Flow Production 10, 196–203, 207–211, 214–222, 227, 232–234, 377

Merits and Demerits of 209, 219

Operational Allowances 117, 119, 200, 321

Operation Functions 115

Operation Rate 96, 113, 204, 220

and Division of Labor 22

Order Point System 386–388

OTED 304–308, 318, 377, 382

Outgoing Fluctuation 103, 104

Outlet Pipe 128

Overall Improvement 17

P

U

Ultimate Purpose of Production 30–32, 206

Unbalanced Process–Operation 15

Underground Sorting 30

Unnecessary Process Delay 97, 99

V

Vacuum Molding 124–130

    Parental Die 132

    Push-out Pin 133

    Side Core 133

Value Engineering 29, 30, 123, 138

Variables 203, 349

Vertical Source Inspection 65

W

Weidmann Plastics Technology 245

Workplace Allowances 117, 119, 321

Work Sampling 120

Publications from Enna and PCS Inc.

Enna and PCS Inc. provide companies with publications that help achieve operational excellence. Enna and PCS Inc. support your efforts to internalize process improvement allowing you to reach your vision and mission. These materials are proven to work in industry. Call toll-free (866) 249-7348 or visit us on the web at www.enna.com to order or request our free product catalog.

Kaizen and the Art of Creative Thinking

Read the book that New York Times Best Selling author of *The Toyota Way*, Jeffrey Liker says, "will help you understand the deep thinking that underlies the real practice of TPS." Dr. Shigeo Shingo's Scientific Thinking Mechanism is the framework from which Toyota and hundreds of other companies have utilized to manage creative problem solving.

ISBN 978-1-897363-59-1 | 2007 | $59.40 | Item: 909

The Idea Generator, Quick and Easy Kaizen

The book discusses the Kaizen mind set that enables a company to utilize its resources of the fullest by directly involving all of its manpower in the enhancement and improvement of the productivity of its operations. Published and co-written by Norman Bodek, the Godfather of Lean.

ISBN 978-0-971243-69-9 | 2001 | $47.52 | Item: 902

The Toyota Mindset

From the brilliant mind of a legend in the LEAN manufacturing world comes the reasoning behind the importance of using your intellect, challenging your workers and why continuous improvement is so important. For anyone who wishes to gain insight into how the Toyota Production System came to be or wants to know more about the person behind TPS this book is a must read!

ISBN 978-1-926537-11-5 | 2009 | $34.99 | Item: 920

Mistaken Kanbans

Let Mistaken Kanbans be your roadmap to guide you through the steps necessary to implement and successful Kanban System. This book will help you to not only understand the complexities of a Kanban System but gives you the tools necessary, and the guidance through real-life lessons learned, to avoid disastrous consequences related to the improper use of such systems.

ISBN 978-1-926537-10-8 | 2009 | $27.99 | Item: 919

The Toyota Way in Sales and Marketing

Many companies today are trying to implement the ideas and principles of Lean into non-traditional environments, such as service centers, sales organizations and transactional environments. In this book Mr. Ishizaka provides insight on how to apply Lean operational principles and Kaizen to these dynamic and complicated environments.

ISBN 978-1-926537-08-5 | 2009 | $28.99 | Item: 918

JIT is Flow

Hirano's *5 Pillars of the Visual Workplace* and *JIT Implementation Manual* were classics. They contained detailed descriptions of techniques and clear instructions. This book highlights the depth of the thought process behind Hirano's work. The clarity which Hirano brings to JIT/Lean and the delineation of the principles involved will be invaluable to every leader and manager aiming for business excellence.

ISBN 978-0-971243-61-3 | 2007 | $47.52 | Item: 903

Kaikaku, The Power and Magic of Lean

Kai ka ku are Japanese characters meaning a 'transformation of the mind.' Norman Bodek brings his vast cross-cultural experience in Japanese manufacturing systems to American industry and creates proven results. With his first-hand knowledge of Lean Manufacturing origins, Norman Bodek chronicles his introduction to Lean in an easy to read, conversational style text.

ISBN 978-0-971243-66-8 | 2006 | $47.52 | Item: 901

Phone: (866) 249-7348   **Fax:** (905) 481-0756   **Email:** info@enna.com

Rebirth of American Industry

The very purpose of this book is to provide modern managers with specific guidelines to be internationally competitive. The book traces the evolution of manufacturing management along two lines: That pioneered by Henry Ford, then furthered by Toyota to its modern level of success; versus that originated by Alfred Sloan and others at General Motors, still in practice in most American companies today.

ISBN 978-0-971243-63-7 | 2005 | $47.52 | Item: 904

All You Gotta Do Is Ask

So, after all the committees, review panels, and head scratching, your company has finally started its Lean transformation. *All You Gotta Do Is Ask* explains how to promote a tidal swell of ideas from your employees. This easy-to-read book will show you why it is important to have a good ideas system, how to set one up, and what it can do for you, your employees, and your organization.

ISBN 978-0-971243-65-1 | 2005 | $37.50 | Item: 906

The Strategos guide to Value Stream & Process Mapping

The Strategos Guide to Value Stream and Process Mapping has proven strategies and helpful tips on facilitating group VSM exercises and puts VSM in the greater Lean context. With photos and examples of related Lean practices, the book focuses on implementing VSM, not just drawing diagrams and graphs.

ISBN 978-1-897363-43-0 | 2007 | $47.00 | Item: 905

SMED - Quick Changeover Solution Package

In today's business environment there is an increasing need to become more agile to accommodate the unique needs of your customers. Enna's *SMED Quick Changeover Package* provides all the information (including a solid five-day training schedule), materials, and techniques needed to effectively lead your own SMED Quick Changeover Program.

ISBN 978-9-973750-94-2 | 2007 | $529.99 | Item: 14

To Order: Enna Corp., 1602 Carolina Street, Unit B3, Bellingham, WA 98229

TPM - Total Productive Maintenance Solution Package

TPM focuses your energies to eliminate down-time and unexpected losses and get productivity back to world-class standards. This training package will allow you to implement a robust system that focuses on systemizing your maintenance needs and developing a customized Total Productive Maintenance system for your company.

ISBN 978-1-926537-05-4 | 2007 | $669.99 | Item: 23

5S Training Package

Our 5S Solution Packages will help your company create a sustainable 5S program that will turn your shop floor around and put you ahead of the competition. All of the benefits that come from Lean Manufacturing are built upon a strong foundation of 5S. Enna's solution packages will show you how to implement and sustain an environment of continuous improvement.

Version 1: Sort, Straighten, Sweep, Standardize and Sustain
ISBN 978-0-973750-90-4 | 2005 | $429.99 | Item: 12
Version 2: Sort, Set In Order, Shine, Standardize and Sustain
ISBN 978-1-897363-25-6 | 2006 | $429.99 | Item: 17

To Order:
Mail orders and checks to:
Enna Products Corporation
ATTN: Order Processing
1602 Carolina Street, Unit B3
Bellingham, WA 98229
USA
Phone: (866) 249-7348
Fax: (905) 481-0756
Email: info@enna.com

We accept checks and all major credit cards.

Notice:
All prices are in US Dollars and are subject to change without notice.